J
3/23

NATIONAL GEOGRAPHIC KiDS

ALMANAC 2023

A zebra foal runs through flowers in Etosha National Park in Namibia.

NATIONAL GEOGRAPHIC KiDS

ALMANAC
2023

NATIONAL GEOGRAPHIC
WASHINGTON, D.C.

National Geographic Kids Books
gratefully acknowledges the following people for their help with the *National Geographic Kids Almanac.*

Stacey McClain of the
National Geographic Explorer Programs

Amazing Animals

Suzanne Braden, Director, Pandas International

Dr. Rodolfo Coria, Paleontologist,
Plaza Huincul, Argentina

Dr. Sylvia Earle, National Geographic
Explorer-in-Residence

Dr. Thomas R. Holtz, Jr., Senior Lecturer,
Vertebrate Paleontology,
Department of Geology, University of Maryland

Dr. Luke Hunter, Executive Director, Panthera

Nizar Ibrahim, National Geographic Explorer

Dereck and Beverly Joubert,
National Geographic Explorers-in-Residence

"Dino" Don Lessem, President, Exhibits Rex

Kathy B. Maher, Research Editor (former),
National Geographic magazine

Kathleen Martin, Canadian Sea Turtle Network

Barbara Nielsen, Polar Bears International

Andy Prince, Austin Zoo

Julia Thorson, Translator, Zurich, Switzerland

Dennis vanEngelsdorp, Senior Extension Associate,
Pennsylvania Department of Agriculture

Space and Earth
Science and Technology

Tim Appenzeller, Chief Magazine Editor, *Nature*

Dr. Rick Fienberg, Press Officer and Director of Communications,
American Astronomical Society

Dr. José de Ondarza, Associate Professor,
Department of Biological Sciences, State University
of New York, College at Plattsburgh

Lesley B. Rogers, Managing Editor (former),
National Geographic magazine

Dr. Enric Sala, National Geographic Explorer-in-Residence

Abigail A. Tipton, Director of Research (former),
National Geographic magazine

Erin Vintinner, Biodiversity Specialist,
Center for Biodiversity and Conservation at the
American Museum of Natural History

Barbara L. Wyckoff, Research Editor (former),
National Geographic magazine

Culture Connection

Dr. Wade Davis, National Geographic
Explorer-in-Residence

Deirdre Mullervy, Managing Editor,
Gallaudet University Press

Wonders of Nature

Anatta, NOAA Public Affairs Officer

Dr. Robert Ballard,
National Geographic Explorer-in-Residence

Douglas H. Chadwick, Wildlife Biologist and Contributor
to *National Geographic* magazine

Susan K. Pell, Ph.D., Science and Public Programs Manager,
United States Botanic Garden

History Happens

Dr. Sylvie Beaudreau, Associate Professor,
Department of History, State University of New York

Elspeth Deir, Assistant Professor, Faculty of Education,
Queens University, Kingston, Ontario, Canada

Dr. Gregory Geddes, Professor, Global Studies,
State University of New York–Orange,
Middletown-Newburgh, New York

Dr. Fredrik Hiebert, National Geographic Visiting Fellow

Micheline Joanisse, Media Relations Officer,
Natural Resources Canada

Dr. Robert D. Johnston,
Associate Professor and Director of the
Teaching of History Program, University of Illinois at Chicago

Dickson Mansfield, Geography Instructor (retired),
Faculty of Education, Queens University,
Kingston, Ontario, Canada

Tina Norris, U.S. Census Bureau

Parliamentary Information and Research Service,
Library of Parliament, Ottawa, Canada

Karyn Pugliese, Acting Director, Communications,
Assembly of First Nations

Geography Rocks

Dr. Kristin Bietsch, Research Associate,
Population Reference Bureau

Carl Haub, Senior Demographer,
Conrad Taeuber Chair of Public Information,
Population Reference Bureau

Dr. Toshiko Kaneda, Senior Research Associate,
Population Reference Bureau

Dr. Walt Meier, National Snow and Ice Data Center

Dr. Richard W. Reynolds, NOAA's National Climatic Data Center

United States Census Bureau, Public Help Desk

Contents

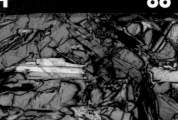

NATIONAL GEOGRAPHIC KIDS
ALMANAC CHALLENGE 2023

THE RESULTS ARE IN!

Which ocean animal won our 2022 Almanac Challenge? *See page 113.*

Want to become part of the 2023 Almanac Challenge? Go to page 112 to find out more.

YOUR WORLD 2023

Festivalgoers enjoy the swing ride at the Hamburg DOM, Germany's longest-running fair that happens three times a year.

3D-PRINTED JET SUITS

Ready, *jet*, go! With a jet suit, you may one day fly right into the future. The creation of British inventor Richard Browning, this suit is powered by arm-mounted turbine engines and a bigger engine that you wear like a backpack. The suit, which is controlled by body movement, can hit some 85 miles an hour (137 km/h) and fly for about five minutes. Browning, who holds a Guinness World Record for fastest speed in a body-controlled jet-engine–powered suit, used a 3D printer to design and create some of the parts that make up the 60-pound (27-kg) suit. But don't expect to see anyone soaring above your house in this suit anytime soon: Right now, it's being tested out by the military and police as a way to swiftly respond to emergencies or chase down criminals.

THE WORLD'S FIFTH OCEAN NAMED

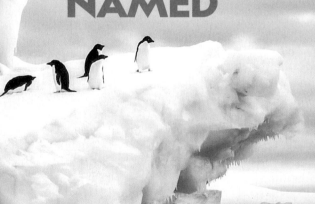

THE SOUTHERN OCEAN IS OFFICIAL! Previously, the large body of water surrounding Antarctica—which is the place where the southernmost stretches of the Pacific, Atlantic, and Indian Oceans meet—was not recognized as a unique ocean. But National Geographic mapmakers ultimately decided to label the Southern Ocean as our planet's fifth ocean on all of their world maps. The new label isn't the only thing that's unique about the Southern Ocean: At some 34 million years old, it's one of Earth's "youngest" oceans. It's also colder and less salty than its four other ocean counterparts.

Welcome to OTTER ISLAND

TWO OTTERS WALK NEAR MARINA BAY, SINGAPORE.

A GROUP OF OTTERS EXPLORES A RESIDENTIAL AREA.

It's hard enough riding a bike on city sidewalks. But in addition to dodging people on walks, runs, or even skateboards, try dodging scampering otters, too! That's life for people in Singapore, a country in Southeast Asia, where smooth-coated river otters live alongside humans.

About 50 years ago, the rivers on the island country of Singapore were so polluted that these native otters could no longer survive there. But thanks to decades of programs that cleaned up the rivers, the otters have made a comeback in this urban environment.

Now biologists are studying the island's otters to learn how the species, found throughout much of Asia, is adapting to city life. For example, these otter pups live with their parents about a year longer than other smooth-coated otters do, since they don't have as much territory to spread out in. Instead of burrowing in the dirt, they make dens in concrete bridges; instead of sleeping in a forest, they snooze between slabs of pavement. This island is now *otterly* wild!

A FAMILY OF OTTERS SWIMS IN MARINA BAY, SINGAPORE.

Wacky Tube Man
Scares Away Dingoes

Here's one way to keep dingoes away: Scare them off with a wiggly inflatable! Scientists in Australia are hoping to prevent the predatory wild dogs from hunting livestock by setting up inflatable objects on farms. In one study, researchers visited a dingo sanctuary, where they set up a bright yellow, 13-foot (4 m)-tall tube man nicknamed Fred-a-Scare near a bowl of dog food. The result? Three out of four times, the dingoes ran away as soon as they spotted Fred wiggling away. While not a foolproof plan—some experts think the dogs will stop fearing tube men after repeated visits— it may be an easy fix for the Australian farmers who routinely lose livestock to hungry dingoes.

BEE INSPIRED

LEMONADE COMPANY'S FOUNDER IS ON A MISSION TO SAVE THE HONEYBEES.

Talk about being buzz-worthy: 17-year-old Mikaila Ulmer has made a big business out of saving honeybees. In 2009, Ulmer created Me & the Bees Lemonade with a special recipe using flaxseed and honey that she plucked from her great-grandma's family cookbook. She eventually bottled it up and started selling it locally, and now, the drink can be found in stores all over the country. But Ulmer's not just about selling lemonade: Part of all Me & the Bees proceeds go to protect bees and their habitats. And aside from running her own company, Ulmer also heads up the Healthy Hive Foundation, a nonprofit organization that supports scientific research aimed at keeping honeybees buzzing around for a long time to come.

Pelican Rescue

Arvy the brown pelican isn't your average bird! When she was just a baby learning the ways of the world in Connecticut, U.S.A., she forgot she needed to fly south for the winter and found herself stranded on a frozen pond. Onlookers found Arvy and took her to a wildlife rehabilitation center in Florida, U.S.A. She was treated for pneumonia and severe frostbite on her webbed feet. Because Arvy lost 30 percent of her feet to frostbite, which impacts her balance, she is unable to return to the wild. So she's now spreading her wings as an ambassador for all brown pelicans at the Busch Wildlife Sanctuary in Florida.

RISE OF THE TITANS

WHEN RESEARCHERS IN AUSTRALIA unearthed fossilized dinosaur bones back in 2006, they didn't realize just how, well, *huge* their discovery was. Now, thanks to new 3D-scanning technology, they know the remains belong to the largest dinosaur species ever found in Australia. Scientists spent years analyzing 3D scans to compare the bones in a database of other species to this new dino, named *Australotitan cooperensis* (casually known as Cooper). Now, the team can say for certain that the dino, which was as long as a basketball court and as tall as a two-story house, is Australia's biggest. Cooper's other characteristics? A long neck and tail, four legs, and a preference for plants. Found in Australia's outback, Cooper's fossils are linked to a lineage of dinosaurs called titanosaurs that were named for their super size. Previously, titanosaurs of this size had only been found in South America's Patagonia region, but now Australia can claim its own titan.

VIKING SHIP
UNCOVERED

Beneath the ground in a spot near Oslo, Norway, sits a Viking ship more than 1,000 years old, and experts are doing everything they can to unearth it. The ship, believed to have been part of a Viking burial site dating back to the 10th century, was discovered by archaeologists using ground penetrating radar (GPR), which revealed that it's more than 60 feet (18 m) long and 16 feet (5 m) wide. Although much of the ship has mostly rotted away, experts hope to excavate the remains so they can use what's left to build a replica and learn more about ancient Viking culture and society. Bringing the boat aboveground is no easy feat, however: The painstaking process will require many hours of slow and careful digging to make sure that what is left of the ancient artifact remains intact.

Colosseum Makeover

In Rome, Italy, a very old building is getting a new look. The Colosseum, the largest amphitheater in the ancient world, is undergoing renovations for a new retractable floor that will allow visitors a different vantage point of the famous landmark. An Italian architectural firm will lead the construction of the floor, which includes installing hundreds of wooden slats that can be rotated to let natural light and air into the chambers below. After archaeologists removed the original floor in the 19th century, visitors could only explore the underground network of tunnels in the ancient site. But once the floor is completed, people will be able to stand in the center of the Colosseum and get a gladiator's view of the surrounding arena.

YARN BOMB!

From street benches to city buses, from tree trunks to trains, nothing is truly safe from yarn bombing. And that's not necessarily a bad thing: Yarn bombing, the act of decorating a space with knitted projects, is a lively way to infuse ordinary objects with pops of color. A type of street art that dates back to the early 2000s, yarn bombing displays have been spotted around the world, from London to Paris to Australia to the United States. Sometimes, yarn bombing is done to bring awareness to hot-button issues, like one display calling for attention to climate change. But many yarn bombers do it simply to bring smiles and brighten up their community one colorful stitch at a time.

sports funnies

World Cup Edition

In 2023, the women's World Cup goes down under! Every four years, the best soccer players on the planet go head-to-head for a chance to claim the world title. In 2019, Team USA came out on top—who will win the 2023 final in Sydney, Australia? Tune in!

Ellen White of Great Britain scores a goal in a match against Chile at the Tokyo 2020 Olympic Games.

Canada's Deanne Rose delivers a penalty kick at the Tokyo 2020 Olympic Games.

Cool Events 2023

WORLD BICYCLE DAY

Spend some of your day on two wheels today—it's fun *and* good for the environment.

June 3

INTERNATIONAL SWEATPANTS DAY

GET COMFY! Throw on your favorite sweats and do something chill and relaxing while you're at it. You deserve it!

January 21

WORLD CHOCOLATE DAY

Need an excuse to eat chocolate? Here's one! Time to treat yourself.

July 7

INTERNATIONAL WOMEN'S DAY

Celebrate all of the amazing women on Earth on this day aimed at raising awareness for the importance of gender equality.

March 8

WORLD ELEPHANT DAY

Pledge to support a world that protects all the awesome elephants on Earth and their habitats.

August 12

EARTH HOUR DAY

Recharge the planet by powering down your electronics from 8:30 p.m. to 9:30 p.m.

March 25

WORLD SINGING DAY

TURN UP THE MUSIC and belt out your favorite tunes!

October 21

WORLD BEE DAY

Show your support for our planet's powerful pollinators, and get to know more about the threats they face.

May 20

INTERNATIONAL CHEETAH DAY

Celebrate the fastest land animal on Earth while helping to raise awareness for these amazing— and vulnerable—big cats.

December 4

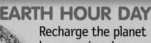

MUPPET GEODE

Cookie Monster, is that you? Scientists were pleasantly surprised to crack open a geode and see a familiar face staring back at them. The rare rock, found in Brazil's Rio Grande do Sul region, sports a deep blue quartz crystal "face," along with two perfectly placed holes bearing an uncanny resemblance to the *Sesame Street* character. Experts say the geode may be worth $10,000. That can get you a lot of cookies!

NEW SUPERHERO: Ratman

MAGAWA, an African giant pouched rat who lived in Cambodia, had a nose for danger. The rodent could sniff out land mines, deadly devices hidden in the countryside. Left over from decades of war in the Southeast Asian country, the land mines are triggered when people accidentally step on them. But Magawa was trained to pick up the scent of the mines and scratch at the ground to signal that he found one so a human could disarm the device. Magawa passed away in 2022, but he found more than a hundred land mines and explosives in five years. What a hero!

Giant pouched rats get their name from the large, hamsterlike pouches in their cheeks, not their body size.

MAGAWA WEARS A MEDAL HE RECEIVED IN 2020 FOR HIS LIFESAVING ACTIONS.

DOG ART GALLERY

This art gallery is for the dogs—literally! In Hong Kong, one artist dedicated an entire collection to canines. The 50-piece collection was part of a temporary exhibit that included interactive pieces like a bouncy water bowl, a giant food bowl ball pit, and other features for pups to play on. There were also boldly colored portraits of dogs positioned close to the floor so the furry friends could get a better look. But humans were just as welcome to, um, *sniff* around.

KIDS vs. PLASTIC

Using rakes and a conveyor belt, Mr. Trash Wheel scoops hundreds of tons of trash out of the Inner Harbor in Baltimore, Maryland, U.S.A., each year.

WHAT IS PLASTIC?

>> **P**lastic can be molded, colored, and textured to make, well, just about anything. That begs the question: What precisely is this wonder product?

THE BASICS
Plastics are polymers, or long, flexible chains of molecules made of repeating links. This molecular structure makes plastic lightweight, hard to break, and easy to mold—all of which makes it extremely useful.

WHERE DO POLYMERS COME FROM?
Polymers can be found in nature, in things like the cell walls of plants, tar, tortoiseshell, and tree sap. In fact, nearly 3,500 years ago, people in what is today Central America used the sap from gum trees to make rubber balls for games. About 150 years ago, scientists began replicating the polymers in nature to improve on them—these are called synthetic polymers.

WHO INVENTED PLASTIC?
In 1869, an American named John Wesley Hyatt created the first useful synthetic polymer. At the time, the discovery was a big deal: For the first time, manufacturing was no longer limited by the resources supplied by nature like wood, clay, and stone. People could create their own materials.

WHAT IS SYNTHETIC PLASTIC MADE FROM?
Today, most plastic is made from oil and natural gas.

WHEN DID IT BECOME POPULAR?
During World War II, from 1939 to 1945, nylon, which is strong and light like silk but made of plastic, was used for parachutes, rope, body armor, and helmet liners. And airplanes used in battle had lightweight windows made of plastic glass, also known as Plexiglas. After the war, plastic became a popular material. Everything from dishes to radios to Mr. Potato Head hit the market. A few decades later, plastic soda bottles became a lightweight nonbreakable alternative to glass bottles, and grocery stores switched from paper bags to cheaper thin plastic ones.

THAT BRINGS US TO TODAY.
Look around: Are you more than a few feet away from something plastic? Probably not! Plastic is all around us.

AMERICANS use an average of ONE plastic grocery bag A DAY. People in DENMARK use an average of FOUR plastic grocery bags A YEAR.

WHERE DOES ALL THE PLASTIC GO?

Only a small percentage of all the plastic that has ever been made has been recycled to make other things. Most has been tossed out and left to slowly biodegrade in landfills, a process that can take hundreds of years. The other option for getting rid of plastic is to burn it. But because plastic is made from fossil fuels, burning it releases harmful pollutants into the air. Here is a breakdown of where all the plastic has gone since people started making it, and how long it takes to biodegrade if it does wind up in a landfill.

9% Recycled

79% Sent to landfills or wound up in the natural environment (like oceans)

12% Burned, releasing toxins into the air

THE LIFE SPAN OF PLASTIC

Plastic that's sent to a landfill doesn't just disappear—it stays there for a really long time. Different types of plastic take different lengths of time to biodegrade.

 PLASTIC BAG
20 YEARS

 PLASTIC-FOAM CUP
50 YEARS

 STRAW
200 YEARS

 BOTTLE
450 YEARS

 SODA SIX-PACK RING **450 YEARS**

 FISHING LINE
600+ YEARS

DEADLY DEBRIS

THE INS AND OUTS OF THE (NOT SO) GREAT PACIFIC GARBAGE PATCH

On a map, the space between California and Hawaii, U.S.A., looks like an endless blue sea, but in person, you'll find a giant floating island—made up of plastic. Plastic can be found in all the oceans of the world, but currents and winds move marine debris around in certain patterns that create huge concentrations, or patches, of plastic in some spots. The biggest one is the Great Pacific Garbage Patch. Scientists estimate that there are about 1.8 trillion pieces of plastic in the patch, and 94 percent of them are microplastics. So, don't try walking on it; it's definitely not solid! Some of the patch is made up of bulky items, including fishing gear like nets, rope, eel traps, crates, and baskets. The patch is also made up of debris washed into the sea during tsunamis. A tsunami is a series of waves caused by an earthquake or an undersea volcanic eruption. It can pull millions of tons of debris—from cars to household appliances to pieces of houses—off coastlines and into the ocean. Scientists and innovators are working on ways to clean up the patch. But with more plastic constantly entering waterways, the effort will inevitably be ongoing.

TANGLED NYLON ROPE THAT HAS WASHED ASHORE OFF THE COAST OF PHUKET, THAILAND

SMASHED-UP SHIPS EVENTUALLY MAKE THEIR WAY TO A SWIRLING MASS OF DEBRIS CALLED THE GREAT PACIFIC GARBAGE PATCH.

GARBAGE PATCH ZONES

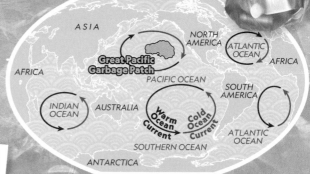

There are five large systems of circulating ocean currents around the world called gyres. Plastic and other trash travel with the currents and get trapped in the gyres. The gyre that the Great Pacific Garbage Patch swirls in is the largest of them all.

Garbage patch area with low concentration of plastics

Garbage patch area with high concentration of plastics

CANADA

PACIFIC OCEAN

UNITED STATES

California

PACIFIC OCEAN

MEXICO

Hawai'i (United States)

THE GREAT PACIFIC GARBAGE PATCH MEASURES 618,000 SQUARE MILES (1.6 MILLION SQ KM).

That's about:

3 TIMES THE SIZE OF FRANCE

2 TIMES THE SIZE OF TEXAS

There are **250 PIECES OF PLASTIC** in the Great Pacific Garbage Patch for **EVERY HUMAN** on Earth.

THERE ARE SOME 5.25 TRILLION PIECES OF PLASTIC WASTE FLOATING AROUND IN THE OCEAN.

In 2018, a group of volunteers removed **4,000 POUNDS** (1,800 kg) of **TRASH** from an **UNINHABITED VOLCANIC ISLAND** off the coast of Alaska, U.S.A.

One Oregon, U.S.A., organization **COLLECTS OCEAN TRASH** to make **COLORFUL SCULPTURES** of **SEA CREATURES.**

Some people take clever steps to sort this messy situation, like installing this giant fish-shaped trash can on a beach in Portugal. Others create art with plastic plucked from the sea, or simply spend time picking up trash to keep our shores clean—and safe.

A FIRE HYDRANT, GARDEN GNOMES, A SKI BOOT, and a RUBBER CHICKEN HAVE ALL WASHED UP ON BEACHES around the world.

FOOD WRAPPERS, CIGARETTE BUTTS, PLASTIC BOTTLES, and PLASTIC BOTTLE CAPS are among the TOP ITEMS COLLECTED during BEACH CLEANUPS.

kids vs. PLASTIC

Do your part to help prevent single-use plastic items from reaching the ocean.
Parents and teachers:
For more information on this topic, you can visit **natgeokids.com/KidsVsPlastic** with your young readers.

CHOOSE THIS

NOT THAT

California, U.S.A., banned restaurants from handing out straws unless customers ask for them.

WHY?

Plastic straws might seem like a small part of the plastic pollution problem, but they can make big trouble for wildlife when they're blown into creeks or rivers and eventually end up in the ocean. A viral video showed rescuers working for nearly 10 minutes to pull just one plastic straw out of the nose of an olive ridley sea turtle—ouch!

So instead, ask your favorite restaurant to provide paper straws, bring your own reusable option, or just skip the straw altogether!

PICK YOUR PERFECT STRAW!

1 I don't want to buy a new straw.
HOLLOW DRY PASTA

2 I want something sturdy yet lightweight.
BAMBOO STRAW

3 I need one that's small and easy to carry.
COLLAPSIBLE STRAW

4 I like to chew on my sippers.
SILICONE STRAW

YOUR PLASTIC-FREE GUIDE TO

SNACKS

Chew on these three ideas for plastic-free snacking.

1 TRAIL MIX

Just mix all your favorite treats from the bulk section of the grocery store together in a bowl, and then eat! You can even sprinkle your mixture with sea salt, cinnamon, or another of your favorite spices for more flavor. Check out these ideas for ingredient inspiration.

- ☐ Pretzels
- ☐ Nuts like almonds, pistachios, or peanuts
- ☐ Pumpkin or sunflower seeds
- ☐ Dried fruit like apricots, raisins, or banana chips
- ☐ Chocolate chips
- ☐ Whole-grain cereal
- ☐ Shredded coconut

2 STOVETOP POPCORN

You'll need a paper bag full of popcorn kernels from the bulk section of the grocery store, some cooking oil, and a big pot with a lid. Make sure to get an adult's help with this recipe.

- ☐ Pour a splash of oil into the pot, using just enough to cover the bottom.
- ☐ Grab an adult and heat the pot on the stovetop over medium heat.
- ☐ Pour in enough popcorn kernels to create one layer along the bottom of the pot.
- ☐ Cover the pot with the lid.
- ☐ After a few minutes, listen for popping sounds. When the popping slows, remove the pot from the burner, take off the lid, and put the popcorn in a bowl.
- ☐ Top off your treat with salt, melted butter, or other spices.

3 BAKED APPLES

Turn this packaging-free fruit into a special snack with brown sugar, butter, and cinnamon. Make sure to get an adult's help with this recipe.

- ☐ Grab an adult and preheat the oven to 350°F (175°C). (You can also use the microwave.)
- ☐ Cut each apple in half, then scoop out its core.
- ☐ Put the apples in an ovenproof baking dish, and then spread a tablespoon of brown sugar and a tablespoon of butter on the inside of each apple half. Then sprinkle the apples with cinnamon.
- ☐ Bake the apples in the oven for about half an hour, or cook in the microwave for about three minutes or until the fruit softens.

DIY Granola Bar Goodies

Plastic food wrappers, like the ones on store-bought granola bars, are a common sight at beach cleanups. Here's a sweet solution: Help keep Earth healthy by ditching the plastic-wrapped snacks and making your own granola bars instead.

PLANET PROTECTOR TIP

Wrap your granola bars in paper or cloth instead of plastic wrap for an on-the-go treat.

YOU'LL NEED

- Medium-size mixing bowl
- Spoon
- 1½ cups (190 g) old-fashioned oats
- 1½ cups (190 g) puffed rice cereal
- ½ cup (65 g) roasted, unsalted sunflower seeds
- ½ teaspoon (1.3 mL) cinnamon
- Medium-size pot
- Knife
- 1 cup (125 g) brown sugar
- ½ cup (65 g) honey
- 3 tablespoons (45 mL) vegetable oil
- ¼ teaspoon (2.5 mL) salt
- ½ teaspoon (1.3 mL) vanilla extract
- ¼ cup (32 g) chocolate chips
- Wax paper
- Square glass baking pan

STEP ONE

Put oats, puffed rice cereal, sunflower seeds, and cinnamon in a mixing bowl and stir with a spoon.

STEP TWO

Grab an adult and combine the brown sugar and honey in a pot.

STEP THREE

Heat the mixture on low and stir for two minutes, or until the mixture is smooth.

STEP FOUR

Mix in oil, salt, and vanilla. Next add the chocolate chips and stir until the chips have completely melted. Then turn off the stove.

STEP FIVE

When the wet mixture in the pot is still warm, pour it into the bowl with the dry ingredients. Stir until the wet and dry ingredients are all combined.

STEP SIX

Place a sheet of wax paper into the glass baking pan so that the paper hangs over the sides of the pan. Pour the mixture on top of the wax paper in the glass pan.

STEP SEVEN

Use your hands to press the granola firmly into the pan. Wait a few hours for the granola to completely cool. (You can put the pan in the refrigerator to cool it more quickly.)

STEP EIGHT

When the granola mixture is fully cooled, carefully lift the wax paper out of the glass pan. Then ask an adult to help cut the snack into bars or bite-size squares. **Enjoy!**

SEA TURTLE RESCUE

RESCUERS SWOOP IN TO HELP A SEA TURTLE THAT SWALLOWED A BALLOON.

A young green sea turtle bobbed along the surface of the water off the coast of Florida, U.S.A. Young turtles usually don't hang out at the surface—that's where predators can easily spot them, plus their food is deeper underwater. But something was keeping this one-foot (30.5-cm)-long turtle from diving.

Luckily, rescuers spotted the struggling turtle and took it back to the Clearwater Marine Aquarium, where they named it Chex. Staff placed Chex in a shallow kiddie pool so that the turtle wouldn't waste energy trying to dive. They tested Chex's blood and ran x-rays but couldn't figure out what was wrong. "Then one day Chex started pooping out something weird," biologist Lauren Bell says. The weird object turned out to be a purple balloon and an attached string.

SOS (SAVE OUR SEAGRASS)!

Sea turtles often mistake floating trash for food. "Even some *people* can't tell the difference between a plastic grocery bag and a jellyfish in the water," Bell says. But plastic doesn't just hurt sea turtles: It also hurts their habitat.

Green sea turtles often hang out close to the shore near seagrass, one of their favorite snacks. Plastic trash left on the beach or coming from rivers that empty into the sea often ends up in this habitat. When it settles on the seagrass, the rubbish can smother the grass, causing it to die. That can mean trouble for green sea turtles like Chex that rely on the seagrass for food and shelter.

During one three-hour cleanup on a beach in Virginia, U.S.A., volunteers collected more than 900 balloons.

TURTLE POWER

BALLOON STRING

PIECE OF BALLOON

1 CHEX THE GREEN SEA TURTLE PROBABLY MISTOOK A TWO-FOOT (0.6-M)-LONG STRING FOR FOOD.

2 CHEX RECOVERED AT THE CLEARWATER MARINE AQUARIUM, SPENDING LOTS OF TIME IN A KIDDIE POOL. ONCE THE TURTLE STARTED EATING SOLID FOODS AGAIN, RESCUERS DECIDED CHEX WAS READY TO RETURN TO THE OCEAN.

GREEN SEA TURTLE
Redington Beach, Florida, U.S.A.

ARCTIC OCEAN

NORTH AMERICA
EUROPE
ASIA
ATLANTIC OCEAN
AFRICA
PACIFIC OCEAN
PACIFIC OCEAN
SOUTH AMERICA
INDIAN OCEAN
AUSTRALIA

Seagrass

SOUTHERN OCEAN
ANTARCTICA

BYE, BALLOON

After several days at the aquarium, Chex started to improve as the balloon made its way through the turtle's digestive system. Chex eventually passed the entire balloon, plus a two-foot (0.6-m)-long string. A few months later, after aquarium staff had successfully introduced solid food back into Chex's diet, rescuers declared the turtle ready to return to the sea.

Bell stood hip deep in the waves as another staff member handed Chex to her. She carefully placed the little turtle in the water and watched it paddle away. "Chex was like, 'Oh, there's the ocean! Okay, bye!'" Bell says. Chex's rescue is worth celebrating … but maybe without the party balloons.

POLLUTION SOLUTION PLASTIC PREDATOR

The ocean is full of trillions of pieces of trash called microplastics that are smaller than the period at the end of this sentence—which makes them really hard to clean up. But the solution might be in tadpole-like creatures called larvaceans (lar-VAY-shuns). These marine animals eat by filtering tiny food particles out of the water and through their bodies. The particles are first trapped in what's called a mucus house—a thin, see-through bubble of, well, mucus that surrounds the larvacean as it travels. Scientists are studying this behavior to see if a similar process could pull harmful microplastics out of the water.

3 BIOLOGIST LAUREN BELL PREPARES TO RELEASE THE LITTLE TURTLE BACK INTO THE SEA.

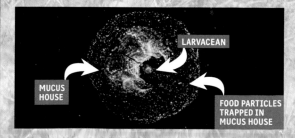

LARVACEAN

MUCUS HOUSE

FOOD PARTICLES TRAPPED IN MUCUS HOUSE

QUIZ WHIZ

What's your eco-friendly IQ? Find out with this quiz!

Write your answers on a piece of paper. Then check them below.

1 **True or false?** Of all plastic ever made, 90 percent has been recycled.

2 There are _____ pieces of plastic in the Great Pacific Garbage Patch for every human on Earth.
- **a.** 2.5
- **b.** 25
- **c.** 250
- **d.** 2,500

3 When was plastic invented?
- **a.** 2009
- **b.** 1769
- **c.** 1969
- **d.** 1869

4 What sea creature's unique way of eating may help pull microplastics out of the ocean?
- **a.** larvacean
- **b.** sea turtle
- **c.** whale shark
- **d.** stingray

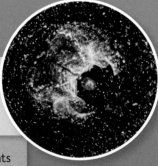

5 **True or false?** Shopping for your favorite treats from the bulk section of the grocery store can prevent plastic items from reaching the ocean.

Not **STUMPED** yet? Check out the *NATIONAL GEOGRAPHIC KIDS QUIZ WHIZ* collection for more crazy **ENVIRONMENT** questions!

ANSWERS: 1. False: Just 9 percent of plastic has been recycled. 2. c; 3. d; 4. a; 5. True

HOMEWORK HELP

Write a Letter That Gets Results

Knowing how to write a good letter is a useful skill. It will come in handy when you want to persuade someone to understand your point of view. Whether you're emailing your congressperson or writing a letter for a school project or to your grandma, a great letter will help you get your message across. Most important, a well-written letter makes a good impression.

CHECK OUT THE EXAMPLE BELOW FOR THE ELEMENTS OF A GOOD LETTER.

Your address

Date

Salutation
Always use "Dear" followed by the person's name; use Mr., Mrs., Ms., or Dr. as appropriate.

Introductory paragraph
Give the reason you're writing the letter.

Body
The longest part of the letter, which provides evidence that supports your position. Be persuasive!

Closing paragraph
Sum up your argument.

Complimentary closing
Sign off with "Sincerely" or "Thank you."

Your signature

Maddie Smith
1234 Main Street
Peoria, Illinois 61525

April 22, 2023

Dear Owner of the Happy Hamburger,

I am writing to ask you to stop using single-use plastic at the Happy Hamburger.

This is my favorite restaurant. My family and I eat there almost every Saturday night. I always order the bacon cheeseburger with mac and cheese on the side. It's my favorite meal, ever!

The other day, my dad brought home a to-go order from your restaurant. The order contained a plastic fork, knife, and spoon, all wrapped in plastic. It also came in a plastic bag. Now that's a lot of plastic!

I am concerned because plastic is a huge problem for the planet. Did you know that nine million tons of plastic waste end up in the ocean every year? Even worse, scientists think that the amount of plastic might triple by 2050.

Some other restaurants in town have cut back on their single-use plastic. The Hotdog Hangout uses paper bags instead of plastic bags for takeout. And servers at the Weeping Onion ask customers if they'd like plastic cutlery, instead of automatically including it in to-go orders.

These are simple changes that I hope you can make at the Happy Hamburger. That way, not only would you be serving the best burgers around, but you'd also be helping to protect the planet.

Thank you very much for your time.

Sincerely,

Maddie Smith

Maddie Smith

COMPLIMENTARY CLOSINGS

Sincerely, Sincerely yours, Thank you, Regards, Best wishes, Respectfully

33

AMAZING
ANIMALS

EXTRAORDINARY ANIMALS

Silly Seal Sniffs Eel

Lisianski Island, Hawaii
This seal *nose* a thing or two about getting into trouble.

The Hawaiian monk seal pup was spotted lounging on the beach—with an eel hanging out of its nostril. Scientists approached the seal, gently held it down with their hands, and then pulled the two-and-a-half-foot (76 cm) dead eel out of its nose in about a minute. "The seal didn't feel any pain," says Charles Littnan, director of the Protected Species Division at the National Oceanic and Atmospheric Administration in Hawaii. "In fact, it didn't seem to care at all."

Scientists have since found three other young seals with eels in their noses—and they don't know why. But since eels are on the seals' menu, the mishap probably happened when the youngsters were hunting. "The pups aren't sure how to handle their food yet," Littnan says. "And they seem to be good at getting into trouble." Looks like these seals need to learn not to play with their food!

DO I HAVE SOMETHING ON MY FACE?

I WISH I HAD A MOTOR FOR THIS THING.

Ape Takes Boat for a Ride!

Tanjung Puting National Park, Borneo

Keep an eye on your vessel when Princess the orangutan is around. The boat-napping buccaneer steals canoes from the dock at Camp Leakey, the orangutan research station where she lives. Princess takes the boats so she can get to the tasty plants that grow downstream. But this sneaky great ape may have another motive: "If people are around, sometimes she does it to show off," says scientist Biruté Mary Galdikas, Camp Leakey's orangutan expert.

Princess's rides can be a royal pain for camp workers, who must retrieve the canoes she abandons. To discourage her, they store the canoes underwater. But Princess simply tips the boats from side to side until the water sloshes out.

All primates are intelligent, but Princess is especially brainy. "I'd say she's one of the smartest orangutans I've ever seen in my life," Galdikas says. Even when Princess is onshore, she eats like a queen: She figured out how to use a key to unlock the camp's dining hall!

I'M ALWAYS IN TUNE.

Singing Dingo

Alice Springs, Australia

He might not have been a famous pop star, but Dinky the dingo sure could belt out a tune! After innkeeper Jim Cotterill helped rescue the young wild dog from a trap in the Australian outback, he noticed that his new pet liked to "sing along" with the piano. When guests would play a song, Dinky would hop on top of the keys and howl a tune to match the notes. "A group of musicians told me that Dinky actually had pretty good pitch," Cotterill said. "When the notes went higher, so did Dinky's voice."

Hippo "Kisses" Hyena

South Luangwa National Park, Zambia

Pucker up! On a safari drive, guide Patrick Njobvu watched as a young hippopotamus emerged from the Luangwa River, walked over to a snoozing spotted hyena, and started to sniff. "The hyena didn't run, and both started sniffing each other, nose to nose, almost like kissing," Njobvu says. The two animals hung out together for about 20 minutes before walking away.

Experts don't know why the hyena didn't run away—some think it might have been too scared to move, while others believe that it could've been feeling very relaxed. And the hippo? It was likely just being curious. Behavioral ecologist Rob Heathcote says that young animals like this hippo are often more curious as they explore the world and learn how to behave.

The "kiss" wasn't true love, but it was definitely cute.

SORRY MY SMOOCHES ARE SANDY!

ANIMAL MYTHS BUSTED

Some people mistakenly think adult opossums hang by their tails or that porcupines shoot their quills. What other misconceptions are out there? Here are some common animal myths.

MYTH Elephants are afraid of mice.

HOW IT MAY HAVE STARTED People used to think that mice liked to crawl into elephants' trunks, which could cause damage and terrible sneezing. So it makes sense that elephants would be afraid of the rodents.

WHY IT'S NOT TRUE An elephant's eyesight is so poor that it could barely even see a mouse. Plus, if an elephant isn't afraid to live among predators such as tigers, rhinos, and crocodiles, a mouse would be the least of its worries!

Who are you again?

MYTH Goldfish only have a three-second memory.

HOW IT MAY HAVE STARTED While an adult human's brain weighs about three pounds (1.4 kg), an average goldfish's brain weighs only a tiny fraction of that. So how could there be any room for memory in there?

WHY IT'S NOT TRUE Research has shown that goldfish are quite smart. Phil Gee of the University of Plymouth in the United Kingdom trained goldfish to push a lever that dropped food into their tank. "They remembered the time of day that the lever worked and waited until feeding time to press it," Gee says. One scientist even trained goldfish to tell the difference between classical and blues music!

MYTH Touching a frog or toad will give you warts.

HOW IT MAY HAVE STARTED Many frogs and toads have bumps on their skin that look like warts. Some people think the bumps are contagious.

WHY IT'S NOT TRUE "Warts are caused by a human virus, not frogs or toads," said dermatologist Jerry Litt. But the wart-like bumps behind a toad's ears *can* be dangerous. These parotoid glands contain a nasty poison that irritates the mouths of some predators and often the skin of humans. So toads may not cause warts, but they can cause other nasties. It's best not to handle these critters—warty or not!

BIG WART

TOE WART CHIN WART NOSE WART FINGER WART

WARTS

Cute Animal SUPERLATIVES

Funky features. Super senses. Sensational speed. No doubt, all animals are cool. But whether they've got goofy grins, funky hair, or endless energy, some species are extra adorable. Here are 15 of the cutest creatures on Earth.

FURRIEST

Thick, white fur helps polar bears blend in with the ice and snow of their Arctic habitat. This fur even grows on the bottom of their paws! It gives them a better grip on the ice and protection from frozen surfaces.

BEST ACROBAT

An inchworm has a funny way of walking: With legs at both ends of its body but none in the middle, it shifts from the front end to go forward, creating an awesome arch with its body as it moves.

MOST COLORFUL

The rainbow finch's funky feathers make this bird a standout on the grasslands of Australia. The hue of its head, which can be black, yellow, red, and orange, varies from bird to bird.

BEST STRETCH

The gerenuk, found in East Africa, is known to stand on its hind legs and stretch its slender neck to get hard-to-reach leaves on bushes and shrubs.

BEST COAT

Blizzard in the forecast? *Snow* problem! The golden snub-nosed monkey, found high in the mountains of central China, has a thick, furry coat and tail. They keep it warm in winter, making this primate ready for any weather.

BEST HAIR DAY

The Polish chicken sometimes goes by the nickname of "top hat" because of the funky feathers at the top of its head, or crest. Its unique appearance made it a prized bird among the rich and royalty in the 1700s. Despite its name, the breed known today comes from the Netherlands.

BEST SPIKES

The lowland streaked tenrec may be tiny, but its spiky exterior poses a big threat to predators. Found only in Madagascar, this mini mammal is about the size of a hedgehog and will shoot its barbs into an animal when under attack.

LONGEST DROP

Talk about a grand entrance: A baby giraffe falls about six feet (1.8 m) from its mom during birth before hitting the ground.

GREAT GLIDER

A Siberian flying squirrel can catch some major air. Using a flap of skin that stretches between its forelegs and hind legs like a parachute and its long, flat tail to balance, the squirrel can cover the length of a football field in one giant leap.

EARLY WALKER

Found in northern Canada, Greenland, Russia, Scandinavia, and Alaska, U.S.A., the sure-footed muskox can stand up, follow its mom, and keep up with its herd just hours after being born. This early start keeps the calf protected from potential predators.

BEST TRANSFORMATION

Think pink! The rosy maple moth may wind up with coloring that looks a lot like a fuzzy pink and yellow tennis ball, but it doesn't begin that way. It actually starts out as a caterpillar known as the greenstriped mapleworm.

BEST SNUGGLER

The smallest raptor in Africa, African pygmy falcons only grow to be about the length of a pencil. To stay warm in winter, these pint-size predators spend up to 15 hours a day snuggling together in their nests.

BEST STRIPES

The ribbon seal's unique black-and-white pattern sets it apart on the sea ice of Alaska, U.S.A., and Russia. Some scientists think the markings may act as camouflage, helping the seals blend into the shadows on ice floes.

BEST WARNING

If you spot a poison dart frog in the wild, watch out! These teeny amphibians are among the world's most toxic animals. Their brightly colored skin—which can be yellow, gold, copper, red, green, blue, or black—sends a message to predators to stay away.

SWEETEST RIDE

When common loon chicks hatch, they're almost immediately on the go—Mom carries her little ones on her back to protect them from predators. Once grown, loons can dive nearly 250 feet (76 m) and hold their breath for up to eight minutes as they fish.

WHAT IS Taxonomy?

Because our planet has billions and billions of living things called organisms, people need a way of classifying them. Scientists created a system called taxonomy, which helps to classify all living things into ordered groups. By putting organisms into categories, we are better able to understand how they are the same and how they are different. There are eight levels of taxonomic classification, beginning with the broadest group, called a domain, followed by kingdom, down to the most specific group, called a species.

Biologists divide life based on evolutionary history, and they place organisms into three domains depending on their genetic structure: Archaea, Bacteria, and Eukarya. (See page 197 for "The Three Domains of Life.")

Where do animals come in?

Animals are a part of the Eukarya domain, which means they are organisms made of cells with nuclei. More than one million species of animals, including humans, have been named. Like all living things, animals can be divided into smaller groups, called phyla. Most scientists believe there are more than 30 phyla into which animals can be grouped based on certain scientific criteria, such as body type or whether or not the animal has a backbone. It can be pretty complicated, so another, less complicated system groups animals into two categories: vertebrates and invertebrates.

HEDGEHOG

SAMPLE CLASSIFICATION
RED PANDA

Domain:	Eukarya
Kingdom:	Animalia
Phylum:	Chordata
Class:	Mammalia
Order:	Carnivora
Family:	Ailuridae
Genus:	*Ailurus*
Species:	*fulgens*

TIP:
Here's a sentence to help you remember the classification order:
Did **K**ing **P**hillip **C**ome **O**ver **F**or **G**ood **S**oup?

BY THE NUMBERS

There are 15,772 vulnerable or endangered animal species in the world. The list includes:

- **1,327 mammals,** such as the snow leopard, the polar bear, and the fishing cat
- **1,481 birds,** including the Steller's sea eagle and the black-banded plover
- **3,280 fish,** such as the Mekong giant catfish
- **1,587 reptiles,** including the Round Island day gecko
- **1,959 insects,** such as the Macedonian grayling

- **2,444 amphibians,** such as the emperor newt
- **And more,** including 218 arachnids, 743 crustaceans, 234 sea anemones and corals, 211 bivalves, and 2,123 snails and slugs

ROUND ISLAND DAY GECKO

Vertebrates
Animals WITH Backbones

Fish are cold-blooded and live in water. They breathe with gills, lay eggs, and usually have scales.

Amphibians are cold-blooded. Their young live in water and breathe with gills. Adults live on land and breathe with lungs.

Reptiles are cold-blooded and breathe with lungs. They live both on land and in water.

Birds are warm-blooded and have feathers and wings. They lay eggs, breathe with lungs, and are usually able to fly. Some birds live on land, some in water, and some on both.

Mammals are warm-blooded and feed on their mothers' milk. They also have skin that is usually covered with hair. Mammals live both on land and in water.

BIRD: MANDARIN DUCK

AMPHIBIAN: POISON DART FROG

Invertebrates
Animals WITHOUT Backbones

Sponges are a very basic form of animal life. They live in water and do not move on their own.

Echinoderms have external skeletons and live in seawater.

Mollusks have soft bodies and can live either in or out of shells, on land or in water.

Arthropods are the largest group of animals. They have external skeletons, called exoskeletons, and segmented bodies with appendages. Arthropods live in water and on land.

Worms are soft-bodied animals with no true legs. Worms live in soil.

Cnidaria live in water and have mouths surrounded by tentacles.

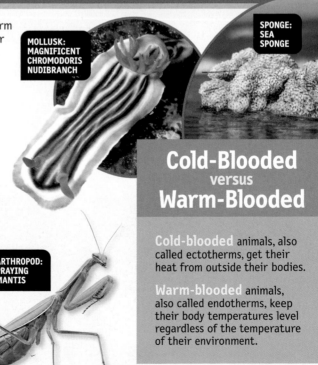

MOLLUSK: MAGNIFICENT CHROMODORIS NUDIBRANCH

SPONGE: SEA SPONGE

ARTHROPOD: PRAYING MANTIS

Cold-Blooded
versus
Warm-Blooded

Cold-blooded animals, also called ectotherms, get their heat from outside their bodies.

Warm-blooded animals, also called endotherms, keep their body temperatures level regardless of the temperature of their environment.

COMEBACK CRITTER:

GOLDEN LION TAMARIN

Scientists help these primates reclaim their forest home.

A family of golden lion tamarins is on the move. With two babies on his back and his mate beside him, the father tamarin reaches for a branch in Brazil's Atlantic Forest. Just a few years ago, this land was a treeless cattle pasture. But conservationists knew that if more forest was lost, then the golden lion tamarins—which live wild nowhere else on Earth—would be gone, too.

DISAPPEARING FORESTS

The Atlantic Forest was once about the size of Egypt. But in the 1500s, European traders and settlers started cutting down the trees to build ships and make room for settlements. Then, over the past century, farmers cut down more trees to clear land for crops until the forest was less than 10 percent of its original size.

Golden lion tamarins spend most of their time in the tree canopy, using branches to travel in search of food and mates. As the forest shrank, habitats became cut off from each other—and so did the primates. By the 1970s, concerned biologists estimated that only about 200 golden lion tamarins were left in the Atlantic Forest.

MONKEY BOOT CAMP

Conservationists gathered at the Smithsonian's National Zoo in Washington, D.C., in 1972 to develop a plan to save the species in the wild. Some zoos already had golden lion tamarins in captivity; all they had to do was breed more tamarins, then prepare some of the families to return to the wild. How? "We sent them to boot camp," says Kenton Kerns, assistant curator of small mammals at the National Zoo.

During several summers following 1972, zookeepers around the world let tamarins out of their enclosures to hang out in the trees. Staff provided each family with a nest to sleep in and sweet potatoes to munch on, and kept watch to

An adult golden lion tamarin is about the size of a squirrel.

GOLDEN LION TAMARIN FATHERS OFTEN CARRY THEIR BABIES ON THEIR BACKS IN BETWEEN FEEDINGS.

GOLDEN LION TAMARIN TWINS HANG ON TO THEIR FATHER AT GERMANY'S DUISBURG ZOO.

ATLANTIC OCEAN

SOUTH AMERICA

PACIFIC OCEAN

Where golden lion tamarins live

BRAZIL

BRAZIL

ATLANTIC OCEAN

ATLANTIC OCEAN

The golden lion tamarin is featured on a banknote in Brazil.

A GOLDEN LION TAMARIN LEAPS FROM ONE BRANCH TO ANOTHER IN ITS BRAZILIAN FOREST HOME.

make sure they didn't leave the grounds. "The free-range lifestyle taught the tamarins how to find insects and navigate branches," Kerns says. In 1983, the first group of tamarins was ready to return to Brazil's forests.

While the monkeys were in training, Brazil's Golden Lion Tamarin Association was busy restoring the tamarins' habitat. The group bought land from private owners and worked with farmers to plant trees on their property, connecting patches of forest and protecting more than 40 square miles (103 sq km) of habitat. The organization also gave local citizens jobs managing tree nurseries and trained teachers on environmental issues. "People were proud to have tamarins on their land," says Denise Rambaldi, former director of the Golden Lion Tamarin Association.

GOING GREEN

About 2,500 golden lion tamarins now live in the Atlantic Forest. About a third of them are descended from 147 captive-born tamarins from the zoo program.

But conservationists aren't done. They continue to reforest the land and inspire young people to protect the animals. Says Lou Ann Dietz, founding director of Save the Golden Lion Tamarin: "Seeing tamarin families chirping and jumping around in the trees overhead, their fur reflecting the sunlight like fire, makes it all worth it."

SUN BEAR RESCUE

How kind caretakers helped an orphaned cub return to the wild

These bears are named for the golden or white "rising sun" patch on their chests, which experts think might help the bears seem bigger than they are.

A three-month-old sun bear huddles alone in a metal cage. A few days ago, poachers snatched the cub from the wild and brought her to a town in Malaysia, an island country in Southeast Asia, where she was sold as a pet, which is illegal. Now the orphan is stressed and hungry. If she stays in the cage, she may not survive.

BEAR AID

That's when caretakers from the Bornean Sun Bear Conservation Centre step in. They give the cub a name—Natalie—and take her in, giving her a special milk with extra protein, plus plenty of comfort and care. Within a few weeks, Natalie grows strong enough to head outside with a caretaker. She even climbs a tree! Soon, she joins three other bears in an outdoor enclosure. Together, the bears lounge, play, and learn to forage for their favorite treats of termites, earthworms, and honey.

WILD AGAIN

After five years at the rescue center, Natalie is ready to be released back into the wild. A team of veterinarians gives the hundred-pound (45-kg) bear one last checkup before fitting her with a tracking collar so that they can watch where she goes for the first few months. Her rescuers fly her by helicopter in a crate to a protected wildlife reserve where people don't live. They use a long rope to open Natalie's crate from afar. She bursts out into the woods—finally a free bear again.

Scientists have spotted mother sun bears cradling cubs in their arms while walking on their hind legs.

WONG SIEW TE FEEDS NATALIE A SPECIAL MILK TO HELP HER GAIN WEIGHT.

WONG WATCHES OVER NATALIE LIKE HER MOTHER WOULD HAVE IN THE WILD.

ASIA
BANGLADESH
INDIA
MYANMAR (BURMA)
LAOS
THAILAND
VIETNAM
CAMBODIA
South China Sea
BRUNEI
MALAYSIA
INDONESIA

ASIA
AREA ENLARGED
PACIFIC OCEAN
INDIAN OCEAN
AUSTRALIA

INDIAN OCEAN

Where sun bears live

SharkFest

Dive in to join the party with these 5 surprising sharks.

Not all sharks are gigantic, toothy eating machines. Among the 500 species, there are a few surprising sharks. Some have teeth so small that they can't take a bite out of anything. Others are practically vegetarian! Discover five species of sharks with mind-blowing traits.

A group of sharks is called a shiver.

TWO LEMON SHARKS HANG OUT NEAR THE BAHAMA ISLANDS.

1 Fishy Friends: Lemon Sharks

Love hanging out with your BFF? So do lemon sharks! Young lemon sharks often stick together for protection from larger sharks and other predators. Scientists say this species hangs out with the same friends for years. And when scientists studied the pups in a predator-free environment, these sharks still chose to swim together rather than alone. Maybe these fish need matching friendship bracelets.

2 Green Glowers: Chain Catsharks

WHAT YOU SEE

WHAT CHAIN CATSHARKS SEE

TO CAPTURE THIS IMAGE, SCIENTISTS BUILT A CAMERA THAT SEES THE WORLD LIKE THIS CATSHARK DOES.

Through your eyes, the chain catshark seems to have brownish yellow skin with black chain-shaped markings. But to another chain catshark swimming 1,600 to 2,000 feet (488 to 610 m) below the surface, the fish glows in the dark! Pigments in the sharks' skin absorb the blue light in the ocean and reflect it as green. These sharks have special cells in their eyes—called receptors—to see it. Because the glow patterns are different for males and females, scientists think these shy sharks use this ability to attract mates.

3 Salad Snackers: Bonnethead Sharks

A BONNETHEAD SHARK EXPLORES THE WATERS OF THE FLORIDA KEYS.

Bonnethead sharks love their greens. Unlike almost all other sharks, which are carnivores, the bonnetheads' digestive system allows them to absorb nutrients from plants. Scientists aren't sure if bonnetheads intentionally snack on plants, or if they're accidentally ingested while scooping up shellfish hiding in the seagrass.

4 Ocean Oldies: Greenland Sharks

A Greenland shark swimming through deep, freezing Arctic water today might have been born when George Washington became the first president of the United States! This shark species can live for nearly 300 years—and possibly as many as 500 years. That's the longest of any vertebrate (an animal with a backbone). Experts think their icy cold habitat and slow lifestyle (a Greenland shark's heart beats only once every 12 seconds; yours beats about once a second) might be their secret to growing seriously old.

A GREENLAND SHARK SWIMS BELOW THE ARCTIC OCEAN ICE, OFF THE COAST OF CANADA.

Sharks have been on Earth longer than trees.

5 Gentle Giants: Whale Sharks

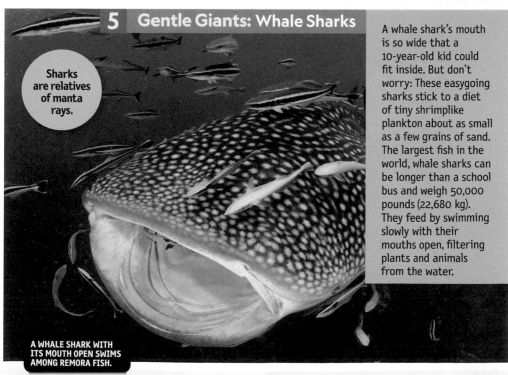

Sharks are relatives of manta rays.

A whale shark's mouth is so wide that a 10-year-old kid could fit inside. But don't worry: These easygoing sharks stick to a diet of tiny shrimplike plankton about as small as a few grains of sand. The largest fish in the world, whale sharks can be longer than a school bus and weigh 50,000 pounds (22,680 kg). They feed by swimming slowly with their mouths open, filtering plants and animals from the water.

A WHALE SHARK WITH ITS MOUTH OPEN SWIMS AMONG REMORA FISH.

UNIC⬤RNS

OF THE SEA

SCIENTISTS TRY TO **SOLVE THE MYSTERY** OF THE NARWHAL'S **GIANT TUSK.**

C hilly water laps against an iceberg in the Arctic Ocean. Suddenly, a pod of narwhals—a species of whale that sports a unicorn-like horn on its head— emerges from the sea near the iceberg's edge.

Narwhals live in the Arctic Ocean. Like most whales, they're jumbo-size—up to 3,500 pounds (1,588 kg)—and surface to breathe. And like some whale species such as orcas, they live in pods. (Narwhals usually have 15 to 20 in a group.) But a narwhal has one thing that no other whale does: a giant tusk growing out of its noggin.

For centuries people have been trying to figure out what this tusk—actually an enlarged tooth—is used for. Scientists have come up with a couple theories that may help solve this gnawing puzzle.

TUSK, TUSK

A narwhal's swordlike tusk first pokes from its jaw through the animal's upper lip when it's about three months old. This is the only tooth the whale develops. Over time, the tusk can grow to be half the length of the whale's body. New research shows that narwhals may use these long appendages to snag prey like arctic cod, using quick jabs to stun the fish before they eat them.

TOOTH SLEUTHS

Another theory is that male narwhals use the tooth to attract females. Similar to a peacock's flashy feathers, the tusk makes them stand out to potential mates. The animals have been observed scraping their tusks together, as though they are in a fencing match. This may be a way for male members of the pod to identify one another.

There's still plenty that scientists don't know about narwhals, and they will continue to look for answers. In the meantime, it appears that these mysterious whales still have a few secrets up their tusks.

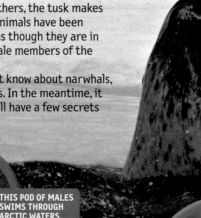

SURFACING ABOVE WATER, A GROUP OF NARWHALS TAKES A BREATH OF AIR.

THIS POD OF MALES SWIMS THROUGH ARCTIC WATERS.

A NARWHAL MOM TRAVELS WITH HER BABY.

4 GNARLY NUDIBRANCHS

1 YOU ARE WHAT YOU EAT

Near the rocky shores of California, U.S.A., and Mexico's Baja California, a neon **Spanish shawl** nudibranch is hard to miss crawling on corals or fluttering through open water. This flashy finger-length slug gets its bright color by recycling pigments from its favorite food, tiny plantlike jellyfish known as hydroids.

LIKE OYSTERS AND CLAMS, NUDIBRANCHS ARE MOLLUSKS. BUT THESE SEA SLUGS DON'T HAVE SHELLS.

2 DEADLY SURFER

The thumbnail-size **blue dragon** cruises tropical oceans, using a stomach bubble to float on the surface while it searches for its favorite snack: Portuguese man-of-wars. But watch out! The dragon stores the poison it ingests from its prey in the tips of its frilly blue fingers.

3 PATTERN PLAY

Fluorescent stripes and polka dots turn the *Nembrotha kubaryana*'s costume into a can't-miss warning sign for potential predators. Distinguished by its often orange edging, this nudibranch lives in tropical western Pacific and Indian Ocean waters and can grow up to 4.7 inches (12 cm) long.

4 SPOTS, HORNS, AND WINGS

Its frilly pigtails, mustache, and daisy-shaped spots make *Bornella anguilla* look more like a cartoon character than a pinkie finger–length sea slug. This nudibranch, named for its eel-like way of swimming (*anguilla* means "eel" in Latin), lives in the tropical waters of the western Pacific and Indian Oceans.

HUMPBACK WHALES RELY ON TEAMWORK TO HUNT, COORDINATING THEIR ACTIONS AS THEY CIRCLE IN ON THEIR PREY.

HUMPBACK WHALES typically **TRAVEL SOLO,** but they do join up during feeding sessions.

Known as the **"SONGSTERS OF THE SEAS,"** male humpback whales **SING COMPLEX SONGS** with repeated patterns.

This behavior, known as bubble-net feeding, allows the whales to disorient their prey by blowing bubbles in a spiral around a school of fish. The ring of bubbles forces the fish to the surface, where other humpbacks await and can then gulp the fish down.

Humpback whales eat up to **3,000 POUNDS** (1,360 kg) **OF FOOD A DAY,** including **SMALL FISH** and **TINY CRUSTACEANS.**

Each summer, Pacific humpbacks **MIGRATE FROM HAWAII , U.S.A.,** to their **FEEDING GROUNDS NEAR ALASKA, U.S.A.—** one of the longest migrations in the animal world.

Sit! Stay! Swim!

Surprising ways sea lions can seem like dogs

Sea lions use their whiskers, called vibrissae (pronounced VEYE-bree-see), to detect the movements of nearby fish.

A PAIR OF AUSTRALIAN SEA LIONS CHECK OUT A PHOTOGRAPHER'S CAMERA NEAR PORT LINCOLN, AUSTRALIA.

Hundreds of Australian sea lions have gathered together along the Australian coast. Some are sprawled out on the beach, sunning themselves. Others bark as they chase one another in the surf. Minus their flippers, these animals could fit right in at a dog park.

These marine mammals actually do remind some people of our furry pooch pals. "Sea lions are curious and playful, which is very doglike," says Deena Weisberg, a researcher who studies human and sea lion interactions on the Galápagos Islands in the Pacific Ocean. "Even when they're in the water, they behave very similarly to dogs." So should sea lions really be called sea *dogs* instead? Check out these five behaviors to decide.

They hang out in packs—er, rafts.

Hundreds of Steller sea lions are squeezed together on a beach in Alaska, U.S.A. Just when you'd think more sea lions couldn't possibly squish themselves into the group, called a raft, another pup wedges itself in. Sea lions are social animals that prefer to spend time in pairs or groups. And like dogs that share a home with cats, sea lions can interact with other animals in their ocean home. They've been spotted swimming with whales and sharing beaches with seals.

A GALÁPAGOS SEA LION BARKS ON A BEACH IN ECUADOR, A COUNTRY IN SOUTH AMERICA.

They bark—loudly.

If you've ever walked by a dog park, you know how loud a few barking dogs can be. When Galápagos sea lions bark, they sound similar—except there are hundreds of them! Like dogs, sea lions bark to get another animal's attention, or because they're excited or angry. But sometimes they bark to see which can be the loudest. The winning sea lion gets the best spot on the beach, which increases a male's chance of mating.

They play "fetch" (sort of).

Dogs chase tennis balls and chew on squeaky bones. Sea lions love to play, too, but their toys are colorful playthings found in the ocean. That could be anything from picking up sea stars, scooping up shells, trying to find an octopus hiding in the rocks, or chasing down fish for lunch. Sea lions love staying active ... just like dogs!

A CALIFORNIA SEA LION PLAYS WITH A SEA STAR IN THE SEA OF CORTEZ NEAR MEXICO.

A CALIFORNIA SEA LION CHECKS OUT A DIVER OFF THE COAST OF MEXICO.

Male sea lions are called bulls, females are called cows, and babies are pups.

They have a *lot* of energy.

When a dog needs to burn energy, its owner takes it for a long walk or a sprint around the yard. Sea lions "porpoise," or swim at fast speeds, zooming out of the water to dive like, well, a porpoise. One of the fastest marine mammals, sea lions go far. They'll swim several miles away and back again on the same day!

They ♥ humans.

Like dogs, sea lions, especially pups, are naturally curious. They'll waddle toward people on beaches or check out swimmers to get a better look. Underwater, sea lions will inspect scuba divers and their gear by nudging them. They can also be aggressive, so if one approaches you, stay calm and keep as much distance as possible until it gets bored and swims away.

FOXES ON ICE

Clever arctic foxes survive snow, ice, and freezing cold temperatures.

Not far from the North Pole, an arctic fox trots across the sea ice on a winter walkabout. It's been days since her last meal, and the whipping wind is relentless. She digs a hollow in the snow, curls up her cat-size body, and wraps her tail across her body and face to stay warm. Her fur acts like a warm sleeping bag, keeping her snug as temperatures dip below 0°F (-18°C). But warm fur alone might not keep this fox alive during the polar winter. Other freeze-defying strategies make this animal a champion of the cold.

FINDING FOOD

Arctic foxes prefer to eat small rodents called lemmings, but when times are tough, they'll take what they can get. This may be scraps of a seal that a polar bear has killed, or crabs and algae stuck to the bottom of ice. Sometimes, they'll stash dead lemmings near their dens for leaner times.

LEMMING

KEEPING WARM

In the toughest temps, this female fox digs a snow den and hunkers down for up to two weeks. She can slow her heart rate and metabolism to avoid burning energy—similar to hibernation but not as long lasting. The fox's short legs provide heat exchange between warm blood flowing down from the body and cold blood flowing up from the legs.

When the fox emerges, she listens for scurrying sounds under the snow. Quietly, she takes a few steps, and then dives into the snow. Her head emerges with a brown fur ball in her mouth. With the energy tank refilled, this arctic fox has a better chance of making it through the long, dark winter.

NINJA GIRAFFES

These animals have some seriously stealthy moves.

You might not think giraffes would have much in common with ninja, skilled combatants who prowled through 15th-century Japan on spy missions. After all, giraffes move awkwardly, and their superlong necks hardly seem stealthy. But these hoofed creatures are surprisingly sleek and agile. Discover how giraffes kick it up a notch, ninja style.

HIDE-AND-SEEK

Often hired by rulers who were competing for power, ninja would dress up as farmers or merchants to spy on their leader's opponent. Giraffes may have a distinctive appearance, but they sport the perfect camouflage for blending into their surroundings. Their brown spots look like the shadows created by sunlight shining through the trees, keeping them protected from predators.

THE NEED FOR SPEED

Ninja trained to become swift runners so they could easily slip away from foes during a chase. Giraffes are also excellent sprinters, using their long, muscular legs. At full gallop, these animals can reach 35 miles an hour (56 km/h), which helps them evade predators, like lions.

SPECTACULAR SENSES

People once believed that ninja could see in the dark and hear tiny movements. This likely wasn't true for ninja, but giraffes really do have superb vision and hearing. Using their keen eyesight, they can spot a moving animal more than a half mile (0.8 km) away. They also hear noises that humans can't detect. Could giraffes be even better warriors than ninja?

WEAPONS MASTERS

When ninja came face-to-face with their rivals, they used swords and daggers to defeat the enemy. Giraffes have their own built-in weapons: hooves with sharp edges. In fact, a giraffe kick can be deadly to other giraffes and predators. Two male giraffes might also fight for dominance by clubbing each other with their heavy heads and necks.

A RED-EYED TREE FROG SITS ON A PLANT SHOOT IN THE SOUTH AMERICAN COUNTRY OF COSTA RICA.

Earth is home to more than 6,000 species of frogs, many of which aren't much bigger than a coin. But these small amphibians possess some big surprises. Check out how five frogs use everything from their ears to their webbed feet to live their best life.

FROG Squad

These awesome amphibian features will turn you into a frog fan.

EYE SURPRISE

Appearing to have its eyes closed, a red-eyed tree frog sits on a branch. The frog, which lives in rainforests ranging from southern Mexico all the way down to the northwestern tip of Colombia in South America, may look like it's asleep, but it is observing its surroundings, thanks to a translucent eyelid. This allows the amphibian to spy on its habitat and look out for predators, like birds, snakes, and large spiders. When the frog senses movement, it opens its special eyelids to reveal its bright red eyeballs—in hopes of startling a hungry predator.

Closed

A SEE-THROUGH EYELID LETS RED-EYED TREE FROGS CHECK OUT THEIR SURROUNDINGS WHILE THEY REST.

Open

OPEN WIDE! RED-EYED TREE FROGS REVEAL THEIR BRIGHT RED EYES TO ALARM PREDATORS.

TINY EARS, BIG NOSE

It's almost impossible to hear anything over a thundering waterfall—unless you're a hole-in-the-head frog living in a rainforest in Southeast Asia. This frog is named for markings that look like, well, holes in its head. But the *actual* holes are for ears that give it super hearing.

The hole-in-the-head frog is one of just two frog species that can croak out and hear ultrasonic calls, or calls at a pitch too high to be heard by humans and other animals. This adaptation likely allows the frogs to communicate above rumbling rivers and streams in their habitat.

HOLE-IN-THE-HEAD FROGS CAN ONLY BE FOUND IN ONE PLACE ON THE PLANET: THE SOUTHEAST ASIAN ISLAND OF BORNEO.

MEGAMOUTH

African bullfrogs have huge mouths! When open, their mouths stretch approximately five inches (13 cm) wide, or over half the size of their eight-inch (20-cm)-long bodies. And these bullfrogs can fit plenty inside those mouths: Using their strong tongues to pull in prey like rodents, birds, and lizards, they pierce the animal with toothlike structures called odontodes, located on their lower jaws. Sharp teeth on the roof of a bullfrog's mouth keep the prey in place. Now the frog can take its time and enjoy the meal. Um, yum?

AN AFRICAN BULLFROG EYES ITS NEXT MEAL: A GIANT AFRICAN MILLIPEDE.

WEBBED FEET TO BEAT

In a rainforest in Southeast Asia, a Wallace's flying frog eyes a lower branch on a nearby tree. Rather than climbing down one tree and up the other to reach the branch, the frog simply takes flight. It splays out its four webbed feet as it leaps down. Membranes between its toes trap air from underneath to form tiny parachute-like shapes. Loose skin flaps on either side of the frog's body catch more air as it falls. It glides to the other tree before making a smooth landing.

Wide, sticky toe pads create cushions to soften the impact as Wallace's flying frogs land. These frogs have been spotted gliding 50 feet (15 m). "They probably glide that far to escape predators," said Phil Bishop, a scientific adviser for the Amphibian Survival Alliance. Traveling the extra distance beats becoming a snack.

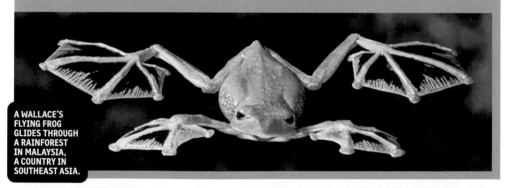

A WALLACE'S FLYING FROG GLIDES THROUGH A RAINFOREST IN MALAYSIA, A COUNTRY IN SOUTHEAST ASIA.

AT CLOSE RANGE, IT'S HARD TO MISS A DYEING POISON FROG'S BOLD COLOR PATTERN.

COOLEST SKIN FOR THE WIN

Up close, a dyeing poison frog's blue, yellow, and black hues are hard to miss. But this amphibian, found in the northeastern rainforests of South America, doesn't have to worry much about predators. Its skin is packed with poison that can paralyze or even kill other animals; the colors are a warning that the frog is toxic if eaten. The poison from certain species historically has been used on the tips of hunting darts, giving poison frogs their other common name, "poison dart frogs." *Yikes.*

SUPER SNAKES

Snakes are masters of disguise, skilled hunters, and champion eaters. More than 3,000 species of these reptiles slither around the world. Check out these surprising facts about snakes.

AMAZON TREE BOA

AFRICAN SAW-SCALED VIPER

SNAKES SMELL WITH THEIR TONGUES.

Smell that mouse? A snake uses its tongue to smell. It flicks its long, forked tongue to pick up chemical molecules from the air, ground, or water. The tongue carries the smelly molecules back to two small openings—called the Jacobson's organ—in the roof of the snake's mouth. Cells in the Jacobson's organ analyze the scent. Mmm, lunch!

SNAKE VENOM CAN KILL.

By sinking two hollow, pointy fangs into their prey, many snakes inject venom to paralyze or kill victims before devouring them. Africa's puff adder is thought to be one of the world's deadliest snakes. Up to six feet (1.8 m) long and weighing as much as 13 pounds (6 kg), the puff adder strikes fast. Its venom can cause severe pain, tissue damage, and even death in humans. It's a snake to be respected ... from a distance.

PUFF ADDER

SNAKES CHANGE THEIR SKIN.

Snakes literally grow out of their skin. Every few months, most start rubbing against the ground or tree branches. Starting at the mouth, a snake slithers out of its too-tight skin. Like a sock, the skin comes off inside out. Voilà—the snake has a fresh, shiny look. Nice makeover.

GOLDEN TREE SNAKE

DIONE RAT SNAKE

CONSTRICTORS GIVE WICKED HUGS.

Boas, anacondas, pythons, and other snakes called constrictors are amazing squeezers. This kind of snake wraps its muscular body around a victim and squeezes until the animal suffocates. The twisted talent comes from muscles attached to 200 or more vertebrae in a snake's backbone. (Humans are born with only 33 vertebrae.)

DEADLY CUTIES

JAVAN SLOW LORIS

Nine species of slow lorises live throughout Southeast Asia.

This adorable animal has some seriously KILLER traits.

Don't be fooled by the crazy-cute slow loris. The snuggly looking creature is the only venomous primate on the planet—and its bite packs enough toxin to kill prey in just a few seconds. The toxin is also powerful enough to kill or severely harm humans, but it's very rare for the slow loris to bite people without first being provoked.

And venom isn't the only killer move the slow loris has. Check out three ways the adorable slow loris is actually downright dangerous.

KILLER LOOKS
A slow loris's sweet face markings might say "Oh, he-ey!" to you, but they say "Danger!" to other animals. To a potential predator like a large snake or hawk-eagle, the markings are like flashing red lights near the loris's mouth, warning that the loris could fight back with its deadly venom.

HIDDEN HUNTER
Huge eyes make slow lorises look harmlessly huggable. But these peepers also make them effective hunters. A special layer behind the retina called a tapetum lucidum (pronounced tuh-PEE-tum loo-SUH-dum) reflects light back through the retina and gives lorises better nighttime vision for nocturnal hunting.

TWICE AS TOXIC
Unlike other venomous animals that produce venom in one place, slow lorises produce toxins in two places: in their saliva and in a gland in their underarms. When lorises lick that gland and mix it with their venomous saliva, they cook up an even more toxic mixture they can inject with a single bite.

A JAVAN SLOW LORIS HANGS OUT IN THE TREE CANOPY OF JAVA, AN ISLAND IN INDONESIA.

SURF Pups

5 WAYS COASTAL WOLVES THRIVE BY THE SEA

Coastal wolves are valued in many Indigenous cultures; some groups consider them ancestors.

Wolves often howl in a chorus.

A wolf steps out onto a sandy beach. Catching a scent, it paws at the wet sand in search of a buried clam. *Crunch!* The wolf crushes the clam in its jaws and swallows. Still hungry, it splashes into the ocean waves and swims to a nearby island to find more food. Wolves on the beach might sound strange, but these special gray wolves have been living seaside for thousands of years. Known as coastal wolves, about 2,000 of these individuals make their homes among the islands and coastal rainforest of western British Columbia in Canada. (Another population lives in Southeast Alaska, U.S.A.) "Their environment is so different from that of any other wolf," wildlife researcher Chris Darimont says. "So they've had to adapt to this unique place." Check out five ways these howlers are living their best life on the beach.

1

BEACH HAIR, DON'T CARE

Unlike most gray wolves, coastal wolves' fur is often streaked with reddish orange highlights. The color matches seaweed found on the shore, likely helping to camouflage these predators as they hunt on the beach.

Coastal wolves also have less underfur than other gray wolves. The cottony fluff helps wolves living in snowy places like Montana, U.S.A., keep warm, but coastal wolves' habitat is so mild that they don't need the extra layer.

2

A wolf's sense of smell is about a hundred times more sensitive than a human's.

SEA SIZE

About the size of a German shepherd, coastal wolves are about 20 percent smaller than gray wolves living in North American forests. Scientists think it could be because these seafood-eaters don't need the extra strength. After all, coastal wolves are wrestling otters, not gigantic moose like their gray wolf cousins. "They aren't chasing massive prey, so they don't need the large body size to take them down," Darimont says.

SWIM TEAM CHAMPS

One small island usually isn't big enough for coastal wolves to find and eat the seven pounds (3 kg) of food they need each day. So the canines dog-paddle from island to island in search of more food. "They swim between islands like we walk on sidewalks," conservationist Ian McAllister says. And these wolves really are super swimmers. Scientists have spotted them on nearly every one of the thousand islands and rocky outcrops in the area, McAllister says, sometimes swimming up to 7.5 miles (12 km) in between each strip of land.

3

Some coastal wolves can get 90 percent of their diet from the sea.

4

5

SPLASHY SURPRISE

Gray wolves that live in open habitats like the tundra often hunt by chasing big, hoofed animals across a wide plain, Darimont says. But that style of hunting doesn't work on a coast that's full of thick rainforest or tiny islands too small to run across. Instead, they often sneak up on prey—then pounce. "The seals haul out of the ocean to get away from killer whales," McAllister says. "But on land, they're not safe from ambushing wolves."

SEAFOOD, PLEASE!

What's to eat? Coastal wolves use their powerful sense of smell to find whatever snacks the ocean served up that day. They might dig in the sand for crabs and clams, feast on fish eggs stuck to kelp, or sneak up on larger animals like sunbathing seals or otters.

Others get their fill of fish just from salmon. "They wait in the shallows where the salmons' backsides are poking out, then snap up the tastiest-looking fish they can find," Darimont says. A coastal wolf might scarf down 10 salmon in one morning. Talk about fish breath!

7 Bee Facts to Buzz About

HONEYBEE

1 Bees have a special **stomach** for **carrying nectar.**

2 Some **bees** may **sleep** on **flowers.**

3 A bee beats its **wings** up to **12,000 times** each **minute.**

4 Male **bees** can't **sting.**

5 In summer, a single **hive** can **house** up to **80,000 honeybees.**

6 The **alkali bee** can visit up to **6,000 flowers** a day.

7 Sweat **bees** like the **taste** of human **perspiration.**

SPIDERWEB STATS

A single spider can eat up to 2,000 insects every year. How do spiders catch all those tasty treats? Using silk from special glands called spinnerets, spiders weave sticky webs to trap their delicious prey. But this silk can do much more than simply catch dinner. Stick around and learn more about the incredible spiderweb.

.00004–.00016
INCH (.001–.004 mm)
Thickness of silk a spider uses to build webs

-76°F TO 302°F
(-60°C to 150°C)
The extreme range of temperatures that a spider's silk can withstand

82
FEET (25 m)
Diameter of webs woven by Darwin's bark spiders—the largest spiderwebs in the world!

ORB WEAVER SPIDER

2–8
Pairs of spinnerets, the glands a spider uses to make silk

5
Number of times stronger a spider's silk is compared to steel of the same diameter

Age of oldest spiderweb ever found embedded in amber

140 MILLION
YEARS OLD

BIG CATS

Not all wild cats are big cats, so what are big cats? To wildlife experts, they are tigers, lions, leopards, snow leopards, jaguars, cougars, and cheetahs. The first five are members of the genus *Panthera*. They can all unleash a mighty roar, and, as carnivores, they survive solely on the flesh of other animals. Thanks to powerful jaws; long, sharp claws; and daggerlike teeth, big cats are excellent hunters.

A lion cub plays on a fallen tree in Botswana.

The National Geographic Big Cats Initiative's goal is to stop the decline of lions and other big cats in the wild through research, conservation, education, and global awareness.
Parents and teachers:
For more information on this initiative, you can visit natgeo.org/bigcats with your young readers.

WHO'S WHO?

BIG CATS IN THE *PANTHERA* GENUS MAY HAVE a lot of features in common, but if you know what to look for, you'll be able to tell who's who in no time.

FUR

SNOW LEOPARD

Most tigers are orange-colored with vertical black stripes on their bodies. This coloring helps the cats blend in with tall grasses as they sneak up on prey. These markings are like fingerprints: No two stripe patterns are alike.

Lions have a light brown, or tawny, coat and a tuft of black hair at the end of their tails. When they reach their prime, most male lions have shaggy manes that help them look larger and more intimidating.

LION

A jaguar's coat pattern looks similar to that of a leopard, as both have dark spots called rosettes. The difference? The rosettes on a jaguar's torso have irregularly shaped borders and at least one black dot in the center.

TIGER

A snow leopard's thick, spotted fur helps the cat hide in its mountain habitat, no matter the season. In winter its fur is off-white to blend in with the snow, and in summer it's yellowish gray to blend in with plants and the mountains.

JAGUAR

LEOPARD

A leopard's yellowy coat has dark spots called rosettes on its back and sides. In leopards, the rosettes' edges are smooth and circular. This color combo helps leopards blend into their surroundings.

JAGUAR
100 to 250 pounds
(45 TO 113 KG)
5 to 6 feet long
(1.5 TO 1.8 M)

BENGAL TIGER
240 to 500 pounds
(109 TO 227 KG)
5 to 6 feet long
(1.5 TO 1.8 M)

LEOPARD
66 to 176 pounds
(30 TO 80 KG)
4.25 to 6.25 feet long
(1.3 TO 1.9 M)

SNOW LEOPARD
60 to 120 pounds (27 TO 54 KG)
4 to 5 feet long (1.2 TO 1.5 M)

AFRICAN LION
265 to 420 pounds
(120 TO 191 KG)
4.5 to 6.5 feet long
(1.4 TO 2 M)

69

Weirdest. Cat. Ever.

THE SERVAL MIGHT LOOK STRANGE, BUT THAT'S A GOOD THING WHEN IT COMES TO HUNTING.

SERVALS CAN CATCH UP TO 30 FROGS IN THREE HOURS WHILE HUNTING IN WATER.

SERVAL KITTENS STAY WITH MOM UP TO TWO YEARS BEFORE LIVING ON THEIR OWN.

Servals can chirp, purr, hiss, snarl, and growl.

A serval sits patiently in a grassy field, swiveling its head back and forth like a watchful owl. The predator is scanning the savanna for a meal not with its eyes, but with its oversize ears. An unseen rodent stirs under the thick brush, and the wild cat tenses. It crouches on its legs and feet before launching up and over the tall grass. Guided only by sound, the serval lands directly on the once invisible rat.

Thanks to its extra-long legs, stretched-out neck, and huge ears, the serval is sometimes called the "cat of spare parts." This wild cat might look weird to some people. "But put together, their bizarre-looking body parts make them really successful hunters," says Christine Thiel-Bender, a biologist who studies servals in their African home.

In fact, servals catch prey in more than half their attempts, making them one of the best hunters in the wild cat kingdom. That's about 20 percent better than lions hunting together in a pride.

ALL EARS

The serval's big ears are key to the animal's hunting success. Servals rely on sound more than any other sense when they're on the prowl. Thanks to their jumbo ears—the biggest of any wild cat's relative to body size—a serval can hear just about any peep on the savanna. (If a person had ears like a serval's, they'd be as big as dinner plates!) To make the most of their super hearing, servals avoid creating noise while hunting. So instead of stalking prey like some cats do, servals squat in clearings and sit still—sometimes for several hours—as they listen for food.

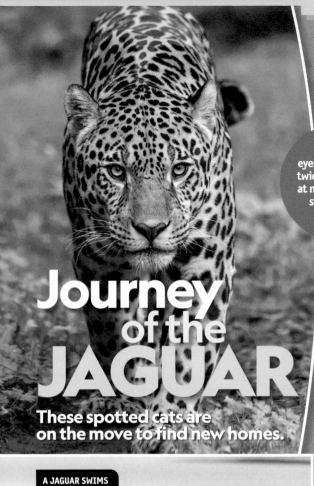

Journey
of the
JAGUAR

These spotted cats are on the move to find new homes.

> A jaguar's eyesight is nearly twice as powerful at night to help it stalk prey in the dark.

The jaguar once prowled through more than seven million square miles (18 million sq km) stretching through North and South America. But in the past century, things like cattle ranching and the growth of cities have cut this territory in half. Few jaguars have been seen in the United States, and their southern range now barely extends into Argentina. The separation of these pockets of jaguars means fewer mates will meet—and fewer cubs will be born each year.

SAFE PASSAGE

Over the past decade or so, special corridors of land were set aside to allow jaguars to get from one habitat to another. But as humans have cleared trees, shrubs, and grass along these corridors, they've become more dangerous for the jaguars as they have nowhere to hide. As a result, wildlife ecologist Alan Rabinowitz launched the Jaguar Corridor Initiative (JCI) to protect the "superhighway" that the jaguars were using—and therefore their entire range.

HOME OF THE RANCH

Another key to keeping the jaguars safe? Educating farmers who live along the corridors. In the past, when jaguars traveled past a pasture of cattle, they may have tried to eat the easy prey, which would make the cats a target for ranchers protecting their herd. But thanks to new guidelines on keeping farm animals fenced in at night, both the cats and the livestock are safer.

A JAGUAR SWIMS ACROSS THE PARAGUAY RIVER IN BRAZIL.

> Jaguar moms typically give birth to two to four cubs at a time.

A JAGUAR STALKS PREY IN BRAZIL'S CUIABÁ RIVER.

TIGERS in the Snow

These wild cats survive the cold of eastern Russia.

Many Amur tigers have beachfront access—they live in Russian forests on the edge of the Sea of Japan.

Silently moving through the trees, a tigress stalks her prey. Deep snow covers the ground, and with each step the big cat sinks to her belly. She knows the snow will muffle any sounds, so she can sneak up on a wild boar that is rooting around for pine nuts. A few yards away, the tiger pauses, crouches, and then launches her 280-pound (127-kg) body toward her prey. Snow sprays up with each leap as she prepares to pounce on the boar with her plate-size paws. A powdery cloud fills the air. Then the snow settles, revealing the three-foot (0.9-m)-long tail and orange, black, and white body. Now stained red, the tigress grasps the boar in her mouth.

She carries her catch behind some larch trees, and her two cubs join her from a nearby hill. Camouflaged in the trees, they were watching their mother hunt. Soon, they'll start hunting for themselves. But for now, they are content with the meal their mother has provided, followed by a nap.

These Siberian, or Amur, tigers live in the eastern reaches of Russia—farther north than any other tiger subspecies. A thick coat of fur insulates their bodies from the freezing winter temps. In summer, their coat blends in with the forest, making them nearly impossible to see.

HUNGER GAMES

The tiger trio is among some 600 Amur tigers that researchers think are left in the wild. As recently as 50 years ago, there were plenty of deer and wild boar, staples of a tiger's diet. Today, these prey animals are harder to find. People hunt

A TIGER CUB STICKS WITH MOM FOR AT LEAST 18 MONTHS.

them, and logging companies and fires destroy the forest where they live. Some tiger habitat is protected, but the cats wander beyond these safe zones in search of prey. Half of all tiger cubs die young because they are sick, killed by hunters, or orphaned. Cubs that survive leave Mom at about 18 months old, relying on the hunting skills they learned growing up. Sometimes a young male must travel far to find unclaimed land that has enough food. And odds are that his journey will take him through areas where people live.

TROUBLESHOOTING

It is late winter when the male tiger leaves his mother's care. When he scratches against a tree, he catches his paw on something. He's walked into a wire snare, and the more he moves, the tighter it gets. A little while later, he hears voices. People. They stay behind the trees, and one of them raises a gun. The tiger roars at the sharp pain in his backside, then lies down and falls asleep. He's been shot by a researcher's tranquilizer gun, not by a hunter. Unable to find enough food in the snowy forest, this tiger started taking livestock and dogs in a nearby town. Dale Miquelle and his team are called in to fix the problem. "Relocating them gives them a second chance," Miquelle says. Otherwise, the farmer would track down the tiger and shoot him.

The researchers quickly weigh and measure the tranquilized tiger. Then they fit a collar with a radio transmitter around his neck. This will let Miquelle's team keep track of the tiger's whereabouts for at least three years.

NEW TERRITORY

Two hours later, the tiger wakes up in the back of a truck about 150 miles (241 km) from the town. The cage gate opens, and the wild cat leaps out. Unfamiliar with the territory, he searches for signs of other tigers. He comes across a birch tree with a strong odor. Another male sprayed the tree and left scrape marks and urine on the ground to tell others "Occupied. Keep moving."

The young tiger walks on. Miquelle's team monitors his movements using signals from the radio collar. They hope he can find food, avoid other males, find his own territory, and eventually mate with a local female. The tiger spots a deer ahead. Melting snow drips from the trees, masking his footsteps as he ambushes his prey. His odds just got a little better.

THIS TIGER'S SCRATCHES ON TREES ARE MESSAGES FOR OTHER TIGERS.

ICE-COLD WATER QUENCHES THIS TIGER'S THIRST.

In the 1930s, only about 30 Amur tigers were left in the wild.

Naughty PETS

THE TUNA I ADDED TO THIS TEA MAKES IT VERY TASTY.

C'MON, LEMME IN. I DIDN'T ROLL IN THE GRASS THAT LONG.

NAME Bella

FAVORITE ACTIVITY
Fishing at teatime

FAVORITE TOY
Squiggly rubber worm bait

PET PEEVE Coffee

NAME Ed

FAVORITE ACTIVITY
Dyeing his fur green with grass stains

FAVORITE TOY Food coloring

PET PEEVE Brown winter grass

IT'S SO FUNNY WHEN THEY THINK I'M LOST IN THE COUCH.

REMOTE LEARNING ISN'T JUST FOR KIDS.

NAME Cullen

FAVORITE ACTIVITY
Playing hide-and-seek without his people knowing it

FAVORITE TOY Toilet paper tube to nibble on

PET PEEVE Locked cage

NAME Ito

FAVORITE ACTIVITY
Changing the virtual background

FAVORITE TOY
Mouse

PET PEEVE
Low battery power

PET TALES

Dog Protects Piglet

Chew Barka   Hairy Pawter

Do pets know their names?

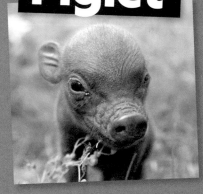

Hörstel, Germany

Roland Adam wasn't sure what to do when he found an orphaned newborn Vietnamese potbellied pig alone and shivering on his farm. But Katjinga the Rhodesian ridgeback did. She snuggled up to the pint-size pig (now called Paulinchen), cleaning the pig with her tongue and nursing her as she would her own puppy. "Katjinga lay down, fed her, and kept her warm," Adam says. In fact, this isn't the first time Katjinga cuddled up with orphaned animals: She's also tended rabbits and ducks. "We even found her warming up one of our sheep that was sick," Adam says. Sounds like Katjinga was one protective pooch!

Yes—kind of. Pets don't speak human, but they do recognize sounds. One study has shown that pets know the difference between the names we've given them and similar-sounding words, even when said by a stranger. Scientists think that dogs and cats learn to listen for the sounds that make up their name because responding often means cuddles and treats. So why does your cat not always come when it's called? It likely knows its name—but it's probably ignoring you.

75

HoW TO SPEAk CaT

Come on, let's play!

Cats are on a roll. All around the globe, kitties now rank as the most popular pet. And no wonder: Everyone feels good when a friendly cat purrs, rubs against their legs, or snuggles in their lap.

But let's get one thing straight. Cats are not dogs! They look, act, and (we're pretty sure) think differently. Dogs depend on us to take care of them; cats maintain a lot of their wildness.

Because they're so independent, cats hide their feelings. Unless you know exactly what to look for, a happy cat and a miserable one can look very much the same. But cats do communicate. Check out how to read your cat's moods by recognizing four ways it "talks" to you.

THE PLAYFUL KITTEN

Kittens are always in the mood for fun. They spend almost every waking minute playing. They love to run and chase, pounce and wrestle, attack and retreat. At about seven weeks old, kittens learn the signs for inviting each other to play. Watch for a kitten with a relaxed, content look. That's its play face. Rolling onto its back or standing up on its hind legs are also signs that a cat's ready for fun. Holding its tail like a question mark and hopping sideways might be other ways of telling a playmate to let the games begin!

Aah. This is the life.

HAPPY CAT

You can tell a happy cat by its relaxed body, half-perked ears, and droopy whiskers. It'll greet you with a chipper "Hi, there" meow and a straight-up tail. Then it'll jump on your lap, purr loudly, and move its body under your hand. Keep your cat happy by petting it—just where it likes it.

All cats, no matter the breed, are born with blue eyes. Their true color appears at about 12 weeks.

Some of the best cat toys are free: a crumpled-up newspaper or a paper bag.

CAT ON THE HUNT

Shh! This cat is after something. You can tell by his intense stare, twitching tail, and forward-pointing ears and whiskers. All his senses are alert as he crouches low to the ground and pads silently toward his prey. Hunting is difficult, dangerous work. Humans have long admired cats for their courage and predatory skills. Without cats, early Egyptians would have lost much of their food supply to rats. So would sailors, who took the little rodent killers with them to sea, spreading the animals around the world. Your cat can hunt pesky houseflies or other insects that sneak into your home—keeping both you and your cat happy.

Cats hunt what they can get: rats in New York City; lizards in Georgia, U.S.A.; and baby turtles on Africa's Seychelles islands.

Heh, heh. He can't hear me coming.

Check out this book!

THE FRUSTRATED FELINE

A frustrated cat will have wide eyes and forward, pricked ears. It'll bat its paws, its teeth might chatter, and it may slowly thrash its tail. Like humans, cats get frustrated when they don't get what they expect. For instance, an indoor cat stares out the window at a bird, but she can't reach the prey outside. The longer the cat sits and watches, the greater her frustration, until she's ready to attack someone.

A cat can get frustrated often. But if you know the signs, you can turn your irritated cat into a contented kitty. When she's annoyed that she can't get to a bird, distract your feline by playing with a fishing-pole toy. Let your kitty catch the "mouse" at the end, and that bird will soon be forgotten.

The word for "cat" is *mao* in Chinese, *gatto* in Italian, *poes* in Dutch, and *kedi* in Turkish.

How to SPEAK CaT

A GUIDE TO DECODING CAT LANGUAGE

I'd rather be hunting.

Prehistoric TIMELINE

HUMANS HAVE WALKED on Earth for some 300,000 years, a mere blip in the planet's 4.5-billion-year history. A lot has happened during that time. Earth formed, and oxygen levels rose in the millions of years of the Precambrian time. The productive Paleozoic era gave rise to hard-shell organisms, vertebrates, amphibians, and reptiles.

Dinosaurs ruled Earth in the mighty Mesozoic. And 66 million years after dinosaurs became extinct, modern humans emerged in the Cenozoic era. From the first tiny mollusks to the dinosaur giants of the Jurassic and beyond, Earth has seen a lot of transformation.

THE PRECAMBRIAN TIME

4.5 billion to 541 million years ago

- Earth (and other planets) formed from gas and dust left over from a giant cloud that collapsed to form the sun. The giant cloud's collapse was triggered when nearby stars exploded.
- Low levels of oxygen made Earth a suffocating place.
- Early life-forms appeared.

THE PALEOZOIC ERA

541 million to 252 million years ago

- The first insects and other animals appeared on land.
- 450 million years ago (mya), the ancestors of sharks began to swim in the oceans.
- 430 mya, plants began to take root on land.
- More than 360 mya, amphibians emerged from the water.
- Slowly, the major landmasses began to come together, creating Pangaea, a single supercontinent.
- By 300 mya, reptiles had begun to dominate the land.

What Killed the Dinosaurs?

It's a mystery that's boggled the minds of scientists for centuries: What happened to the dinosaurs? Although various theories have bounced around, a recent study confirms that the most likely culprit is an asteroid or comet that created a giant crater. Researchers say that the impact set off a series of natural disasters like tsunamis, earthquakes, and temperature swings that plagued the dinosaurs' ecosystems and disrupted their food chains. This, paired with intense volcanic eruptions that caused drastic climate changes, is thought to be why half of the world's species—including the dinosaurs—died in a mass extinction.

DINO TIMES

THE MESOZOIC ERA

252 million to 66 million years ago

The Mesozoic era, or the age of the reptiles, consisted of three consecutive time periods (shown below). This is when the first dinosaurs began to appear. They would reign supreme for more than 150 million years.

TRIASSIC PERIOD

252 million to 201 million years ago

- The first mammals appeared. They were rodent-size.
- The first dinosaur appeared.
- Ferns were the dominant plants on land.
- The giant supercontinent of Pangaea began breaking up toward the end of the Triassic.

JURASSIC PERIOD

201 million to 145 million years ago

- Giant dinosaurs dominated the land.
- Pangaea continued its breakup, and oceans formed in the spaces between the drifting landmasses, allowing sea life, including sharks and marine crocodiles, to thrive.
- Conifer trees spread across the land.

CRETACEOUS PERIOD

145 million to 66 million years ago

- The modern continents developed.
- The largest dinosaurs developed.
- Flowering plants spread across the landscape.
- Mammals flourished, and giant pterosaurs ruled the skies over small birds.
- Temperatures grew more extreme. Dinosaurs lived in deserts, swamps, and forests from the Antarctic to the Arctic.

THE CENOZOIC ERA—TERTIARY PERIOD

66 million to 2.6 million years ago

- Following the dinosaur extinction, mammals rose as the dominant species.
- Birds continued to flourish.
- Volcanic activity was widespread.
- Temperatures began to cool, eventually ending in an ice age.
- The period ended with land bridges forming, which allowed plants and animals to spread to new areas.

DINO Classification

Classifying dinosaurs and all other living things can be a complicated matter, so scientists have devised a system to help with the process. Dinosaurs are put into groups based on a very large range of characteristics.

Scientists put dinosaurs into two major groups: the bird-hipped ornithischians and the lizard-hipped saurischians.

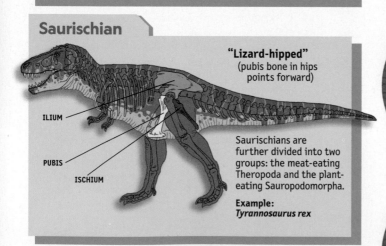

Ornithischian

"Bird-hipped"
(pubis bone in hips points backward)

ILIUM

PUBIS

ISCHIUM

Ornithischians have the same-shaped pubis as birds of today, but today's birds are actually more closely related to the saurischians.

Example: *Styracosaurus*

Saurischian

"Lizard-hipped"
(pubis bone in hips points forward)

ILIUM

PUBIS

ISCHIUM

Saurischians are further divided into two groups: the meat-eating Theropoda and the plant-eating Sauropodomorpha.

Example: *Tyrannosaurus rex*

Within these two main divisions, dinosaurs are then separated into orders and then families, such as Stegosauria. Like other members of the Stegosauria, *Stegosaurus* had spines and plates along its back, neck, and tail.

VELOCIRAPTOR **MEANS "SPEEDY THIEF."**

THERE WERE NO *T. REX* IN SOUTH AMERICA.

TRICERATOPS **HAD 800 TEETH.**

IT TOOK A DINOSAUR EGG UP TO SIX MONTHS TO HATCH!

4 NEWLY DISCOVERED DINOS

Humans have been searching for—and discovering—dinosaur remains for hundreds of years. In that time, at least 1,000 species of dinos have been found all over the world, and thousands more may still be out there waiting to be unearthed. Recent finds include a *Yamatosaurus izanagii*, a hadrosaur discovered by an amateur fossil hunter in Japan.

1

Llukalkan aliocranianus
(Saurischian)

Name Meaning: *Llukalkan* means "one who causes fear" in the Mapuche Indigenous language.

Length: 16 feet (5 m)

Time Range: Late Cretaceous

Where: Argentina

2

Yamatosaurus izanagii
(Ornithischian)

Name Meaning: *Yamato* is the name for ancient Japan and *Izanagi* is the god who created the Japanese islands according to Japanese mythology.

Length: 23–26 feet (7–8 m)

Time Range: Late Cretaceous

Where: Japan

3

Tlatolophus galorum
(Ornithischian)

Name Meaning: *Tlatolophus* is a mix of two words—"word" in the Indigenous language Nahuatl and "crest" in Greek.

Length: 26.2–39.4 feet (8–12 m)

Time Range: Late Cretaceous

Where: Mexico

4

Arackar licanantay
(Saurischian)

Name Meaning: Atacameña bones in the Kunza Indigenous language

Length: 26 feet (8 m)

Time Range: Late Cretaceous

Where: Chile

DINO SECRETS REVEALED

Cool technology shows surprising discoveries about dinosaurs.

It's been 66 million years since the dinosaurs went extinct. And we're *still* learning new things about them, thanks to cutting-edge technology like lasers, 3D models, x-rays, and even robotics. For instance, experts are able to run extinct bones through a computer program to reconstruct missing bits and better understand how these animals actually functioned. Want to find out more? Check out three surprising dino discoveries that modern technology has helped scientists unearth.

SPINOSAURS HUNT PREHISTORIC SAWFISH.

River Beast

The Sahara seems like a strange place for a river-dwelling dinosaur. But more than 95 million years ago in what is now Morocco, a country in northern Africa, today's giant desert was actually lush with waterways deep enough for car-size fish to swim in. That's where *Spinosaurus*—a predator longer than *T. rex*—made its home.

At first, scientists believed that the sail-backed creature had some kind of watery lifestyle, perhaps hunting fish like a bear would. But after finding a partial skeleton in 2014, experts assessed that the dinosaur probably spent a lot of time in water.

And the paleontologists didn't stop there. Returning to the site in 2018, they dug up a 17-foot (5-m) *Spinosaurus* tail—one vertebra at a time. (These are the same bones that make up your spine.) Using high-speed cameras and robots, they created an eight-inch (20-cm)-long mechanical tail, which they watched paddle in an enclosed waterway.

They discovered that the beast swam through rivers like a crocodile and could propel itself with eight times more power than related land dinosaurs. In fact, *Spinosaurus* is the first large dino found that had a tail designed for swimming.

A YOUNG *MUSSAURUS* CHECKS OUT TWO RHYNCHOSAURS (PRONOUNCED REEN-KOH-SOARS) AS AN ADULT LOOKS ON.

Baby Steps

Dinosaurs lumbered on all fours like a *Stegosaurus* or scrambled around on two legs like a *Tyrannosaurus*. But not all dinosaurs moved the same way as they grew up.

Paleontologist Alejandro Otero found that out by using a high-tech machine called a CT scanner to take x-rays of *Mussaurus* bones (pronounced moo-SOAR-us). He then turned the x-rays into 3D models using a computer program and then simulated how the dinosaur stood at different ages.

What'd the simulations show? It turns out that, like human babies, *Mussaurus* hatchlings walked on all fours—but started walking on their two hind limbs as they grew older.

A NEWLY HATCHED *DEINONYCHUS* CHICK IS WATCHED OVER BY DAD.

Cracking the Case

A fossilized dinosaur egg looks kind of like a rock. So scientists were surprised to discover that the eggs of *Deinonychus* (pronounced die-NAHN-uh-kus) were probably blue!

When exposed to heat and pressure, microscopic dino remains can transform into stuff that can last for millions of years. This lets scientists take a closer look. When paleobiologist Jasmina Wiemann struck the *Deinonychus* eggs with a laser, the light reflecting back revealed compounds that give modern eggs bright colors and speckling.

This helped her figure out the blue color, but it also suggested something else: Like modern birds with similarly colorful eggs, *Deinonychus* likely sat on open-air nests to hatch its eggs.

QUIZ WHIZ

Explore just how much you know about animals with this quiz!

Write your answers on a piece of paper. Then check them below.

1 An adult golden lion tamarin is about the size of a _____ .

a. squirrel
b. golden retriever
c. beaver
d. hamster

2 **True or false?** A pack of sea lions is called a raft.

3 Scientists think narwhals use their tusks to _____ .

a. jab and stun prey
b. stand out to potential mates
c. identify each other
d. all of the above

4 A kitten standing up on its hind legs is ready to _____ .

a. fight
b. play
c. run away
d. pounce

5 Which of the following is FALSE about arthropods?

a. They live in water and on land.
b. They have external skeletons, called exoskeletons.
c. They have segmented bodies with appendages.
d. They are the smallest group of animals.

Not **STUMPED** yet? Check out the *NATIONAL GEOGRAPHIC KIDS QUIZ WHIZ* collection for more crazy **ANIMAL** questions!

ANSWERS: 1. a; 2. True; 3. d; 4. b; 5. d

Wildly Good Animal Reports

Seahorse

Your teacher wants a written report on the seahorse. Not to worry. Use these organizational tools so you can stay afloat while writing a report.

STEPS TO SUCCESS: Your report will follow the format of a descriptive or expository essay (see page 129 for "How to Write a Perfect Essay") and should consist of a main idea, followed by supporting details and a conclusion. Use this basic structure for each paragraph, as well as the whole report, and you'll be on the right track.

1. Introduction
State your **main idea.**
Seahorses are fascinating fish with many unique characteristics.

2. Body
Provide **supporting points** for your main idea.
Seahorses are very small fish.
Seahorses are named for their head shape.
Seahorses display behavior that is rare among almost all other animals on Earth.

Then **expand** on those points with further description, explanation, or discussion.
Seahorses are very small fish.
Seahorses are about the size of an M&M at birth, and most adult seahorses would fit in a teacup.
Seahorses are named for their head shape.
With long, tubelike snouts, seahorses are named for their resemblance to horses.
A group of seahorses is called a herd.
Seahorses display behavior that is rare among almost all other animals on Earth.
Unlike most other fish, seahorses stay with one mate their entire lives. They are also among the only species in which dads, not moms, give birth to the babies.

3. Conclusion
Wrap it up with a **summary** of your whole paper.
Because of their unique shape and unusual behavior, seahorses are among the most fascinating and easily distinguishable animals in the ocean.

KEY INFORMATION

Here are some things you should consider including in your report:

What does your animal look like?
To what other species is it related?
How does it move?
Where does it live?
What does it eat?
What are its predators?
How long does it live?
Is it endangered?
Why do you find it interesting?

SEPARATE FACT FROM FICTION: Your animal may have been featured in a movie or in myths and legends. Compare and contrast how the animal has been portrayed with how it behaves in reality. For example, penguins can't dance the way they do in *Happy Feet*.

PROOFREAD AND REVISE: As you would do with any essay, when you're finished, check for misspellings, grammatical mistakes, and punctuation errors. It often helps to have someone else proofread your work, too, as that person may catch things you have missed. Also, look for ways to make your sentences and paragraphs even better. Add more descriptive language, choosing just the right verbs, adverbs, and adjectives to make your writing come alive.

BE CREATIVE: Use visual aids to make your report come to life. Include an animal photo file with interesting images found in magazines or printed from websites. Or draw your own! You can also build a miniature animal habitat diorama. Use creativity to help communicate your passion for the subject.

THE FINAL RESULT: Put it all together in one final, polished draft. Make it neat and clean, and remember to cite your references.

A volcano erupts in
Geldingadalur, Iceland.

SPACE and EARTH

15 COOL THINGS ABOUT PLANETS

A billion Earths could fit inside one of **SATURN'S thousands of rings.**

A planet is **a LARGE BODY of rock, gas, and other material** that **travels** around a **star (like our sun).**

JUPITER is our **solar system's BIGGEST PLANET—** all seven of the other **planets** could **fit inside it.**

Pieces of **MARS** have been found on **EARTH.**

Earth's name comes from the **Middle English word** *ertha,* meaning **"ground."**

The **surface temperature** on **Venus** is hot enough to **melt lead.**

PLUTO used to be our solar system's ninth planet. But in 2006, scientists reclassified it as a **DWARF PLANET.**

EARTH was **created** 4.5 billion years ago from a **mass** of **DUST** and **ROCK.**

EARTH moves around the **SUN** at **67,000** miles an hour—
(107,826 km/h)
that's more than **100 TIMES THE SPEED** of the fastest passenger airplane.

The Great Red Spot— a **hurricanelike storm** wider than **Earth**— has been blowing on **Jupiter** for **centuries.**

THE GREAT RED SPOT

Uranus has only **two seasons: summer**

and **winter.** Each lasts **42 Earth years.**

EUROPA, one of Jupiter's **79 known moons,** has **a salty, ice-covered OCEAN** that's almost 10 times deeper than **EARTH'S OCEANS.**

TITAN, one of **SATURN'S MOONS,** is **LARGER** than the planet **MERCURY.**

Olympus Mons— the highest peak on Mars— is **three times the size of Mount Everest.**

Because it's **closest** to the **sun, Mercury has the shortest year of our solar system's planets**— about **88 Earth days.**

89

PLANETS

MERCURY

VENUS

EARTH

MARS

CERES

JUPITER

SUN

MERCURY

Average distance from the sun:
  35,980,000 miles (57,900,000 km)

Position from the sun in orbit: 1st

Equatorial diameter: 3,030 miles
  (4,878 km)

Length of day: 59 Earth days

Length of year: 88 Earth days

Known moons: 0

VENUS

Average distance from the sun:
  67,230,000 miles (108,200,000 km)

Position from the sun in orbit: 2nd

Equatorial diameter: 7,520 miles
  (12,100 km)

Length of day: 243 Earth days

Length of year: 224.7 Earth days

Known moons: 0

EARTH

Average distance from the sun:
  93,000,000 miles (149,600,000 km)

Position from the sun in orbit: 3rd

Equatorial diameter: 7,900 miles
  (12,750 km)

Length of day: 24 hours

Length of year: 365 days

Known moons: 1

MARS

Average distance from the sun:
  141,633,000 miles (227,936,000 km)

Position from the sun in orbit: 4th

Equatorial diameter: 4,221 miles
  (6,794 km)

Length of day: 25 Earth hours

Length of year: 1.9 Earth years

Known moons: 2

This artwork shows the eight planets and five known dwarf planets in our solar system. The relative sizes and positions of the planets are shown but not the relative distances between them.

SATURN

URANUS

NEPTUNE

PLUTO
· HAUMEA
· MAKEMAKE
ERIS

JUPITER

Average distance from the sun:
483,682,000 miles (778,412,000 km)

Position from the sun in orbit: 6th

Equatorial diameter: 88,840 miles
(142,980 km)

Length of day: 9.9 Earth hours

Length of year: 11.9 Earth years

Known moons: 79*

SATURN

Average distance from the sun:
890,800,000 miles (1,433,600,000 km)

Position from the sun in orbit: 7th

Equatorial diameter: 74,900 miles
(120,540 km)

Length of day: 10.7 Earth hours

Length of year: 29.5 Earth years

Known moons: 82*

URANUS

Average distance from the sun:
1,784,000,000 miles (2,871,000,000 km)

Position from the sun in orbit: 8th

Equatorial diameter: 31,760 miles
(51,120 km)

Length of day: 17.2 Earth hours

Length of year: 84 Earth years

Known moons: 27

NEPTUNE

Average distance from the sun:
2,795,000,000 miles (4,498,000,000 km)

Position from the sun in orbit: 9th

Equatorial diameter: 30,775 miles
(49,528 km)

Length of day: 16 Earth hours

Length of year: 164.8 Earth years

Known moons: 14

*Includes provisional moons which await confirmation
and naming from the International Astronomical Union.

For information about dwarf planets,
see page 92.

DWARF PLANETS

Haumea

Eris

Pluto

Thanks to advanced technology, astronomers have been spotting many never-before-seen celestial bodies with their telescopes. One recent discovery? A population of icy objects orbiting the sun beyond Pluto. The largest, like Pluto itself, are classified as dwarf planets. Smaller than the moon but still massive enough to pull themselves into a ball, dwarf planets nevertheless lack the gravitational "oomph" to clear their neighborhood of other sizable objects. So, although larger, more massive planets pretty much have their orbits to themselves, dwarf planets orbit the sun in swarms that include other dwarf planets, as well as smaller chunks of rock or ice.

So far, astronomers have identified five dwarf planets in our solar system: Ceres, Pluto, Haumea, Makemake, and Eris. There are many more newly discovered dwarf planets that will need additional study before they are named. Astronomers are observing hundreds of newly found objects in the frigid outer solar system. As time and technology advance, the family of known dwarf planets will surely continue to grow.

CERES
Position from the sun in orbit: 5th
Length of day: 9.1 Earth hours
Length of year: 4.6 Earth years
Known moons: 0

PLUTO
Position from the sun in orbit: 10th
Length of day: 6.4 Earth days
Length of year: 248 Earth years
Known moons: 5

HAUMEA
Position from the sun in orbit: 11th
Length of day: 3.9 Earth hours
Length of year: 282 Earth years
Known moons: 2

MAKEMAKE
Position from the sun in orbit: 12th
Length of day: 22.5 Earth hours
Length of year: 305 Earth years
Known moons: 1*

ERIS
Position from the sun in orbit: 13th
Length of day: 25.9 Earth hours
Length of year: 561 Earth years
Known moons: 1

*Includes provisional moons, which await confirmation and naming from the International Astronomical Union.

BLACK HOLES

BLACK HOLE →

A black hole really seems like a hole in space. Most black holes form when the core of a massive star collapses, falling into oblivion. A black hole has a stronger gravitational pull than anything else in the known universe. It's like a bottomless pit, swallowing anything that gets close enough to it to be pulled in. It's black because it pulls in light. Black holes come in different sizes. The smallest known black hole has a mass about three times that of the sun. The biggest one scientists have found so far has a mass about 66 billion times greater than the sun's. Really big black holes at the center of galaxies probably form by swallowing enormous amounts of gas over time. In 2019, scientists released the first image of a black hole's silhouette (left). The image, previously thought impossible to record, was captured using a network of telescopes.

What's the farthest we've sent something into space?

About 13.8 billion miles (22.2 billion km)! In 1977, NASA scientists launched two spacecraft, Voyager 1 and Voyager 2, to study the outer planets of our solar system and beyond. Today, Voyager 1 is the farthest thing we've sent into the universe, while Voyager 2 is a still impressive 11.5 billion miles (18.5 billion km) away. Each far-flung vessel carries a gold-plated disc with messages for extraterrestrials. What would a traveling alien get out of us Earthlings? Music, whale calls, greetings in 55 languages, and photos of astronauts, airplanes, and kids in classrooms. Each disc also has playing instructions in case aliens ever find this high-tech message in a bottle.

Hello!

Zdravstvuyte!

Konnichiwa!

¡Hola!

Bonjour!

Saluti!

EARTH'S GREATEST HITS

DESTINATION SPACE

ALIEN SEA

Orange haze blurs the view outside your spaceship's window. You're descending to Titan, the largest of Saturn's 82 moons and 1.5 times bigger than Earth's moon. The smog beneath you thins, and you gasp in amazement: On the alien surface below, rivers flow through canyons. Waves crash in oceans. But Titan is nothing like home.

Your special spacecraft splashes down in Kraken Mare, Titan's largest sea. The pumpkin orange coastline is lined by craggy cliffs. Rocks dot the shore. But because it's a frigid minus 290°F (-179°C) here, the rocks are made of solid ice.

Rain begins to fall. It isn't water—it's methane and ethane. On Earth these are polluting gases. On Titan they form clouds and fall as rain that fills the rivers and oceans. You scoop up a sample of ocean liquid for a closer look: Scientists think there's a chance that Titan's seas might be home to alien life.

It'd be very strange if something did live here. On Earth everything living is partly made of water. Because there's no liquid water on Titan's surface, creatures here would be formed of methane or ethane. And because it's so cold, they'd move in slow motion.

Before you can get a good look at your sample, you hear a rumble. It's an ice volcano, thousands of feet tall. It shoots out a slurry of ice and ammonia (a chemical used as a cleaning product on Earth). You'd better get away before the icy blasts sink your spacecraft!

Destination
Titan

Location
Orbiting the planet Saturn

Distance
886 million miles
(1.43 billion km)
from Earth

Time to reach
3 years

Weather
minus 290°F (-179°C),
with scattered methane
rainstorms

THE MOON TITAN

At minus 290°F (-179°C), Titan seems way too cold for alien life. But it might not be. Even on Earth, creatures called **cryophiles thrive in below-freezing** temperatures. *Brr!*

Sky Calendar
2023

Jupiter

Annular solar
eclipse

Supermoon

- **JANUARY 3-4**
QUADRANTIDS METEOR SHOWER PEAK.
Featuring up to 40 meteors an hour, it is
the first meteor shower of every new year.

- **MAY 6-7**
ETA AQUARIDS METEOR SHOWER PEAK.
View about 30 to 60 meteors an hour.

- **JUNE 4**
VENUS AT GREATEST EASTERN
ELONGATION. Visible in the western sky
after sunset, Venus will be at its highest
point above the horizon in the evening sky.

- **JULY 3**
SUPERMOON, FULL MOON. The moon
will be full and closer to Earth in its orbit,
likely appearing bigger and brighter than
usual. Look for two more supermoons on
August 31 and September 29.

- **AUGUST 12-13**
PERSEID METEOR SHOWER PEAK.
One of the best—see up to 90 meteors
an hour! Best viewing is in the direction
of the constellation Perseus.

- **OCTOBER 14**
ANNULAR SOLAR ECLIPSE. The moon
is too far away to completely cover the
sun, so this eclipse appears as a ring
of light around a dark circle created by
the moon. Visible in southern Canada,
the southwestern United States, Central
America, Colombia, and Brazil. A partial
eclipse can be viewed throughout most
of North and South America.

- **OCTOBER 21-22**
ORIONID METEOR SHOWER PEAK.
View up to 20 meteors an hour. Look toward
the constellation Orion for the best show.

- **OCTOBER 28**
PARTIAL LUNAR ECLIPSE. Look for part
of the moon to darken as it passes through
Earth's penumbra—or partial shadow.
It will be visible in Europe, Asia, Africa, and
western Australia.

- **NOVEMBER 3**
JUPITER AT OPPOSITION. This is your best
chance to view Jupiter in 2023. The gas
giant will appear bright in the sky and be
visible throughout the night. Got a pair
of binoculars? You may be able to spot
Jupiter's four largest moons as well.

- **DECEMBER 13-14**
GEMINID METEOR SHOWER PEAK.
A spectacular show—see up to 120
multicolored meteors an hour!

- **2023—VARIOUS DATES**
VIEW THE INTERNATIONAL SPACE
STATION (ISS). Parents and teachers: You
can visit https://spotthestation.nasa.gov
to find out when the ISS will be flying over
your neighborhood.

*Dates may vary slightly depending on your
location. Check with a local planetarium for
the best viewing times in your area.*

A LOOK INSIDE

The distance from Earth's surface to its center is some 4,000 miles (6,437 km) at the Equator. There are four layers: a thin, rigid crust; the rocky mantle; the outer core, which is a layer of molten iron and nickel; and finally the inner core, which is believed to be mostly solid iron.

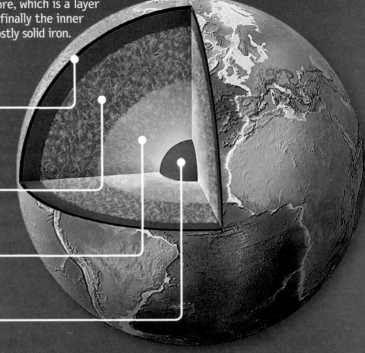

The **CRUST** includes tectonic plates, land-masses, and the ocean. Its average thickness varies from 5 to 25 miles (8 to 40 km).

The **MANTLE** is about 1,800 miles (2,900 km) of hot, thick, solid rock.

The **OUTER CORE** is liquid molten rock made mostly of iron and nickel.

The **INNER CORE** is a solid center made mostly of iron and nickel.

What if you could dig to the other side of Earth?

Got a magma-proof suit and a magical drill that can cut through any surface? Then you're ready to dig some 7,900 miles (12,714 km) to Earth's other side. First you'd need to drill about 25 miles (40 km) through the planet's ultra-tough crust to its mantle. The heat and pressure at the mantle are intense enough to turn carbon into diamonds—and to, um, crush you. If you were able to survive, you'd still have to bore 1,800 more miles (2,897 km) to hit Earth's Mars-size core that can reach 11,000°F (6093°C). Now just keep drilling through the core and then the mantle and crust on the opposite side until you resurface on the planet's other side. But exit your tunnel fast. A hole dug through Earth would close quickly as surrounding rock filled in the empty space. The closing of the tunnel might cause small earthquakes, and your path home would definitely be blocked. Happy digging!

ROCK STARS

Rocks and minerals are everywhere on Earth! And it can be a challenge to tell one from the other. So what's the difference between a rock and a mineral? A rock is a naturally occurring solid object made mostly from minerals. Minerals are solid, nonliving substances that occur in nature—and the basic components of most rocks. Rocks can be made of just one mineral or, like granite, of many minerals. But not all rocks are made of minerals: Coal comes from plant material, while amber is formed from ancient tree resin.

Igneous

Named for the Greek word meaning "from fire," igneous rocks form when hot, molten liquid called magma cools. Pools of magma form deep underground and slowly work their way to Earth's surface. If they make it all the way, the liquid rock erupts and is called lava. As the layers of lava build up, they form a mountain called a volcano. Typical igneous rocks include obsidian, basalt, and pumice, which is so chock-full of gas bubbles that it actually floats in water.

ANDESITE

GRANITE PORPHYRY

Metamorphic

Metamorphic rocks are the masters of change! These rocks were once igneous or sedimentary, but thanks to intense heat and pressure deep within Earth, they have undergone a total transformation from their original form. These rocks never truly melt; instead, the heat twists and bends them until their shapes substantially change. Metamorphic rocks include slate as well as marble, which is used for buildings, monuments, and sculptures.

MICA SCHIST

BANDED GNEISS

Sedimentary

When wind, water, and ice constantly wear away and weather rocks, smaller pieces called sediment are left behind. These are sedimentary rocks, also known as gravel, sand, silt, and clay. As water flows downhill, it carries the sedimentary grains into lakes and oceans, where they are deposited. As the loose sediment piles up, the grains eventually get compacted or cemented back together again. The result is new sedimentary rock. Sandstone, gypsum, limestone, and shale are sedimentary rocks that have formed this way.

LIMESTONE

HALITE

Identifying Minerals

With so many different minerals in the world, it can be a challenge to tell one from another. Fortunately, each mineral has physical characteristics that geologists and amateur rock collectors use to tell them apart. Check out the physical characteristics below: color, luster, streak, cleavage, fracture, and hardness.

Color

When you look at a mineral, the first thing you see is its color. In some minerals, this is a key factor because their colors are almost always the same. For example, azurite, below, is always blue. But in other cases, impurities can change the natural color of a mineral. For instance, fluorite, above, can be green, red, violet, and other colors as well. This makes it a challenge to identify by color alone.

FLUORITE

AZURITE

Luster

"Luster" refers to the way light reflects from the surface of a mineral. Does a mineral appear metallic, like gold or silver? Or is it pearly like orpiment, or brilliant like diamond? "Earthy," "glassy," "silky," and "dull" are a few other terms used to describe luster.

ORPIMENT

DIAMOND

Streak

The "streak" is the color of a mineral's powder. When minerals are ground into powder, they often have a different color than when they are in crystal form. For example, the mineral pyrite usually looks gold, but when it is rubbed against a ceramic tile called a "streak plate," the mark it leaves is black.

PYRITE

Cleavage

"Cleavage" describes the way a mineral breaks. Because the structure of a specific mineral is always the same, it tends to break in the same pattern. Not all minerals have cleavage, but the minerals that do, like this microcline, break evenly in one or more directions. These minerals are usually described as having "perfect cleavage." But if the break isn't smooth and clean, cleavage can be considered "good" or "poor."

MICROCLINE

GOLD

Fracture

Some minerals, such as gold, do not break with cleavage. Instead, geologists say that they "fracture." There are different types of fractures, and, depending on the mineral, the fracture may be described as jagged, splintery, even, or uneven.

Hardness

The level of ease or difficulty with which a mineral can be scratched refers to its "hardness." Hardness is measured using a special chart called the Mohs Hardness Scale. The Mohs scale goes from 1 to 10. Softer minerals, which appear on the lower end of the scale, can be scratched by the harder minerals on the upper end of the scale.

RATING	MINERAL NAME	EXAMPLES
1	TALC	BAR OF SOAP
2	GYPSUM	FINGERNAIL
3	CALCITE	COPPER PENNY
4	FLUORITE	SOFT IRON NAIL
5	APATITE	STEEL POCKETKNIFE BLADE
6	ORTHOCLASE	WINDOW GLASS
7	QUARTZ	HARDENED STEEL FILE
8	TOPAZ	TOPAZ
9	CORUNDUM	RUBY, SAPPHIRE
10	DIAMOND	DIAMOND

A NEW TYPE OF ROCK WAS RECENTLY DISCOVERED SOME FIVE (8 KM) MILES BENEATH THE SURFACE OF THE PACIFIC OCEAN.

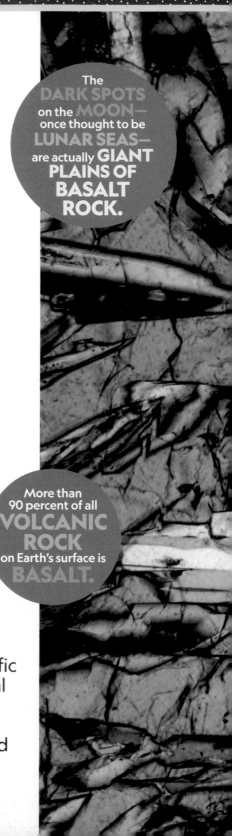

The **DARK SPOTS** on the **MOON**— once thought to be **LUNAR SEAS**— are actually **GIANT PLAINS OF BASALT ROCK.**

More than 90 percent of all **VOLCANIC ROCK** on Earth's surface is **BASALT.**

The never-before-seen basalt rock, found by drilling deep into the Pacific Ocean floor, has a different chemical and mineral makeup than anything ever discovered on Earth. Scientists think it was formed during huge and extra-hot volcanic eruptions some 50 million years ago.

BASALT forms when **VOLCANIC LAVA COOLS**— and it can take days to months for the rock to **SOLIDIFY.**

Experts say the **NEW ROCK** formed at the same time as the **RING OF FIRE**— the large horseshoe-shaped zone in the Pacific that's home to around 75 percent of the **PLANET'S VOLCANOES.**

A HOT TOPIC

WHAT GOES ON
INSIDE A STEAMING, BREWING VOLCANO?

If you could look inside a volcano, you'd see something that looks like a long pipe, called a conduit. This leads from inside the magma chamber under the crust up to a vent, or opening, at the top of the mountain. Some conduits have branches that shoot off to the side, called fissures.

When pressure builds from gases inside the volcano, the gases must find an escape, and they head up toward the surface! An eruption occurs when lava, gases, ash, and rocks explode out of the vent.

CRATER

VENT

CONDUIT

FISSURE

MAGMA CHAMBER

HARDENED LAVA AND ASH LAYERS

TYPES OF VOLCANOES

CINDER CONE VOLCANO
Eve Cone, Canada

Cinder cone volcanoes look like an upside-down bowl. They spew cinder and hot ash. Some of these volcanoes smoke and erupt for years at a time.

COMPOSITE VOLCANO
Licancábur, Chile

Composite volcanoes, or stratovolcanoes, form as lava, ash, and cinder from previous eruptions harden and build up over time. These volcanoes spit out pyroclastic flows, or thick explosions of hot ash that travel at hundreds of miles an hour.

SHIELD VOLCANO
Mauna Loa, Hawaii, U.S.A.

The gentle, broad slopes of a shield volcano look like an ancient warrior's shield. Its eruptions are often slower. Lava splatters and bubbles rather than shooting forcefully into the air.

LAVA DOME VOLCANO
Mount St. Helens, Washington, U.S.A.

Dome volcanoes have steep sides. Hardened lava often plugs the vent at the top of a dome volcano. Pressure builds beneath the surface until the top blows.

RING OF FIRE

Although volcanoes are found on every continent, most are located along an arc known as the Ring of Fire. This area, which forms a horseshoe shape in

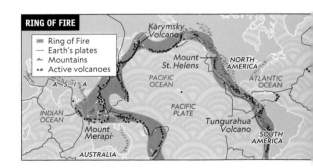

the Pacific Ocean, stretches some 24,900 miles (40,000 km). Several of the large, rigid plates that make up Earth's surface are found here, and they are prone to shifting toward each other and colliding. The result? Volcanic eruptions and earthquakes—and plenty of them. In fact, the Ring of Fire hosts 90 percent of the world's recorded earthquakes and about 75 percent of its active volcanoes.

BLUE VOLCANO

A strange eruption creates a dazzling light show.

The night is pitch-black. But the dark slopes of a hill inside the crater of Kawah Ijen volcano in Indonesia are lit up like a holiday light show. Tourists flock to the volcano to see what look like glowing blue rivers of lava. But they aren't rivers of lava. They're rivers of glowing sulfur.

Burning Blue

Glowing red lava flowing from an erupting volcano isn't unusual. Glowing sulfur is. Hot, sulfur-rich gases escape constantly from cracks called fumaroles in Kawah Ijen's crater. The gases cool when they hit the air. Some condense into liquid sulfur, which flows down the hillside. When the sulfur and leftover gases ignite, they burn bright blue and light up the night sky.

Scientists were told that sulfur miners on the volcano sometimes use torches to ignite the sulfur. The blue flames make Kawah Ijen popular with tourists, who watch from a safe distance. Scientists have also confirmed that some of the sulfur and gases burn naturally.

Volcano Miners

Sulfur is a common volcanic gas, and its chemical properties are used to manufacture many things, such as rubber. But sulfur is so plentiful in Kawah Ijen's crater that miners make a dangerous daily trek into the crater to collect it from a fumarole near an acid lake.

"The local people pipe the gases from the fumarole through ceramic pipes," says John Pallister, a retired geologist with the Cascades Volcano Observatory in Washington, U.S.A. He has walked into the crater himself, wearing a gas mask for protection against the clouds of acid that rise from the lake. "They spray the pipes with water from a spring," he says. This cools the gases and causes them to condense into molten sulfur. The sulfur then cools and hardens into rock.

Using this method, miners get more usable rock faster than if they just collected scattered pieces. They smash up the rock with metal bars, stuff the pieces into baskets, and carry them out of the crater on their backs. The loads are heavy—between 100 and 200 pounds (45 to 91 kg) apiece.

Reading the Danger Zone

Miners face another danger: a huge eruption. Kawah Ijen's last big eruption was almost 200 years ago, but the volcano is still active. A big eruption could endanger both miners and tourists.

Indonesian scientists want to find a way to predict a big eruption in time to keep everyone safe. But the deep acid lake makes it difficult to pick up the usual signals that warn of a coming volcanic eruption.

As scientists search for ways to predict this unusual volcano's behavior, Kawah Ijen's blue fires continue to attract audiences who appreciate the volcano's amazing glow.

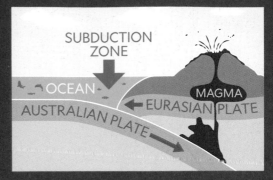

SUBDUCTION ZONE

OCEAN

AUSTRALIAN PLATE

EURASIAN PLATE

MAGMA

How Kawah Ijen Erupts

Earth's outer shell is broken into a jigsaw puzzle of several tectonic plates, or gigantic slabs of rock, that move constantly. In Indonesia, the oceanic **Australian plate** slips under the **Eurasian plate** at a **subduction zone.** As the Australian plate slides deep down, heat generated in Earth's interior makes the plate superhot, and parts of it melt. This melted rock, called **magma,** rises toward Earth's surface. Pressure on the magma lessens as it rises, allowing gases inside to expand, which can lead to explosive volcanic eruptions.

FUN FACTS ABOUT INDONESIA

Indonesia is a group of more than 17,500 islands off the coast of Southeast Asia. It's the largest country in the region.

When the volcano on the tiny Indonesian island of Krakatau erupted in August 1883, it could be heard thousands of miles away.

The *Rafflesia arnoldii,* the largest single flower in the world, grows in Indonesia. The flower smells like rotting meat, can grow to 3 feet (0.9 m) across, and weighs up to 24 pounds (10.9 kg).

Nearly 11 million people live in Jakarta, Indonesia's most populated city. That's almost 2.5 million more people than are living in New York City.

QUIZ WHIZ

Are your space and Earth smarts out of this world? Take this quiz!

Write your answers on a piece of paper. Then check them below.

1 **True or false?** Gravel, sand, silt, and clay are all ways to describe sedimentary rocks.

2 **In which ocean can you find the Ring of Fire?**
a. Pacific
b. Atlantic
c. Indian
d. Arctic

3 **Fill in the blank.** Indonesia is a group of more than 17,500 _____ off the coast of Southeast Asia.

4 An annular solar eclipse occurs as a ring of light around a dark circle created by _____.
a. the sun
b. the moon
c. Saturn
d. Venus

5 **True or false?** Earth moves around the sun at a pace that's more than 100 times the speed of the fastest passenger airplane.

Not **STUMPED** yet? Check out the *NATIONAL GEOGRAPHIC KIDS QUIZ WHIZ* book collection for more crazy **SPACE AND EARTH** questions!

ANSWERS: 1. True; 2. a; 3. islands; 4. b; 5. True

HOMEWORK HELP

ACE YOUR SCIENCE FAIR

You can learn a lot about science from books, but to really experience it firsthand, you need to get into the lab and "do" some science. Whether you're entering a science fair or just want to learn more on your own, there are many scientific projects you can do. So put on your goggles and lab coat, and start experimenting.

Most likely, the topic of the project will be up to you. So remember to choose something that is interesting to you.

THE BASIS OF ALL SCIENTIFIC INVESTIGATION AND DISCOVERY IS THE SCIENTIFIC METHOD. CONDUCT YOUR EXPERIMENT USING THESE STEPS:

Observation/Research—Ask a question or identify a problem.

Hypothesis—Once you've asked a question, do some thinking and come up with some possible answers.

Experimentation—How can you determine if your hypothesis is correct? You test it. You perform an experiment. Make sure the experiment you design will produce an answer to your question.

Analysis—Gather your results, and use a consistent process to carefully measure the results.

Conclusion—Do the results support your hypothesis?

Report Your Findings—Communicate your results in the form of a paper that summarizes your entire experiment.

Bonus!

Take your project one step further. Your school may have an annual science fair, but there are also local, state, regional, and national science fair competitions. Compete with other students for awards, prizes, and scholarships!

EXPERIMENT DESIGN
There are three types of experiments you can do.

MODEL KIT—a display, such as an "erupting volcano" model. Simple and to the point.

DEMONSTRATION—shows the scientific principles in action, such as a tornado in a wind tunnel.

INVESTIGATION—the home run of science projects, and just the type of project for science fairs. This kind demonstrates proper scientific experimentation and uses the scientific method to reveal answers to questions.

A woman climbs Grossvenediger, a glacier-covered mountain in the Austrian Alps.

AWESOME
EXPLORATION

THIS CLIFF
IS COVERED WITH
TENS OF THOUSANDS
OF DRAWINGS OF
ANCIENT ANIMALS
AND HUMANS,
DATING BACK MORE THAN
12,000 YEARS.

Experts say the **ARTWORK** was **COMPLETED** at the end of the ICE AGE, likely by the first humans to live in the western Amazon.

Scientists discovered the artwork on a cliff that extends for some eight miles (13 km) in the Amazon rainforest in Colombia. The drawings showcase now extinct animals that were alive and well at the time, as well as plants, humans, and geometric shapes.

There are also images of the **MASTODON,** the elephant's prehistoric relative, **GIANT SLOTHS,** and **ICE AGE HORSES.**

Also discovered in the area? The **REMAINS** of **FOOD** eaten by the artists, like **FRUITS, ALLIGATORS,** and **ARMADILLOS.**

Some of the **IMAGES** are so **HIGH ON THE CLIFF** that researchers **USED DRONES** to take pictures of them.

GET TO KNOW OUR
MIGHTY TREES!

As an "arbornaut," Dr. Meg Lowman spends much of her time in the treetops, studying life high in the branches. Here, the National Geographic Explorer and real-life Lorax shares more about her career and why she implores everyone to save the trees.

What is an arbornaut?

Like an astronaut explores outer space, an arbornaut explores the tops of the trees. It's a new science, but it's an essential one because half of the land species on our planet live in the treetops and never come to the ground. Trees are essential for our life in so many ways.

Have you always liked to climb trees?

Yes! As a kid, I built tree forts with my friends, and I have always just loved trees. Even though I do have a high respect for heights, I have an even bigger curiosity and amazement at the life up there.

What is one of your coolest discoveries in the treetops?

I have played a role in a lot of discoveries of new species of insects. I have even had some species named after me. There is a "Meg mite" out there, which is found in the forests of Ethiopia.

And it's not a discovery, but one of my proudest accomplishments is helping to create

and design canopy walkways, which can now be found all over the world. These walkways allow everyone, including people with mobility limitations, to have access to the treetops and discover their beauty.

Where is your favorite place to study trees?

The upper Amazon in Peru. It's so far from the mouth of the Amazon River that it is still fairly pristine. It hasn't been hit by poachers who cut down trees. I love it there because it has the highest biodiversity in the world.

What are your arbornaut essentials while in the field?

Water and Oreos! Just kidding, although I do love my cookies. I usually have a bucket dangling from my waist with a carabiner that holds tools like a tape measure, pencils, a notebook, a camera, binoculars, and little vials to collect important insects along the way. Oh, and I'll have a pooter, which is a tool that has a straw you suck on to grab bugs up without squishing them.

Why is it important to study trees?

They are the home to all of these species, and we have learned things like how leaves control climate for us, and how pollination occurs, and how it all impacts the environment. Trees literally keep us alive. We cannot survive on this planet without keeping our trees healthy.

THIS YEAR'S CHALLENGE

Trees take care of humans, so let's be good neighbors by taking care of trees in return! That starts by paying attention to them, which is the inspiration for this year's Almanac Challenge: Me as a Tree.

Discover your inner arbornaut! Have fun learning about different kinds of trees through reading, researching, and hands-on observation. Explore the arboreal world from roots to canopy to unearth the various features of different species. Think about which features you most appreciate and would want to have. Once you've imagined the kind of tree you'd want to be, tell us about your creation by writing a brief tree autobiography and drawing a tree selfie.

HINT: The more you understand trees, the more creative your tree autobiography can be!

➡ Get details and the official rules at **natgeokids.com/almanac.**

LAST YEAR'S CHALLENGE

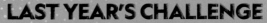

Kids care about the ocean and were eager to share the wonders of their favorite marine animals in last year's Our Awesome Ocean challenge. Here's what we learned from hundreds of stellar submissions:

• 86 percent were SHOW (drawing) and 14 percent were TELL (writing) and about half of those were both!

• The most popular creatures represented were dolphins, orcas, whales, sharks, sea turtles, sea otters, octopuses, and jellyfish.

• Less common favorites included coral, clown frogfish, flying fish, cuttlefish, catfish, snowflake clownfish, anglerfish, peacock mantis shrimp, and hermit crabs.

• Protecting ocean animals and their ecosystem is important to readers—and for the planet!

SHOW Grand Prize Drawing Winner, Aditi Sundar, age 10
TELL Grand Prize Writing Winner (featuring the vaquita),
    Oola Breen-Ryan, age 10

SEA TURTLE: ADITI'S DRAWING ENTRY INCLUDED A POEM ABOUT PRESERVING THE TURTLE'S OCEAN HABITAT.

See more entries online at **natgeokids.com/almanac.**

DARE TO EXPLORE

How quick-thinking scientists help protect the planet

A SLOW LORIS SPENDS TIME IN ITS RAINFOREST HOME ON THE INDONESIAN ISLAND OF SUMATRA.

SCIENTISTS FIT THIS MATSCHIE'S TREE KANGAROO WITH A TRACKING COLLAR SO THEY CAN STUDY ITS MOVEMENTS.

THE BIOLOGIST

Lisa Dabek studies endangered Matschie's tree kangaroos to learn how to better protect them in the wild. She talks about tracking one on the island of New Guinea.

"Even the most difficult challenges always have solutions. I have asthma, but I figured out how to hike the mountains of Papua New Guinea."

"I was with our local research team, trying to capture a tree kangaroo in a cloud forest, which is a rainforest high in the mountains. Like regular kangaroos, tree kangaroos have pouches and can hop, but they live in trees. We wanted to put a camera on one so we could see what it did in the treetops.

"To find one, we looked for claw marks on bark and kangaroo poop on the ground. We finally spotted a kangaroo 60 feet (18 m) up in a tree. Then one of the locals climbed up. We knew the tree kangaroo would react by leaping down as if a predator were close. I held my breath. From way up high, the tree kangaroo spread its limbs, glided down, and landed on the soft, mossy ground. She let us gently put a camera collar on her before she hopped away. When the collar fell off five days later, we retrieved it and had footage of her munching on orchids and cleaning her pouch a hundred feet (30 m) up in a tree!

"Little is known about these animals, and I want more people to discover them so we can save them together."

WANT TO BE A BIOLOGIST?

STUDY Biology, chemistry
WATCH *FernGully: The Last Rainforest*
READ *Quest for the Tree Kangaroo* by Sy Montgomery

THE WILDLIFE WARRIOR

Onkuri Majumdar is a wildlife conservationist who works to save animals stolen from the wild in parts of Asia and Africa. She recalls rescuing slow lorises seized by smugglers.

"We should strive to make the world a better place, especially for wild animals that can't stand up for themselves."

"When I was working in Thailand, my team heard that slow lorises—primates that live throughout Asia—were being poached, or illegally taken, from the wild. They were being sold so tourists could take photos with them and share the images on social media. Poachers also sell the shy, small animals as pets.

"To catch the criminals, we trained a local police team to track them. I was there for the arrest and rescue operation to make sure the animals were recovered safely. You could tell the lorises hadn't been well cared for. We wrapped them in blankets to keep them warm, but they were so stressed, they chewed up the cloth. I was relieved to deliver the animals to a wildlife rescue center where caregivers would help the lorises get healthy again.

"Moments like saving those lorises are why I do my job. I want to help catch poachers and encourage lawmakers to pass laws against these terrible crimes."

WANT TO BE A WILDLIFE WARRIOR?
STUDY Veterinary science, law enforcement
WATCH *The Fox and the Hound*
READ *A Wolf Called Wander* by Rosanne Parry

THE ADVENTURER

Carsten Peter is a biologist who climbs sizzling volcanoes to photograph eruptions. He describes getting caught in the middle of a days-long eruption.

PHOTOGRAPHER CARSTEN PETER SNAPPED THIS PHOTO OF AN EXPLOSION ON MOUNT ETNA, A VOLCANO IN ITALY.

"Every volcano is as different as every human. Each one has its own character."

"A group of us were on an expedition on Mount Etna, a volcano in Italy. We hoped to photograph a paroxysm (pronounced puh-ROKS-ism). They're massive eruptions that produce fire mountains, or wild sprays of magma.

"We camped out halfway up the peak and waited. In the middle of the night a fissure, or crack, suddenly appeared in front of us. Ash and dust started swirling around, stinging our eyes. The smell of volcanic gases filled our noses, and volcanic lightning cracked in the air. The ground was so hot, the bottom of my friend's shoes melted.

"The eruption lasted for days. We decided to stay so we could document everything, even though we hadn't brought enough food. We saw several paroxysms. During calmer moments, we dug under cooled ash to find snow we could melt for drinking water.

"It's one thing to understand the science of volcanoes, but it's crazy to feel it up close. Not everyone can sleep on a volcano. That's why I do what I do—to show people the awesome power of nature."

WANT TO BE AN ADVENTURER?
STUDY Photography, environmental studies, geography
WATCH The documentary *Volcanoes: The Fires of Creation*
READ *Extreme Planet: Carsten Peter's Adventures in Volcanoes, Caves, Canyons, Deserts, and Beyond!* by Carsten Peter and Glen Phelan

The Explorer's Lens

Meet conservation photographer Gab Mejia

As a conservation photographer and National Geographic Explorer, Gab Mejia shares powerful images of places, people, and animals in an effort to educate others on issues like climate change, pollution, and other challenges impacting Earth. Mejia was born and raised in the Philippines, and many of his images showcase his country—especially its endangered species and Indigenous people. Here, Mejia shares more about his message as a visual storyteller and what it's like being behind the lens.

PHILIPPINE EAGLE

Q: What inspired you to become a photographer?

A: When I was 13, my dad brought me on a trek in the rainforest in the Philippines, and it opened my eyes to a different world. One where I was able to witness nature and its beauty and rawness, and I wanted to share it with others. I also loved to travel and visit new places, and photography became my passport to see the rest of the world.

Q: What is the trickiest part of being a photographer?

A: Chasing the light! Many people don't realize that in order to get that perfect shot, you need the right lighting. So, I'll be up very early to get that golden light of the sunrise, or I'll wake up in the middle of the night to capture the stars. When I'm in the field, I don't get much sleep.

Q: What's one standout moment you've experienced in your career?

A: Photographing the Philippine eagle. It's such a beautiful creature, and the whole time I was taking photos I kept thinking, "I just can't believe I'm face-to-face with this majestic bird." Also, because they are on the brink of extinction, it gives my work more purpose. It's not just taking pictures of the eagle—it's capturing their images and showing everyone just how amazing they are.

Q: Any scary moments in the field?

A: One night, while I was shooting Monte Fitz Roy, a mountain in Patagonia, I went back to my tent late at night—and alone. Suddenly, I see these bright white, glowing eyes in the bush across from my tent. It was straight out of a horror movie. I thought for sure the eyes belonged to a mountain lion, and I freaked out. I grabbed my headlamp and shone it into the bush and saw it was actually a South Andean deer, which is a very rare species in Argentina. So what was a scary moment turned into a fascinating and memorable one.

Q: Part of your focus as a photographer has been to raise awareness about Indigenous communities. What has that experience been like?

A: They are private people, but they do want their story to be told. Their homes are being destroyed by logging and climate change—and they need our help. As far as actually being with the tribes, I spend time with them and gain their trust before I even bring out my camera. They respect that I am a fellow Filipino sharing their story, and I've become good friends with the tribe leaders.

Q: What message do you want to send through your photography?

A: Never stop exploring! I share my photos to inspire others to seek out their own adventures. To look for the wildlife, visit amazing natural places, and hopefully be inspired to use your voice to make a positive change. Also, I hope my photos are a reminder to all that our world is so beautiful, and we need to protect it for future generations.

EPiC SCIENCE FAiLS

Nat Geo Explorers spill their most embarrassing moments.

Even supersmart scientists mess up sometimes! These Nat Geo Explorers reveal some of their wildest slipups—and what they learned from them.

ICE... POPS!

THE SCIENTIST:
Anne Jungblut

COOL JOB:
Environmental microbiologist

THE LOCATION:
South Georgia Island, in the southern Atlantic Ocean near Antarctica

ANNE JUNGBLUT LOOKS FOR SOIL SAMPLES AMONG THOUSANDS OF KING PENGUINS ON SOUTH GEORGIA ISLAND.

LAZY LIONS

THE SCIENTIST:
Rae Wynn-Grant

COOL JOB:
Large carnivore ecologist

THE LOCATION:
Tanzania, a country in Africa

"I was studying the movement and hunting behavior of lions in the savanna. When I found my first subject, he was snoozing. I noticed that his belly was huge—he'd just eaten a big meal. I watched the lion do nothing but sleep for hours until it got dark. And then when I came back the next morning, the lion still hadn't moved.

"In four months, I found seven other lions ... just lying around, full of food. I never arrived in time to see the behavior I was there to study. Instead, I had to interview local people about the lions' movements for my paper—something I didn't need to spend months in Africa to do!

"I learned that wild animals don't always do things on my schedule. But at least I got to see these predators behaving naturally: Lions definitely spend most of their time asleep."

UNFORTUNATELY FOR RAE WYNN-GRANT, LIONS LIKE THIS ONE SLEEP OR REST UP TO 20 HOURS A DAY.

"I study too-small-to-see organisms that live in little pools of water on top of glaciers. I have to use special ice shoes, rope, and an ice axe to climb to collection sites since the ice sheet has deep cracks that could be deadly. So once I'm finally at the site, I'm eager to get started.

"One time I was so excited to gather as much evidence as possible and filled my sampling tubes to the top with water and sediment from the glaciers. Even though I'm an ice and soil scientist, I ignored the fact that water increases by 20 percent when it freezes. So when we put all my test tubes into the freezer for safekeeping, one totally shattered! Luckily, we quickly put the samples in new containers, but that day I learned to respect science—it's not going to change for me."

SNAKE MISTAKE

THE SCIENTIST:
Ruchira Somaweera

COOL JOB:
Herpetologist

THE LOCATION:
Northern Australia

RUCHIRA SOMAWEERA HOLDS AN ARAFURA FILE SNAKE IN AUSTRALIA.

"I was catching snakes so I could study their health. We kept the snakes in fabric bags for the night so we could examine them the next day. Mosquitoes and ants were everywhere, and I didn't want the snakes to be uncomfortable, so I brought the bagged animals into my insect-proof tent.

"At about 3 a.m., I woke up to the most horrible smell. It turns out that a Stimson's python had escaped and crawled into my warm sleeping bag. I'd rolled over onto it, causing the snake to vomit parts of a half-digested frog!

"The snake was fine—we released it the next day—and now I always check that the snake bags are totally tied up."

SCRATCHY CHASE

THE SCIENTIST: Patrícia Medici

COOL JOB: Conservationist

THE LOCATION: Pantanal, Brazil

"We shot a tranquilizer dart at a large male tapir so that we could study its health. Sometimes, the animal sprints off into the forest, and we have to chase after it no matter where it goes. It can be dangerous for the tapir because if it falls asleep in water, we wouldn't be able to get it out. (An adult tapir can weigh over 500 pounds [227 kg]!)

"So we raced after this tapir straight into a sea of thorns and stickers. Most of us were wearing pants and long-sleeve shirts, but one member of the team was in shorts, and wound up covered in scratches by the time we caught up with the tapir. We named the tapir 'Band-Aid,' and I'm sure that my shorts-wearing teammate now always remembers to dress for a wild chase!"

MYSTERY BONE

THE SCIENTIST: Daniel Dick

COOL JOB: Paleontologist

THE LOCATION: Colombia, a country in South America

PALEONTOLOGISTS DANIEL DICK (LEFT) AND ERIN MAXWELL LOOK FOR ICHTHYOSAUR FOSSILS IN COLOMBIA.

"We were examining an eight-foot (2.4-m)-long skeleton of an ichthyosaur (a huge extinct marine reptile). It was my first day in the field, and I wanted to impress the other scientists. As I examined the skull, I spotted an unusual bone that the others had missed and began to describe it—the bone might be proof that this animal is an entirely new species!

"'That's mud,' my teacher said. I was so embarrassed, but science is about learning. And now I'm really good at spotting the difference between mud and bone."

PATRÍCIA MEDICI FEEDS A CAPTIVE BABY TAPIR AT A WILDLIFE REHABILITATION CENTER IN BRAZIL.

Keep Earth WILD

A National Geographic photographer gives you a behind-the-scenes look at his quest to save animals.

Joel Sartore has squealed like a pig, protected his camera from a parakeet, and suffered through a stink attack—all to help save animals through photography. "I hope people will look these animals in their eyes and then be inspired to protect them," says Sartore, a National Geographic photographer.

Sartore is on a mission to take pictures of more than 15,000 animal species living in captivity through his project, the National Geographic Photo Ark. During each photo shoot, he works with zookeepers, aquarists, and wildlife rehabbers to keep his subjects safe and comfortable. But things can still get a little, well, wild! Read on for some of Sartore's most memorable moments.

Moment of SNOOZE

GIANT PANDAS, *native to China*

Zoo Atlanta, Atlanta, Georgia, U.S.A.
" These giant pandas were just a few months old when I put the football-size twins in a small, white photo tent and snapped a few pics as they tumbled on top of each other. But the youngsters were tiring out, and I knew I was losing my chance to get a memorable photo before they drifted off to sleep. One cub put his head on the back of the other, and I managed to capture an awesome shot just seconds before the two cubs fell asleep. "

> Some arctic fox dens are 300 years old.

Moment of HA

ARCTIC FOX, *native to the Arctic regions of Eurasia, North America, Greenland, and Iceland*

Great Bend Brit Spaugh Zoo, Great Bend, Kansas, U.S.A.

" Todd the arctic fox wanted to sniff everything, but he was moving too quickly for me to get a good picture. I needed to do something surprising to get his attention, so I squealed like a pig! The weird sound made the fox stop, sit down, and tilt his head as if he were thinking, What's the matter with you? Good thing I was fast, because the pig noise only worked once. The next time I squealed, Todd completely ignored me. "

More WILDNESS! Photo Ark spotlights all kinds of animals. Meet some of Joel Sartore's strangest subjects.

BUDGETT'S FROG

ORANGE SPOTTED FILEFISH

MEDITERRANEAN RED BUG

NORTH AMERICAN PORCUPINE

Sartore uses black or white backgrounds because he wants the focus to be on the animals. That way a mouse is as important as an elephant.

Newborn giant pandas are about the size of a stick of butter.

A single colony of gray-headed flying foxes can include a million bats.

Giraffes sometimes use their tongues to clean their ears.

Moment of YAY

GRAY-HEADED FLYING FOX, *native to southeastern Australia*

Australian Bat Clinic, Advancetown, Australia

When I arrived at the clinic, I was amazed to see all sorts of bats just hanging from laundry racks all over the rescue center. They sleepily watched me as I walked through the room and asked a staff member for a friendly flying fox to photograph. She scooped up a sweet bat and placed its feet on a wire rack in front of my backdrop. The calm bat didn't seem to mind being in front of the camera. The best part? This clinic rehabilitates bats that have torn their wings, and my subject was eventually released back into the wild.

Moment of YUM

RETICULATED GIRAFFE, *native to Africa*

Gladys Porter Zoo, Brownsville, Texas, U.S.A.

You definitely can't make a giraffe do anything it doesn't want to do. So to get this animal to be part of our photo shoot, we combined the activity with one of the giraffe's favorite things: lunch. We hung the huge black backdrop from the rafters in the part of the giraffe's enclosure where it gets fed. The giraffe ambled in, not minding me at all. For about 10 minutes, while the animal munched on bamboo leaves, I could take all the pictures I wanted. But as soon as lunch was over, the giraffe walked out, and our photo shoot was done.

GETTING THE SHOT

Capturing good photographs of wild animals can be tough. To get amazing pictures of them, nature photographers often tap into their wild side, thinking and even acting like the creatures they're snapping. Whether tracking deadly snakes or swimming with penguins, the artists must be daring—but they also need to know when to keep their distance. Three amazing photographers tell their behind-the-scenes stories of how they got these incredible shots.

Check out this book!

FANG FOCUS

PHOTOGRAPHER: Mattias Klum
ANIMAL: Jameson's mamba
SHOOT SITE: Cameroon, Africa

"The Jameson's mamba is beautiful but dangerous. It produces highly toxic venom. My team searched for weeks for the reptile, asking locals about the best spots to see one. At last we came across a Jameson's mamba peeking out from tree leaves. Carefully, I inched closer. It's important to make this kind of snake think that you don't see it. Otherwise it might feel threatened and strike you. At about four and a half feet (1.4 m) away, I took the picture. Then I backed up and the snake slid off."

SECRETS FROM AMAZING WILDLIFE PHOTOGRAPHERS

Usually solitary creatures, oceanic whitetip sharks have been observed swimming with pods of pilot whales.

SHARK TALE

PHOTOGRAPHER: Brian Skerry
ANIMAL: Oceanic whitetip shark
SHOOT SITE: The Bahamas

"I wanted to photograph an endangered oceanic whitetip shark. So I set sail with a group of scientists to an area where some had been sighted. Days later, the dorsal fin of a whitetip rose from the water near our boat. One scientist was lowered in a metal cage into the water to observe the fish. Then I dived in. Because I wasn't behind the protective bars, I had to be very careful. These nine-foot (2.7-m) sharks can be aggressive, but this one was just curious. She swam around us for two hours and allowed me to take pictures of her. She was the perfect model."

LEAPS and BOUNDS

PHOTOGRAPHER: Nick Nichols
ANIMAL: Bengal tiger
SHOOT SITE: Bandhavgarh National Park, India

"While following a tiger along a cliff, I saw him leap from the edge to his secret watering hole and take a drink. I wanted a close-up of the cat, but it wouldn't have been safe to approach him. Figuring he'd return to the spot, I set up a camera on the cliff that shoots off an infrared beam. Walking into the beam triggers the camera to click. The device was there for three months, but this was the only shot I got of the cat. Being near tigers makes the hair stand up on my arm. It was a gift to encounter such a magnificent creature."

About 3,000 Bengal tigers are left in the wild.

WILD VET
ADVENTURE
WITH ONE WILDLIFE DOCTOR

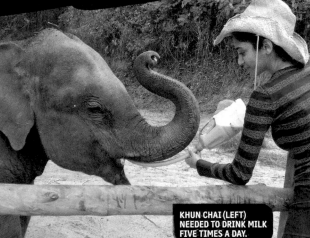

KHUN CHAI (LEFT) NEEDED TO DRINK MILK FIVE TIMES A DAY.

Animals can't tell their doctors when they aren't feeling well. So that makes the job of a wildlife veterinarian a little ... well, wild. Meet Gabby Wild, who travels the world to provide medical care for animals in zoos, shelters, national parks, and rescue centers. Here, the wildlife vet tells you how she treated one animal in need of a little medicine—and a lot of care.

ELEPHANT CALF GETS SOME TLC

"In Thailand, a country in Southeast Asia, people sometimes use elephants as work animals to help on their farms. One farmer illegally stole an elephant calf from the forest, which he thought would be cheaper than buying an adult elephant. But soon the calf was close to dying. The farmer realized the young elephant needed medical help.

"He brought the youngster to a wildlife hospital where I was working, and we named the calf Khun Chai, which means 'prince' in Thai. We observed that he didn't want to play with the other elephants and refused to drink the milk we offered him.

"I had studied some elephant behavior, and I thought that maybe he just didn't want to be bothered. So when I went into his enclosure, I sat quietly on the ground and only looked at him out of the corner of my eye. About a half hour later, I could feel a light tap on my shoulder—Khun Chai was patting me with his trunk!

"From that moment on, Khun Chai followed me all around the rescue center. I fed him milk five times a day, walked him three times a day, and bathed him a few times a week. As he ate and gained weight, he became a healthy elephant.

"We decided that because people had raised Khun Chai, it would be dangerous to release him back into the forest. So eventually we moved him to a local conservation center where he could live with other elephants. I'm glad I could help him grow up to be healthy and happy."

A male Asian elephant usually lives with its mother for about five years.

Extreme Job!

There's not much normal about John Stevenson's job. A volcanologist, Stevenson evaluates eruptions, follows lava flows, and travels to remote locations to learn more about volcanoes. Read on for more details on his risky but rewarding career.

TESTING NEW RESEARCH EQUIPMENT

SCIENCE-MINDED "As a kid, I really liked science and nature, and in college I pursued chemical engineering but studied geology as well. Having a background in all of the sciences gave me a better understanding of the bigger picture, from volcano monitoring to understanding eruptions."

BIG DIG "I once spent ten days collecting pumice and ash samples from a 4,200-year-old eruption in Iceland. We'd dig in the soil until we found the layer of ash that we wanted, then spend up to two hours photographing and taking samples. At night, we'd find a nice spot by a stream, eat dinner, and camp out."

DANGER IN THE AIR "Being exposed to the edge of a lava flow can be dangerous. The air is hot and can be thick with poisonous sulfur dioxide gas. Once, while working at the active Bárðarbunga volcano in Iceland, we had to wear gas masks and use an electronic gas meter as dust swirled around us."

RAINING ASH "When I worked at Volcán de Colima in Mexico, we camped a few miles from the crater. One night, I woke up to a whooshing sound. This quickly changed to a *patter-patter-patter* that sounded like heavy rain falling on the tent. When I put my hand out to feel the rain, it was covered in coarse gray sand. The volcano had erupted, and ash was raining down on us. We quickly packed up our stuff and headed to a safer spot."

JOB PERKS "I get to play with fun gadgets in cool locations. If I didn't have to work, I would still go hiking and camping and play with gadgets and computers in my spare time anyway. I enjoy trying to solve the problems of getting the right data and finding a way to process it so that it can tell us about how the world works."

WORKING IN THE FIELD

awes8me

Duh! Don't try these tricks on your own.

1 FLIPPING OUT

Freeride mountain biking sends riders down routes that look impossible to most people. Besides trails, bikers ride on wood planks, platforms, and even off cliffs! U.S. biker Cameron Zink impressed the crowd at a freeride mountain bike competition in Utah, U.S.A., when he completed a 78-foot (24-m)-long backflip, one of the longest in history.

THIS IMAGE IS A MASH-UP OF SEVERAL PHOTOGRAPHS OF CAMERON ZINK'S 78-FOOT (24-M)-LONG BACKFLIP.

SOARING SPORTS

YOU'D BETTER LIKE HEIGHTS IF YOU PLAN TO PLAY THESE GAMES.

TOKYO 2020

2 DEFYING GRAVITY

Gymnasts use strength, agility, coordination, and balance to leap and flip in the air. Considered the world's best gymnast, Simone Biles of the United States (left) won four gold medals, one silver, and two bronze after competing at two Olympic Games. She even has four original moves named after her. Go, Simone!

3 ALLEY-OOP

Now here's a way to guarantee a dunk—**trampoline basketball,** or basketball with some assists by trampolines. Sometimes going by the name SlamBall, the game has increased in popularity as more trampoline parks open across the United States.

4 DIVE IN

Look out below! This cliff diver takes a big leap in Mazatlán, Mexico. People have been **cliff diving** for centuries: It's said that Hawaiian warriors jumped from cliffs on the island of Lanai to prove their loyalty and bravery.

5 FLIGHT OF THE FUTURE

Hoverboards might become old school if **flyboards** (like the one shown here) ever take off. Still in development, this flyboard has four engines operated by a handheld remote. It's fueled by kerosene and will be able to cover more than 7,000 feet (2,134 m) without stopping. Up next: flyboard races in the sky!

SPRINGS FOR FEET 6

This super bouncer from California can jump more than six feet (1.8 m) in the air on his **pogo stick.** Traditionally, pogo sticks get their bounce from springs, but this one works with compressed air, which increases height.

7 OFF THE WALL

You literally bounce off the walls with this pastime. Part gymnastics, part parkour, **wall trampoline** jumpers improvise flips and twists midair. Some circus acrobats have been doing a version of wall trampoline for years, and now jumpers are hoping to turn it into a competitive sport.

TWO PEOPLE PRACTICE WALL TRAMPOLINE AT THE QUEBEC CIRCUS SCHOOL IN CANADA.

8 GO FLY A KITE

Talk about catching some air. A **kiteboarder** uses the wind to his advantage on the waters near the island nation of Mauritius, off the coast of Madagascar. Kiteboarders move along the water and make jumps of up to 50 feet (15 m) by using strength and coordination to control the kite that they're attached to.

QUIZ WHIZ

Discover just how much you know about exploration with this quiz!

Write your answers on a piece of paper. Then check them below.

1 Fueled by _____, the flyboard can cover more than 7,000 feet (2,134 m) without stopping.
a. gasoline
b. kerosene
c. plant power
d. solar power

2 True or false? Poachers sell slow lorises as pets.

3 Oceanic whitetip sharks have been observed swimming with groups of what other sea animals?
a. walruses
b. greenback turtles
c. orcas
d. pilot whales

4 A cliff in Colombia is covered with some 70,000 drawings of ancient animals, including _____.
a. giant sloths
b. ice age horses
c. mastodons
d. all of the above

5 Male Asian elephants usually live with their mothers for about _____ years.

Not **STUMPED** yet? Check out the *NATIONAL GEOGRAPHIC KIDS QUIZ WHIZ* collection for more crazy **EXPLORATION** questions!

ANSWERS: 1. b; 2. True; 3. d; 4. d; 5. 5

HOMEWORK HELP

How to Write a Perfect Essay

Need to write an essay? Does the assignment feel as big as climbing Mount Everest? Fear not. You're up to the challenge! The following step-by-step tips will help you with this monumental task.

1 **BRAINSTORM.** Sometimes the subject matter of your essay is assigned to you, sometimes it's not. Either way, you have to decide what you want to say. Start by brainstorming some ideas, writing down any thoughts you have about the subject. Then read over everything you've come up with and consider which idea you think is the strongest. Ask yourself what you want to write about the most. Keep in mind the goal of your essay. Can you achieve the goal of the assignment with this topic? If so, you're good to go.

2 **WRITE A TOPIC SENTENCE.** This is the main idea of your essay, a statement of your thoughts on the subject. Again, consider the goal of your essay. Think of the topic sentence as an introduction that tells your readers what the rest of your essay will be about.

3 **OUTLINE YOUR IDEAS.** Once you have a good topic sentence, you then need to support that main idea with more detailed information, facts, thoughts, and examples. These supporting points answer one question about your topic sentence—"Why?" This is where research and perhaps more brainstorming come in. Then organize these points in the way you think makes the most sense, probably in order of importance. Now you have an outline for your essay.

4 **ON YOUR MARK, GET SET, WRITE!** Follow your outline, using each of your supporting points as the topic sentence of its own paragraph. Use descriptive words to get your ideas across to readers. Go into detail, using specific information to tell your story or make your point. Stay on track, making sure that everything you include is somehow related to the main idea of your essay. Use transitions to make your writing flow.

5 **WRAP IT UP.** Finish your essay with a conclusion that summarizes your entire essay and restates your main idea.

6 **PROOFREAD AND REVISE.** Check for errors in spelling, capitalization, punctuation, and grammar. Look for ways to make your writing clear, understandable, and interesting. Use descriptive verbs, adjectives, and adverbs when possible. It also helps to have someone else read your work to point out things you might have missed. Then make the necessary corrections and changes in a second draft. Repeat this revision process once more to make your final draft as good as you can.

FUN and GAMES

A tokay gecko grips onto a tree.

What do you get if you cross a pastry with a snake?

A pie-thon.

CRITTER CHAT

ARE YOU AMOOSED?

If animals used social media, what would they say? Follow this moose's day as it updates its feed.

Moose

LIVES IN: Northern regions of North America, Europe, and Asia
SCREEN NAME: OhDeer
FRIENDS: ⌄

SPRUCE GROUSE
WoodBird

CANADA LYNX
CoolCat

SNOWSHOE HARE
SnowHopper

7 a.m.

OhDeer It's about time to say goodbye to my magnificent antlers. Before I shed them next month, let's all admire these six-foot-wide bad boys.

 Those antlers seem like a lot of trouble just to fight for a mate. All my guy had to do was show off some fluffy feathers. (Isn't he handsome?) **WoodBird**

CoolCat I'll take my ear tufts over your 40-pound antlers—and I don't need them to impress a mate. I just found another lynx that lives nearby.

You'll look so different without your antlers! But not as different as I'll look in a few months when I'm wearing my grayish brown summer coat. 😊 **SnowHopper**

12:00 p.m.

OhDeer Before this lake freezes over, I'm going to swim a few laps. #SwimSelfie

I'll hop in the water to avoid **@CoolCat** when she wakes up at sundown, but I'd much rather take a bath in dust. **SnowHopper**

 WoodBird I bet wet moose smells pretty bad. I'll stick to the trees to keep safe from **@CoolCat**.

You guys are no fun. I just want to play hide-and-seek ... and eat. 😊 **CoolCat**

6:00 p.m.

OhDeer First flurry of the season! Doesn't the snow look good on me?

Woot! If this keeps up, I'll finally be able to relax in a deep burrow under the snow. #SnowDaySleepIn **WoodBird**

 CoolCat Hide all you want. But I'm more interested in where **@SnowHopper**'s hanging out.

Ha! Good luck— my winter coat matches the snow, so you'll never find me. #HareMagic **SnowHopper**

 OhDeer Hey, where'd **@SnowHopper** go?

START

132

WHAT IN THE WORLD?

SQUIRMY WORMY

These photos show close-up views of creepy little critters. On a separate sheet of paper, unscramble the letters to identify what's in each picture.

ANSWERS ON PAGE 354

DIEPSR

RCSOOINP

ELETEB

RETITMSE

NEIECTEDP

HRACKCOCO

OMWSR

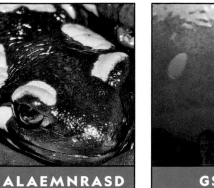

ALAEMNRASD

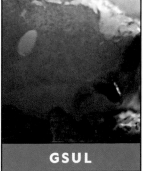

GSUL

133

SIGNS OF THE TIMES

Seeing isn't always believing. Two of these funny signs are not real. Can you spot which two are fake?

ANSWERS ON PAGE 354

1 NEXT 8km

2 AMERICAN WAY

3

4 212 Boring

7 IGUANA CROSSING
CRUCE DE IGUANAS

5 NO NAME ST

6

FUNNY FILL-IN

Ask a friend to give you words to fill in the blanks in this story and write them on a separate sheet of paper. Then read the story out loud and fill in the words for a laugh.

_____ and I set sail on the famous pirate ship the _____ _____ for
    friend's name   adjective   animal

our summer vacation. After _____ out to sea, Captain _____ beard gave
                                     verb ending in –ing   color

us a tour. Suddenly the sky turned dark and it started to _____ . A bolt of _____
                                                          verb   noun

streaked across the sky as a large wave filled with _____ crashed over the side of the
                                                       noun, plural

ship. Fish were flying everywhere—one even landed on my _____ . The first mate,
                                                             body part

_____ , took cover with _____ . The captain was taking down the sail when a(n)
  celebrity   historical figure

_____ gust of wind sent him flying through the air. He held on to the _____ but his
  adjective   noun

trousers flew off the ship, showing _____-_____ underpants! After he landed back
                                       color   noun

on the deck, we all went below until the storm ended. But we didn't find the captain's pants until

_____ days later—when we spotted them on a(n) _____ 's fin.
  large number   ocean animal

NOUN TOWN

This city is full of nouns, or people, places, and things. But 12 compound nouns—nouns made up of two or more words, or two words combined to make one word—have been drawn exactly as they're named. Can you guess the compound nouns illustrated in each of the numbered scenes? Here's a hint: The answer to number 1 is "sleeping bag."

ANSWERS ON PAGE 354

FIND THE HIDDEN ANIMALS

Animals often blend in with their environment for protection. Find each animal listed below in one of the pictures. On a separate sheet of paper, write the letter of the correct picture and the animal's name.

ANSWERS ON PAGE 354

1. stargazer (a type of fish)
2. arctic fox
3. pygmy seahorse
4. harlequin crab
5. katydid
6. common chameleon

WHAT IN THE WORLD?

DOWN UNDER

These photographs show close-up and faraway views of things in Australia. On a separate sheet of paper, unscramble the letters to identify what's in each picture.

ANSWERS ON PAGE 354

DRSRBFUOSA

RTEGA ARERIBR FREE

ORNGAAKO

AWSCYSAOR

NREMBOGAO

RULUU

LAFG

OAAKL

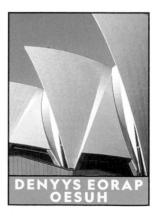

DENYYS EORAP OESUH

FROM THE PAGES OF *QUIZ WHIZ:*

STUMP
YOUR PARENTS

Answer the questions on a separate sheet of paper. If your parents can't answer these questions, maybe they should go to school instead of you!

ANSWERS ON PAGE 354

1 Which of these wacky festivals is real?
a. the Lumberjack World Championships in Hayward, Wisconsin, U.S.A.
b. the Okie Noodling Tournament in Pauls Valley, Oklahoma, U.S.A.
c. the Rainbow Gathering in Santa Fe, New Mexico, U.S.A.
d. all of the above

2  _____ is the planet farthest from the sun.
a. Earth   c. Mercury
b. Neptune d. Saturn

3 The first compasses were made in _____.
a. China
b. Portugal
c. Peru
d. Zimbabwe

4 A person who studies trees is called a(n)_____.
a. dendrologist
b. etymologist
c. treeologist
d. geologist

5 Before graduating high school, the average U.S. kid will have eaten _____ peanut butter and jelly sandwiches.
a. 800
b. 1,500
c. 2,600
d. 3,500

6 Which statement is false? Two-toed sloths _____.
a. are often covered in algae
b. climb upside down
c. shiver
d. eat leaves

7 A group of grasshoppers is called a _____.
a. cloud
b. pod
c. bloat
d. scrum

8 A _____ is the world's largest rodent.
a. chipmunk
b. New York City rat
c. capybara
d. marmot

9 Alfred Nobel, the man for whom the Nobel Peace Prize is named, invented _____.
a. lightbulbs
b. sleeping bags
c. hot chocolate
d. dynamite

10  Match each country to the currency it uses:
a. Canada   1. metical
b. England   2. euro
c. Poland   3. dollar
d. Spain   4. pound
e. Mozambique   5. zloty

FUNNY FILL-IN

Ask a friend to give you words to fill in the blanks in this story and write them on a separate sheet of paper. Then read the story out loud and fill in the words for a laugh.

_____! I just received _____ billion dollars from my _____
  silly expression   large number   adjective

great-great-great-great-aunt for my birthday. I know exactly what I'll do with the _____.
                                                                                       noun

First I'll buy the _____. Maybe I could hire _____ to be my
                   favorite sports team   famous athlete

_____! I'm going to have all my _____ made of _____
  type of job   article of clothing, plural   noun, plural

and build a roller coaster in my new _____. I'll ride a(n) _____
                                     room of a house   verb ending in –ing

_____ to school—no more bus rides for me. And now I can get _____
    noun   female friend's name

a(n) _____ like she always wanted. I think I'll even _____ a charity to save
      noun   verb

the _____. I'm so rich, I can give my parents an allowance.
    animal, plural

LAUGH OUT LOUD

"DO YOU HAVE ANYTHING
FOR DRY, SCALY SKIN?"

"NO THANKS."

"I DON'T KNOW WHY HE DOESN'T
HONK LIKE THE REST OF US."

"I'M NOT OVER
HALLOWEEN YET."

"I KNOW THIS IS GOING TO SOUND WEIRD
BUT ... I'M KINDA THIRSTY."

"FORGET THE GPS—LET'S
JUST FOLLOW THEM."

WHAT IN THE WORLD?

BEACH DAZE

These photographs show close-up views of objects you see at the beach. On a separate sheet of paper, unscramble the letters to identify what's in each picture.

ANSWERS ON PAGE 354

AMLP ETER

DASNELASCT

KOSLNER NAD KAMS

USMTIWSI

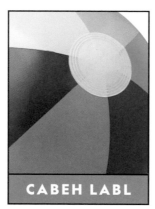

CABEH LABL

DEWAESE

LASLEHES

HEBAC WOLTE

LEBUMRAL

FIND THE HIDDEN ANIMALS

Animals often blend in with their environment for protection. Find each animal listed below in one of the pictures. On a separate sheet of paper, write the letter of the correct picture and the animal's name.

ANSWERS ON PAGE 354

1. walking leaf insect
2. flounder
3. walruses
4. island fox
5. cowrie*
6. leaf-tailed gecko

__HINT:__ A cowrie is a sea snail.

143

FUNNY FILL-IN

Ask a friend to give you words to fill in the blanks in this story and write them on a separate sheet of paper. Then read the story out loud and fill in the words for a laugh.

For summer break, my family took a trip to a(n) _____ town. I was excited to look
_____ historical era

for people wearing old-fashioned _____ and _____ . My brother
_____ article of clothing, plural _____ noun, plural

only cared about seeing _____ . We were _____ by a bank when a
_____ animal, plural _____ verb ending in –ing

man dressed in all _____ _____ out of the building. He threw some bags of
_____ color _____ past-tense verb

_____ over his shoulders before _____ off down the street. "Stop, thief!"
_____ noun, plural _____ verb ending in –ing

a(n) _____ yelled behind us. I ran to the _____ next to the bank and
_____ type of job _____ animal, plural

_____ climbed on top of one. My brother tossed me a(n) _____ as I rode off
_____ adverb ending in –ly _____ noun

after the crook. I twirled it in the air, _____ it around the _____ thief. I caught
_____ verb ending in –ing _____ adjective

him! The _____ gave my brother and me special badges as a thank-you for our help.
_____ same type of job

Officer _____ —I like the sound of that.
_____ your name

144

FROM THE PAGES OF *QUIZ WHIZ:*

STUMP
YOUR PARENTS

Answer the questions on a separate sheet of paper. If your parents can't answer these questions, maybe they should go to school instead of you!

ANSWERS ON PAGE 354

1 What does mucus do?
a. helps your lungs take in oxygen
b. makes flavors taste stronger
c. filters harmful bacteria from your body
d. stops your nose from collapsing

2 Ostriches cannot do which of the following?
a. lay eggs
b. run
c. kick
d. fly

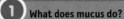

3 Which is the world's highest waterfall?
a. Niagara Falls, in Canada and the United States
b. Angel Falls, in Venezuela
c. Victoria Falls, in Zambia and Zimbabwe
d. Iguazú Falls, in Argentina and Brazil

4 Which of these TV families first appeared in a 1938 magazine cartoon?
a. the Addams family
b. the Flintstones
c. the Brady Bunch
d. the Munsters

5 Which of the following terms would *not* be used to refer to a young lion?
a. whelp
b. lionet
c. cub
d. calf

6 Which ancestor do all dog breeds have in common?
a. dinosaur
b. hyena
c. wolf
d. Scooby-Doo

7 The scarab was a sacred insect in ancient Egypt. What is a scarab?
a. a cockroach
b. a beetle
c. a wasp
d. a dragonfiy

8 What does Earth have that the moon does not?
a. water
b. rocks
c. an atmosphere
d. aluminum

9 In which century was the first macaroni and cheese recipe printed?
a. 13th century
b. 15th century
c. 17th century
d. 21st century

10 Which Disney princess kissed a frog?
a. Ariel
b. Rapunzel
c. Tiana
d. Jasmine

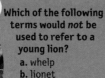
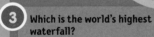
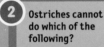
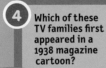

WHAT IN THE WORLD?

RED ALERT

These photographs show close-up views of red things. On a separate sheet of paper, unscramble the letters to identify what's in each picture.

ANSWERS ON PAGE 354

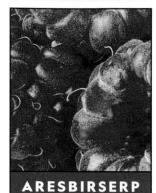

ARESBIRSERP

IELCYBC

BYRU

EVSLGO

EDR XFO

PEPSRPE

EKRNAES

NAERGEMPAOT

AARDNLCI

CRITTER CHAT

I'M JUST THINKIN' ABOUT 'ROO!

If animals used social media, what would they say? Follow this eastern gray kangaroo's day as it updates its feed.

Eastern Gray Kangaroo

LIVES IN: Eastern Australia
SCREEN NAME: HopAlong
FRIENDS: ⌄

PLATYPUS	COASTAL PEACOCK SPIDER	COMMON BLUE-TONGUED SKINK
DuckBeaver	SparkleSpider	TongueSurprise

START

7 a.m.

 HopAlong
Has anybody seen my joey? I just let him out of the pouch for the first time, and he's already hopped off on an adventure.

 SparkleSpider
I'll keep all eight eyes out!

 DuckBeaver
I remember when that little 'roo was the size of a cherry! That was when my lima bean–size babies were still in their eggs. (That's right, I'm a mammal that lays eggs!)

 TongueSurprise
Oh yeah, I saw your joey not too long ago. He spooked me so much that I flashed my bright blue tongue at him to scare him off. #SorryNotSorry

 HopAlong
Thanks, everybody! He's back in the pouch— and he's grounded.

3:00 p.m.

 HopAlong
Woot—29 feet! My best long jump ever! #GoldMedalForMe

 DuckBeaver
OK, but I'd lap you in a swimming contest. Meet me in the lagoon any time, any day.

 SparkleSpider
That's nothing. Watch me shimmy-shake to impress a special lady spider.

 TongueSurprise
That's one delicious-looking dance. 😊

4:55 p.m.

 HopAlong
It's FINALLY cooling off. Time to feast on grass with my mob!

 DuckBeaver
That sounds like too many party animals—I like to splash solo.

TongueSurprise
Bedtime for me. And since I just lost my tail to a falcon, I need my beauty sleep to start growing it back. TTYL!

 SparkleSpider
Now that the lizard's snoozing, I can get in one last hunt without worrying. Look out, crickets!

STRIKA ENTERTAINMENT

UnLeaShed

1

DOES THAT MEAN WHAT I *THINK* IT MEANS?

IT *SURE DOES!* IT MEANS WE COULD MEET A *REAL ALIEN!*

THOUGH IT HAS *NOT* BEEN CONFIRMED, SOME SCIENTISTS THINK *LIFE* COULD EXIST ON *OTHER PLANETS* ...

2

DO YOU THINK *ALIENS* HAVE *PETS?* THEIR CHEW TOYS MUST BE *OUT OF THIS WORLD!*

3

I'M SURE *ALIENS* WOULD TREAT *ME* LIKE *ROYALTY!* I *WISH* WE COULD *CONTACT* THEM.

4

LET'S BUILD A *SPACE RADIO* TO *COMMUNICATE* WITH THEM!

5

THE PETS GET TO WORK ...

CAN WE USE MY *WATER DISH* FOR THE *SATELLITE DISH?*

NO WAY! THAT BOWL IS TOO *SMALL!*

6

HOW ABOUT THE *TRASH CAN LID?*

BANG! BANG! BANG!

THAT'S *PERFECT!*

7

FINALLY ...

GREETINGS, *ALIEN LIFE-FORMS!* THIS IS NEVILLE, ATLAS, AND *PRINCESS TALLULAH*—

IT'S JUST *LULU!*

148

BONUS!

20 THINGS
TO MAKE YOU
HAPPY

Looking at cute pictures of animals can make you happy, but there are other benefits, too! A study in Japan found that looking at pictures of cute baby animals may also boost your attention to detail and overall work performance.

What makes YOU HAPPY?

Rice Krispies Treats?
Jumping on a trampoline?
Reading comic books?

Make a "Happy List" of all the things that lift your spirits and refer to it when you need **a pick-me-up.**

PLAY WITH a puppy

There's actually a chemical reason you feel happier after snuggling a sweet pooch. When a person pets a dog, a hormone called oxytocin is released. It is a chemical that helps lower blood pressure and reduce stress.

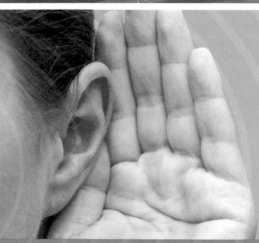

BECOME AN AWESOME LISTENER

TIP 1

TRY TO UNDERSTAND. Instead of thinking about **what you'll say next,** or whether you agree with the speaker, try to listen to what the person is telling you, why it's important to them, and **how it makes them feel.**

TIP 2

ASK FOLLOW-UP QUESTIONS. When someone is telling a story or sharing their feelings, **don't immediately change the subject** when they stop talking. To show that you're interested, **ask questions** about what they've told you. For example: Then what happened? How did that make you feel?

APPRECIATE SIMPLE PLEASURES

Take a bubble bath, watch the sun set, or eat a warm cookie.

Call a friend

GET MOVING!

- PLAY BASKETBALL
- ROLLER-SKATE
- RIDE A BICYCLE
- SWIM
- JUMP ROPE
- HAVE A DANCE PARTY
- JUMP ON A TRAMPOLINE
- PUNCH A PUNCHING BAG
- PLAY TAG, KICKBALL, OR CAPTURE THE FLAG
- TRY MARTIAL ARTS, LIKE KARATE OR TAE KWON DO

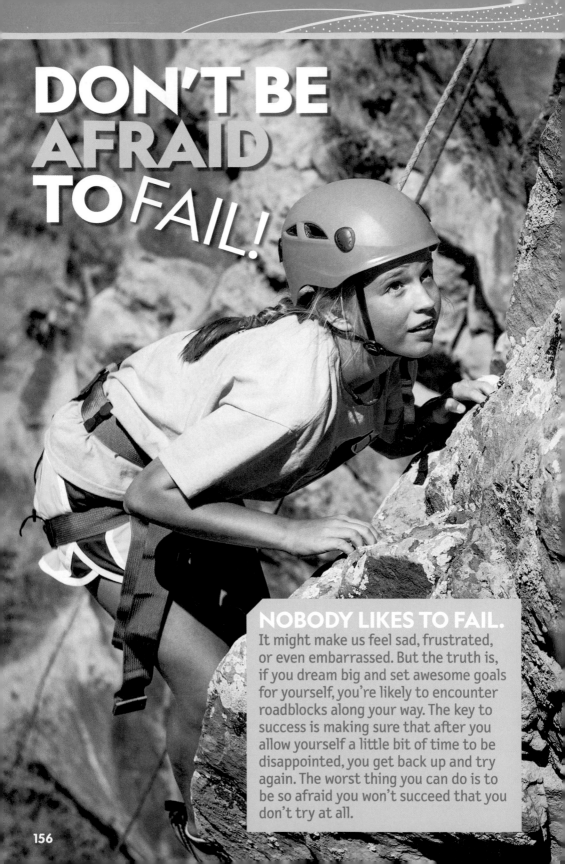

DON'T BE AFRAID TO FAIL!

NOBODY LIKES TO FAIL.

It might make us feel sad, frustrated, or even embarrassed. But the truth is, if you dream big and set awesome goals for yourself, you're likely to encounter roadblocks along your way. The key to success is making sure that after you allow yourself a little bit of time to be disappointed, you get back up and try again. The worst thing you can do is to be so afraid you won't succeed that you don't try at all.

Meditate

5 Awesome Facts About Meditation:

1 Meditation is a practice to train and quiet the mind.

2 Studies have found that after eight weeks of meditating daily, people experience neuroplasticity, which means their brains physically change. So cool!

3 Meditation has been shown to lower physical pain, anxiety, and blood pressure, as well as boost memory, alertness, and creativity.

4 Meditation is not about clearing or ridding your mind of thoughts; in fact, thoughts are a normal part of practicing meditation. As the doctor, author, and meditator Deepak Chopra said, "Meditation is not a way of making your mind quiet. It is a way of entering into the quiet that is already there—buried under the 50,000 thoughts the average person thinks every day."

5 Meditation isn't a religious practice—people from all different walks of life meditate.

Discover A HOBBY you love

Be resilient.

THINK HAPPY THOUGHTS

JUST THINKING ABOUT HAPPY EXPERIENCES AND MEMORIES CAN MAKE YOU HAPPIER, SO WHY NOT GIVE THESE SOME THOUGHT?

- The last time you laughed really hard
- A time when you made someone else really, really happy
- Something you're looking forward to in the future
- The best meal you've ever eaten

Never, ever give up!

TRY yoga

WHAT IS YOGA?

Yoga is a practice that brings together our body, breath, and mind so that these different parts of us are all working together.

Happy Activity

Try the cat-cow yoga pose to get started and pump up your happiness.

STEP 1: To begin the pose, get down on your hands and knees. Place your hands right underneath your shoulders on the floor and your knees beneath your hips. Spread your fingers out nice and wide.

STEP 2: Inhale deeply and arch your back. Then pull your shoulders down while you look up at the ceiling so that your whole spine has a beautiful arch to it.

STEP 3: As you breathe out, round your back, spread out your shoulder blades, and look toward your belly.

STEP 4: Flow back and forth between these movements three to five times, or however many you like. Make sure you move slowly and breathe fully with each movement.

STEP 5: Check in with yourself to see if anything has shifted or changed. You've gotten oxygen into your system, regulated your breath and nervous system, and set the stage for happiness to unfold.

160

F♥RGIVE

WHEN SOMEONE HURTS **YOUR FEELINGS,**

or treats you badly, it can be hard to move forward. But holding on to that anger and bitterness is actually hurting *you*, not them. And studies have found that forgiving someone can reduce depression, anxiety, and anger. So for your health and happiness, learn to let go and forgive.

KEEP

AN OPEN MIND

When you're willing to see things from a different angle, cool things start happening— you meet interesting people, make amazing discoveries, and embark on awesome adventures.

TAKE CARE
OF SOMETHING

Whether it be a puppy or a plant, if something relies on you to be there and nurture it, that gives you purpose. And having purpose makes people happy.

Pick Flowers

(though not from your neighbor's garden)!

LISTEN TO MUSIC

STUDIES HAVE FOUND THAT MUSIC CAN LESSEN ANXIETY, RELIEVE STRESS, AND BOOST LISTENERS' MOODS. SO TURN UP THOSE HAPPY TUNES!

Sleep soundly

Sleep is the body's way of recharging every night, and it's very important to your overall health. Sleep increases your ability to learn new things, improves your memory, and boosts your attention span. It also helps you be more alert, keep your emotions steady, and feel happier. With all of sleep's great benefits, it's no wonder experts recommend getting between 8½ and 9¼ hours of sleep a night.

Five Keys to Better Z's

- Turn off TVs, computers, cell phones, and other gadgets at least one hour before bedtime.

- Try to go to sleep and wake up around the same time each day.

- Avoid caffeine after noon each day.

- Exercise regularly.

- Try to decrease stress. If you are feeling anxious, try guided meditation, positive visualization, or a breathing exercise before bed.

BE GRATEFUL

Keep a Gratitude Journal

Every night, for about five minutes, take time to reflect on your day and all the parts of it that you're thankful for. If you're having trouble thinking of good things, try answering these questions.

- What went well today?
- Who are the people in my life I love? What do I love about them?
- What parts of my body are healthy and working well?
- What makes me laugh?
- Did I see anything, do anything, or eat anything today that made me smile?

Write a Thank-You Note

You know what's even better than thinking of why you're grateful? Telling someone that you're grateful for them or for something they did. Try writing someone a note, whether it be to a parent, teacher, sister, brother, or friend, and tell them that you appreciate them in your life, and why. Be specific about what it is they do that you're grateful for and how these things make you feel. Not only will you be making whoever you send it to feel happy, you'll feel happier, too!

GO outside

Humans need to be outside, in the sunlight, breathing fresh air into our lungs and being inspired by nature. So turn off that glowing screen and step outside!

5 THINGS TO DO OUTSIDE

1. Go for a hike or nature walk.
2. Climb a tree.
3. Roller-skate or in-line skate.
4. Make up a synchronized swimming routine, or play Marco Polo, in a pool.
5. Check out a field guide from the library and try to identify a flower, tree, or bird.

Costumed performers entertain a crowd with a traditional lion dance during a Lunar New Year celebration in London, England.

CULTURE
CONNECTION

CELEBRATIONS

LUNAR NEW YEAR
January 22

Also called Chinese New Year, this holiday marks the new year according to the lunar calendar. Families celebrate with parades, feasts, and fireworks. Young people may receive gifts of money in red envelopes.

NAURYZ
March 21

This ancient holiday is a major moment on the Kazakhstan calendar. To usher in the start of spring, the people of this Asian country set up tentlike shelters called yurts, play games, go to rock concerts, and feast on rich foods.

EASTER
April 9⁺

A Christian holiday that honors the resurrection of Jesus Christ, Easter is celebrated by giving baskets filled with gifts, decorated eggs, or candy to children.

THE WHITE NIGHTS FESTIVAL
Second week of June through the first week of July

In St. Petersburg, Russia, during the "white nights" of summer the sun stays just above the horizon at night ... and the city comes alive. Festivities held under the midnight sun include the Scarlet Sails celebration, featuring a tall red-sailed ship and a brilliant fireworks display on the Neva River.

MEDELLÍN FLOWER FESTIVAL
(LA FERIA DE LAS FLORES)
Late July/Early August

Each year, Colombia showcases the work of local farmers by displaying their beautiful blooms throughout the city of Medellín. The weeklong festival is complete with competitions and a parade featuring flower-covered floats, horses, antique cars, and more.

ROSH HASHANAH
September 15*–17

A Jewish holiday marking the beginning of a new year on the Hebrew calendar. Celebrations include prayer, ritual foods, and a day of rest.

Around the World

THIMPHU TSHECHU
September 24–26

This colorful three-day Buddhist festival in Thimphu, Bhutan, features bustling markets, religious devotion, and entertainment that includes dances performed wearing traditional masks.

DIWALI
November 12

To symbolize the inner light that protects against spiritual darkness, people light their homes with clay lamps for India's largest and most important holiday.

HANUKKAH
December 7*–15

This Jewish holiday is eight days long. It commemorates the rededication of the Temple in Jerusalem. Hanukkah celebrations include the lighting of menorah candles for eight days and the exchange of gifts.

CHRISTMAS DAY
December 25

A Christian holiday marking the birth of Jesus Christ, Christmas is usually celebrated by decorating trees, exchanging presents, and having festive gatherings.

*Begins at sundown.
† Orthodox Easter is April 16.

2023 CALENDAR

JANUARY
S	M	T	W	T	F	S
1	2	3	4	5	6	7
8	9	10	11	12	13	14
15	16	17	18	19	20	21
22	23	24	25	26	27	28
29	30	31				

FEBRUARY
S	M	T	W	T	F	S
			1	2	3	4
5	6	7	8	9	10	11
12	13	14	15	16	17	18
19	20	21	22	23	24	25
26	27	28				

MARCH
S	M	T	W	T	F	S
			1	2	3	4
5	6	7	8	9	10	11
12	13	14	15	16	17	18
19	20	21	22	23	24	25
26	27	28	29	30	31	

APRIL
S	M	T	W	T	F	S
						1
2	3	4	5	6	7	8
9	10	11	12	13	14	15
16	17	18	19	20	21	22
23	24	25	26	27	28	29
30						

MAY
S	M	T	W	T	F	S
	1	2	3	4	5	6
7	8	9	10	11	12	13
14	15	16	17	18	19	20
21	22	23	24	25	26	27
28	29	30	31			

JUNE
S	M	T	W	T	F	S
				1	2	3
4	5	6	7	8	9	10
11	12	13	14	15	16	17
18	19	20	21	22	23	24
25	26	27	28	29	30	

JULY
S	M	T	W	T	F	S
						1
2	3	4	5	6	7	8
9	10	11	12	13	14	15
16	17	18	19	20	21	22
23	24	25	26	27	28	29
30	31					

AUGUST
S	M	T	W	T	F	S
		1	2	3	4	5
6	7	8	9	10	11	12
13	14	15	16	17	18	19
20	21	22	23	24	25	26
27	28	29	30	31		

SEPTEMBER
S	M	T	W	T	F	S
					1	2
3	4	5	6	7	8	9
10	11	12	13	14	15	16
17	18	19	20	21	22	23
24	25	26	27	28	29	30

OCTOBER
S	M	T	W	T	F	S
1	2	3	4	5	6	7
8	9	10	11	12	13	14
15	16	17	18	19	20	21
22	23	24	25	26	27	28
29	30	31				

NOVEMBER
S	M	T	W	T	F	S
			1	2	3	4
5	6	7	8	9	10	11
12	13	14	15	16	17	18
19	20	21	22	23	24	25
26	27	28	29	30		

DECEMBER
S	M	T	W	T	F	S
					1	2
3	4	5	6	7	8	9
10	11	12	13	14	15	16
17	18	19	20	21	22	23
24	25	26	27	28	29	30
31						

awes8me

1 NIGHT LIGHTS Boca Ciega Bay in St. Petersburg, Florida, U.S.A., comes alive with lighted boats during a floating celebration of the winter holidays. Participants in the annual St. Pete Beach holiday boat parade also donate toys to kids in need. Sounds like a perfect parade!

Festive Parades

THESE SUPER SPECTACLES WILL PUT YOU IN A PARTY MOOD.

2 FLOWER POWER

For more than a century, fantastic flower-covered floats and marching bands have dazzled crowds at the annual Rose Parade in Pasadena, California, U.S.A., on New Year's Day. Not a fan of flowers? Stick around for a college football game that follows the parade.

3
BLAZING BOAT

The Up Helly Aa festival in Lerwick, Scotland, ends every January in a blaze. Harking back to a Viking ritual, hundreds of torchbearers march through the town's streets before setting a 30-foot (9-m)-long galley—a type of ship—on fire.

4 COLORFUL RITUAL

Millions of people of the Hindu faith come together to take a ritual dip in one of four sacred rivers in India as part of the Kumbh Mela festival. The religious procession can include elephants and camels, and festival organizers often provide music and dance performances.

5 BALLOON BONANZA

More than three million people lined the streets of New York City to watch the debut of this Hello Kitty balloon in the Macy's Thanksgiving Day Parade. The parade has been held on the morning of Thanksgiving almost every year since 1924.

DANCE PARTY 6

With fancy headdresses and costumes, dancers perform the samba, an Afro-Brazilian group dance, in front of a crowd at the Carnival parade in Rio de Janeiro, Brazil. Carnival, a festival of merrymaking and feasting, allows people to let loose.

7 FLOATING FESTIVAL

People in Venice, Italy, take their parades to the water. That's because this city is built in a lagoon with canals for streets. Revelers float down the Grand Canal in decorated gondolas and other boats, like this giant mouse gondola, during the annual Carnival festival.

8 CLOWN REVELRY

Giant jesters parade through the streets of the historic French Quarter in New Orleans, Louisiana. During the annual Mardi Gras celebration, nearly a hundred krewes—or festive groups—toss goodies, including toys, stuffed animals, and Mardi Gras beads, to the people who come to watch.

What's Your Chinese Horoscope?
Locate your birth year to find out.

In Chinese astrology, the zodiac runs on a 12-year cycle, based on the lunar calendar. Each year corresponds to one of 12 animals, each representing one of 12 personality types. Read on to find out which animal year you were born in and what that might say about you.

RAT
1972, '84, '96, 2008, '20
Say cheese! You're attractive, charming, and creative. When you get mad, you can have really sharp teeth!

RABBIT
1975, '87, '99, 2011, '23
Your ambition and talent make you jump at opportunity. You also keep your ears open for gossip.

HORSE
1966, '78, '90, 2002, '14
Being happy is your *mane* goal. And though you're smart and hardworking, your teacher may ride you for talking too much.

ROOSTER
1969, '81, '93, 2005, '17
You crow about your adventures, but inside you're really shy. You're thoughtful, capable, brave, and talented.

OX
1973, '85, '97, 2009, '21
You're smart, patient, and as strong as an ... well, you know. Though you're a leader, you never brag.

DRAGON
1988, 2000, '12, '24
You're on fire! Health, energy, honesty, and bravery make you a living legend.

SHEEP
1967, '79, '91, 2003, '15
Gentle as a lamb, you're also artistic, compassionate, and wise. You're often shy.

DOG
1970, '82, '94, 2006, '18
Often the leader of the pack, you're loyal and honest. You can also keep a secret.

TIGER
1974, '86, '98, 2010, '22
You may be a nice person, but no one should ever enter your room without asking—you might attack!

SNAKE
1977, '89, 2001, '13
You may not speak often, but you're very smart. You always seem to have a stash of cash.

MONKEY
1968, '80, '92, 2004, '16
No "monkey see, monkey do" for you. You're a clever problem-solver with an excellent memory.

PIG
1971, '83, '95, 2007, '19
Even though you're courageous, honest, and kind, you never hog all the attention.

Bet You Didn't Know!

6 Spooky Facts for Halloween

1 Cat **urine** can **glow** under **black light.**

2 **Phasmophobia** is the **fear of ghosts.**

3 A man **sculpted a statue** of himself using his own **hair, teeth,** and **nails.**

4 **Vampire bats** don't actually **suck blood—** they **lap it up** with their **tongues.**

5 Mike the **chicken** set a world record by living for **18 months** without a head, from **1945 to 1947.**

6 In ancient Egypt, **a mummy's brain** was removed through the **nose.**

THE WORLD'S LARGEST SANDCASTLE STANDS AS TALL AS A SIX-STORY BUILDING.

The **CASTLE IN DENMARK** beat the previous **RECORD-HOLDING CASTLE,** built in Germany, by about **10 FEET.** (3 m)

IMAGES of **WINDSURFING** and **KITESURFING**— two popular activities in the beach town where it was built— **ARE CARVED INTO THE CASTLE.**

Built in Denmark in 2021 by a squad of 30 sculptors, the sizable sandcastle is solid enough to stand tall through stormy weather. The secret ingredient to get it to stay put? A little bit of clay and a layer of glue.

As a nod to the pandemic, the castle is **TOPPED** with a **REPLICA** of the **CORONAVIRUS WEARING A CROWN.**

The **COLOSSAL CASTLE** is made of more than **5,000 TONS** (4,536 t) of **SAND.**

Cake Fakes

How bakers cook up these desserts in disguise

According to cake artists, the best thing about baking fancy cakes isn't eating them—it's delivering their awesome creations to customers. "In the 50 years I've been doing this, the thing I most look forward to is someone's reaction when I present them with their cake," cake decorator Serdar Yener says. Cake artists like Yener use some cool tricks to inspire these reactions from customers—and to make their baked goods look extra-realistic. A few of these artists spill their secrets here.

TOILET PAPER ... YUM?

Baker Kate Pritchett knew her toilet-paper-roll cake looked like the real deal when her husband found it in the fridge and tried to take it out. "He thought it was actual toilet paper and didn't know why it was in the refrigerator!" she says. The fake TP is actually a three-layer chocolate cake topped with marshmallow-flavored icing. Pritchett used several tools to scratch patterns on the icing to give it a toilet paper–like appearance.

SWEET TOOTH, ER, TEETH

Makeup artist Molly Robbins decided to try painting cakes instead of people's faces after making desserts that resembled her customers' pets. She eventually moved on to crafting complicated wild animals, such as sloths, giraffes, and, yup, sharks. To give this predator its sharp-looking teeth, Robbins sculpted cubes of sugar into some 30 individual shark teeth—only a 10th as many as the 300 a real great white shark would have.

THE PERFECT PIZZA

Bite into this greasy-looking slice of pepperoni pizza and you'll get a sugary surprise: chocolate cake, vanilla buttercream, and pieces of chocolate painted to look like pepperoni. Baker Ben Cullen drizzled a sugary glaze over the "cheese" to make it look oily, plus he curled up the edges of the chocolate pepperonis with a tweezer for a just-out-of-the-oven appearance. To get the crust color right, he experimented with yellow, red, and brown food dyes for a slightly burnt look.

ONE SCOOP OF CAKE, PLEASE

This sundae actually *is* as sweet as it looks! But the entire treat is made of mostly cake, and not, well, ice cream. Decorator BethAnn Goldberg uses a special icing called fondant that's easy to mold and creates a smooth surface. The cherry on top? A hunk of fondant. The bowl and spoon? Also fondant. "Working with fondant is sort of like playing with edible Play-Doh," Goldberg says. She did include *some* cake in the dish: The "scoops" of ice cream are cake—they're flavored to taste like the ice cream they represent.

TIGER-LICIOUS

This 10-pound (4.5-kg) tiger cake gets its real-life look from colored airbrushing: orange-and-white fur that was airbrushed on, then finished with airbrushed black stripes. Its eyeballs are actually white-sugar spheres that have been painted to look like a real tiger's eyes. To keep the heavy cake head from falling off, Yener stuck chopsticks on both sides of the tiger's neck to hold the head in place.

SNEAKY SNEAKERS

Goldberg scuffed up these kicks on purpose, like new-but-ripped jeans. "That's what makes it look like it's *really* a shoe," she says. Goldberg started with a block of vanilla sponge cake that she carved into a sneaker shape. Then she molded fondant over the sneaker structure. Finally, she brushed powdered edible paint over the fondant to look like fabric and added gray scuff marks with a tiny paintbrush.

EAT THE BEAT

You can strum this guitar cake—but you'd have to lick your fingers afterward. Except for the flexible cords used to mimic real guitar strings, this 2.8-foot (0.9-m)-long instrument is completely edible. Plus, the whole thing is coated in a sweet glaze to make it shine. To make the neck, Yener used a sugar paste that dries superhard; the body of the guitar is made of sponge cake that Yener covered with colored fondant. "The hardest part of making any cake is always delivering it," he says. "You're like an airline pilot that has to land *very* carefully."

177

THE SECRET HISTORY OF
CHOCOLATE

THESE FACTS WILL MELT IN YOUR MOUTH.

Deep in the South American rainforest is ... a chocolate tree? One-foot (0.3-m)-long bright yellow pods hang from its branches. Inside are small, bitter seeds that give the tree its name: cacao (kuh-KOW). (The first part of the seed's scientific name, *Theobroma cacao*, translates to "food of the gods" in Greek.) These seeds are how we make chocolate.

The seeds—which grow only near the Equator—don't look or taste delicious.

But ancient people figured out how to use them to make tasty treats. Check out this timeline for the sweet scoop on the history of chocolate.

1 3300 B.C.

The earliest people known to have used the cacao plant are the ancient Mayo-Chinchipe people of what's now Ecuador, a country in South America. Experts aren't sure whether these people used the plant for food, drink, or medicine. But they do know the culture used cacao often, because they found traces of theobromine—a natural chemical compound that comes from the plant—in artifacts found at archaeological sites throughout the region.

2 ca 1800 B.C.

The ancient Olmec people of Mesoamerica (what's now Mexico and Central America) begin using cacao seeds—also called cocoa beans—to brew warm, flavored drinks. Historians aren't sure how the Olmec figured out that the plant's bitter beans would make tasty beverages. But one guess is that when they ate the fruit surrounding the seeds, they'd spit the seeds into a fire, which gave off a pleasing smell.

CACAO BEANS GROW INSIDE PODS LIKE THESE. THE COLOR OF THE POD CHANGES BASED ON SEVERAL THINGS, LIKE THE PLANT'S LOCATION.

Historians don't always know the exact dates of historical events. That's why you'll see a "ca" next to some of the years on these pages. It stands for "circa," meaning "around."

Chocolate bars have been taken on every American and Russian space voyage.

3 ca EIGHTH CENTURY A.D.

Cha-ching! The Maya, another group of ancient people from Mesoamerica, start using cocoa beans as money. Archaeologists have even found counterfeit beans made of clay that people tried to pass off as the real deal.

4 1500s

Many Aztec—ancient people who lived in what's now central Mexico—are drinking cacao every day, mixing the seeds with chilies to make a spicy, frothy beverage. In 1519, Spanish explorer Hernán Cortés reported that Aztec ruler Montezuma II drank 50 cups a day. Cortés brings the drink back to Spain in 1528, and the Spaniards make one big change—adding sugar.

5 1600s–1700s

Chocolate houses—similar to coffeehouses today—become popular gathering spots for rich Europeans and Americans to meet over a hot chocolate drink. During the Revolutionary War, which lasts from 1775 to 1783, wounded soldiers are given the beverage to warm them and provide an energy boost, and troops are sometimes paid with cocoa beans. In 1785, Thomas Jefferson predicts that hot chocolate will become as popular as tea or coffee.

6 1800s

A company called J. S. Fry & Sons of England adds extra cacao butter to liquid chocolate, turning it solid and creating the first mass-produced chocolate bars. Over the next several decades, chocolate makers add milk powder to their recipes to create milk chocolate.

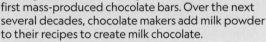

Chocolate is still kind of ... chewy. So in 1879, Rodolphe Lindt of Switzerland comes up with a process called conching, in which a machine stirs the chocolate until it gets that melt-in-your-mouth texture. Dozens of different brands start making their own chocolate bars with the conching process.

A chemical in cacao releases feel-good chemicals in the brain.

7 EARLY 1900s

At the beginning of the 20th century, the main ingredient in chocolate—cocoa—becomes much cheaper. Chocolate is no longer a treat for just rich people, and stores around the world are stocked with affordable chocolate bars for everyone.

8 2023

Chocolate can now be found in grocery stores, candy shops ... and on the runway. Salon du Chocolat, the world's biggest chocolate festival, features a chocolate fashion show in Paris, France, every year, with clothes made of the sweet treat. The outfits are too fragile to be sold, so after the festival some are put on display in what must be the best-smelling museum exhibit ever.

MONEY AROUND THE WORLD!

The Southern Cross constellation appears on **Brazilian coins.**

ACCORDING to some **PEOPLE, CANADA'S $100 BANKNOTE** gives off the scent of **MAPLE SYRUP.**

A British businessman created his own currency —named the **PUFFIN—** for an island he owned off England.

IN FEBRUARY 2015, SCUBA DIVERS OFF ISRAEL FOUND MORE THAN 2,600 GOLD COINS DATING BACK AS FAR AS THE NINTH CENTURY.

Bank of **BOTSWANA**

This note is legal tender for **Ten Pula**

Botswana's currency is named **PULA,** meaning **"RAIN,"** which is **VALUABLE** in this **ARID NATION.**

A **JANITOR** at a **GERMAN LIBRARY** found and turned in a **BOX OF RARE COINS** thought to be worth **HUNDREDS OF THOUSANDS OF DOLLARS.**

ANCIENT GREEKS believed that PLACING A COIN IN A DEAD PERSON'S MOUTH would pay for the ferry ride to the afterlife.

COINS CREATED IN **1616** FOR WHAT IS NOW **BERMUDA** WERE NICKNAMED **"HOGGIES"** BECAUSE THEY HAD IMAGES OF **HOGS** ON THEM.

More than **$5 TRILLION** in **MONOPOLY MONEY** has been printed since 1935.

IN INDIA, the SLANG TERM for **100,000 RUPEES** IS *PETI*, OR SUITCASE. You might need one to carry that much money!

KING TUT APPEARS ON THE EGYPTIAN 1-POUND COIN.

A BRITISH ARTIST MADE A DRESS OUT OF USED BANKNOTES FROM AROUND THE WORLD.

MONEY TIP! CLIP COUPONS FOR YOUR PARENTS. Ask if they'll put the money they save into your piggy bank.

SAVING
Languages At Risk

Today, there are more than 7,000 languages spoken on Earth. But by 2100, more than half of these may disappear. In fact, some experts say one language dies every two weeks, as a result of the increasing dominance of languages such as English, Spanish, and Mandarin.

So what can be done to keep dialects from disappearing altogether? To start, several National Geographic Explorers have embarked on various projects around the planet. Together, they are part of the race to save some of the world's most threatened languages, as well as to protect and preserve the cultures they belong to. Here are some of the Explorers' stories.

The Explorer: Tam Thi Ton
The Language: Bahnar

TON IN A BAHNAR CLASSROOM

The Work: By gathering folklore like riddles and comics, Ton is creating bilingual learning materials for elementary students to teach them Bahnar, the language of an ethnic group living in Vietnam's Central Highlands.

NARAYANAN SHARES STORIES FROM THE FIELD AT NATIONAL GEOGRAPHIC'S HEADQUARTERS IN WASHINGTON, D.C., U.S.A.

The Explorer: Sandhya Narayanan
The Languages: Quechua and Aymara

The Work: By immersing herself in the Indigenous languages of the Andean region along the Peru-Bolivia border, Narayanan aims to understand how interactions among Indigenous groups affect language over time.

HARRISON DOING AN INTERVIEW

The Explorer: K. David Harrison
The Language: Koro-Aka

The Work: Harrison led an expedition to India that identified Koro-Aka, a language which was completely new to science. He is also vice president of the Living Tongues Institute for Endangered Languages, dedicated to raising awareness and revitalizing little-documented languages.

The Explorer: Susan Barfield
The Language: Mapudungun

The Work: Barfield shines a light on the language of the Mapuche people of southern Chile with her trilingual children's book, *El Copihue*. The book is based on a Mapuche folktale and is illustrated by Mapuche students.

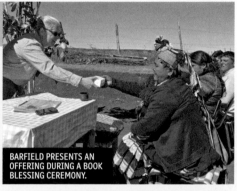

BARFIELD PRESENTS AN OFFERING DURING A BOOK BLESSING CEREMONY.

PERLIN INTERVIEWS A VILLAGE LEADER.

The Explorer: Ross Perlin
The Language: Seke

The Work: In an effort to preserve the Seke language of northern Nepal, Perlin has been working closely with speakers both in their villages and in New York, where many now live, including young speakers determined to document their own language.

The Explorer: Lal Rapacha
The Language: Kiranti-Kõits

The Work: As the founder and director of the Research Institute for Kiratology in Kathmandu, Nepal, Rapacha carries out research on the lesser known languages of Indigenous Himalayan people, including Kiranti-Kõits, his endangered mother tongue.

RAPACHA WORKING IN THE FIELD IN NEPAL

MYTHOLOGY

GREEK

EGYPTIAN

The ancient Greeks believed that many gods and goddesses ruled the universe. According to this mythology, the Olympians lived high atop Greece's Mount Olympus. Each of these 12 principal gods and goddesses had a unique personality that corresponded to particular aspects of life, such as love or death.

Egyptian mythology is based on a creation myth that tells of an egg that appeared on the ocean. When the egg hatched, out came Ra, the sun god. As a result, ancient Egyptians became worshippers of the sun and of the nine original deities, most of whom were the children and grandchildren of Ra.

THE OLYMPIANS

Aphrodite was the goddess of love and beauty.

Apollo, Zeus's son, was the god of the sun, music, and healing. Artemis was his twin.

Ares, Zeus's son, was the god of war.

Artemis, Zeus's daughter and Apollo's twin, was the goddess of the hunt and of childbirth.

Athena, born from the forehead of Zeus, was the goddess of wisdom and crafts.

Demeter was the goddess of fertility and nature.

Hades, Zeus's brother, was the god of the underworld and the dead.

Hephaestus, the son of Hera and Zeus, was the god of fire.

Hera, the wife and older sister of Zeus, was the goddess of women and marriage.

Hermes, Zeus's son, was the messenger of the gods.

Poseidon, the brother of Zeus, was the god of the seas and earthquakes.

Zeus was the most powerful of the gods and the top Olympian. He wielded a thunderbolt and was the god of the sky and thunder.

THE NINE DEITIES

Geb, son of Shu and Tefnut, was the god of the earth.

Isis (Ast), daughter of Geb and Nut, was the goddess of fertility and motherhood.

Nephthys (Nebet-Hut), daughter of Geb and Nut, was protector of the dead.

Nut, daughter of Shu and Tefnut, was the goddess of the sky.

Osiris (Usir), son of Geb and Nut, was the god of the afterlife.

Ra (Re), the sun god, is generally viewed as the creator. He represents life and health.

Seth (Set), son of Geb and Nut, was the god of the desert and chaos.

Shu, son of Ra, was the god of air.

Tefnut, daughter of Ra, was the goddess of rain.

All cultures around the world have unique legends and traditions that have been passed down over generations. Many myths refer to gods or supernatural heroes who are responsible for occurrences in the world. For example, Norse mythology tells of the red-bearded Thor, the god of thunder, who is responsible for creating lightning and thunderstorms. And many creation myths, especially those from some of North America's native cultures, tell of an earth-diver represented as an animal that brings a piece of sand or mud up from the deep sea. From this tiny piece of earth, the entire world takes shape.

NORSE

ROMAN

Norse mythology originated in Scandinavia, in northern Europe. It was complete with gods and goddesses who lived in a heavenly place called Asgard that could be reached only by crossing a rainbow bridge.

Although Norse mythology is lesser known, we use it every day. Most days of the week are named after Norse gods, including some of these major deities.

NORSE GODS

Balder was the god of light and beauty.

Freya was the goddess of love, beauty, and fertility.

Frigg, for whom Friday was named, was the queen of Asgard. She was the goddess of marriage, motherhood, and the home.

Heimdall was the watchman of the rainbow bridge and the guardian of the gods.

Hel, the daughter of Loki, was the goddess of death.

Loki, a shape-shifter, was a trickster who helped the gods—and caused them problems.

Skadi was the goddess of winter and of the hunt. She is often represented as the "Snow Queen."

Thor, for whom Thursday was named, was the god of thunder and lightning.

Tyr, for whom Tuesday was named, was the god of the sky and war.

Wodan, for whom Wednesday was named, was the god of war, wisdom, death, and magic.

Much of Roman mythology was adopted from Greek mythology, but the Romans also developed a lot of original myths as well. The gods of Roman mythology lived everywhere, and each had a role to play. There were thousands of Roman gods, but here are a few of the stars of Roman myths.

ANCIENT ROMAN GODS

Ceres was the goddess of the harvest and motherly love.

Diana, daughter of Jupiter, was the goddess of hunting and the moon.

Juno, Jupiter's wife, was the goddess of women and fertility.

Jupiter, the patron of Rome and master of the gods, was the god of the sky.

Mars, the son of Jupiter and Juno, was the god of war.

Mercury, the son of Jupiter, was the messenger of the gods and the god of travelers.

Minerva was the goddess of wisdom, learning, and the arts and crafts.

Neptune, the brother of Jupiter, was the god of the sea.

Venus was the goddess of love and beauty.

Vesta was the goddess of fire and the hearth. She was one of the most important of the Roman deities.

World Religions

A round the world, religion takes many forms. Some belief systems, such as Christianity, Islam, and Judaism, are monotheistic, meaning that followers believe in just one supreme being. Others, like Hinduism, Shintoism, and most native belief systems, are polytheistic, meaning that many of their followers believe in multiple gods.

All of the major religions have their origins in Asia, but they have spread around the world. Christianity, with the largest number of followers, has three divisions—Roman Catholic, Eastern Orthodox, and Protestant. Islam, with about one-quarter of all believers, has two main divisions—Sunni and Shiite. Hinduism and Buddhism account for almost another one-fifth of believers. Judaism, dating back some 4,000 years, has nearly 15 million followers, less than one percent of all believers.

CHRISTIANITY

Based on the teachings of Jesus Christ, a Jew born some 2,000 years ago in the area of modern-day Israel, Christianity has spread worldwide and actively seeks converts. Followers in Switzerland (above) participate in an Easter season procession with lanterns and crosses.

BUDDHISM

Founded about 2,400 years ago in northern India by the Hindu prince Gautama Buddha, Buddhism spread throughout East and Southeast Asia. Buddhist temples have statues, such as the Mihintale Buddha (above) in Sri Lanka.

HINDUISM

Dating back more than 4,000 years, Hinduism is practiced mainly in India. Hindus follow sacred texts known as the Vedas and believe in reincarnation. During the festival of Navratri, which honors the goddess Durga, the Garba dance is performed (above).

Spreading Light

Sisters in traditional Indian clothing celebrate Diwali by placing clay lamps on rangoli—decorative patterns created on the floor with materials such as colored powders or sand. Diwali is a five-day Hindu festival celebrating the triumph of light over darkness.

ISLAM

Muslims believe that the Quran, Islam's sacred book, records the words of Allah (God) as revealed to the Prophet Muhammad beginning around A.D. 610. Believers (above) circle the Kaaba in the Grand Mosque in Mecca, Saudi Arabia, the spiritual center of the faith.

JUDAISM

The traditions, laws, and beliefs of Judaism date back to Abraham (the patriarch) and the Torah (the first five books of the Old Testament). Followers pray before the Western Wall (above), which stands below Islam's Dome of the Rock in Jerusalem.

QUIZ WHIZ

How vast is your knowledge about the world around you? Quiz yourself!

Write your answers on a piece of paper. Then check them below.

1 In ancient Egypt, how was a mummy's brain removed?
a. through the mouth
b. through the belly button
c. through the nose
d. It wasn't removed.

2 In which city does an annual Mardi Gras parade with giant jesters take place?
a. New York, New York
b. New Orleans, Louisiana
c. New Delhi, India
d. Lerwick, Scotland

3 In India, the slang term for 100,000 rupees is _____.
a. treasure
b. penny
c. token
d. peti

4 The earliest people known to have used the cacao plant are the _____.
a. Mayo-Chinchipe
b. Chinese
c. Egyptian
d. Olmec

5 **True or false?** Everything in this sneaker, pictured to the right, is edible—down to the shoelaces!

Not **STUMPED** yet? Check out the *NATIONAL GEOGRAPHIC KIDS QUIZ WHIZ* collection for more crazy **CULTURE** questions!

ANSWERS: 1. c; 2. b; 3. d; 4. a; 5. True

Explore a New Culture

STAMPS OF BRAZIL

CURRENCY AND COINS OF BRAZIL

FLAG OF BRAZIL

YOU'RE A STUDENT, but you're also a citizen of the world. Writing a report on another country or your own country is a great way to better understand and appreciate how different people live. Pick the country of your ancestors, one that's been in the news, or one that you'd like to visit someday.

Passport to Success

A country report follows the format of an expository essay because you're "exposing" information about the country you choose.

The following step-by-step tips will help you with this international task.

1 **RESEARCH.** Gathering information is the most important step in writing a good country report. Look to internet sources, encyclopedias, books, magazine and newspaper articles, and other sources to find important and interesting details about your subject.

2 **ORGANIZE YOUR NOTES.** Put the information you gather into a rough outline. For example, sort everything you found about the country's system of government, climate, etc.

3 **WRITE IT UP.** Follow the basic structure of good writing: introduction, body, and conclusion. Remember that each paragraph should have a topic sentence that is then supported by facts and details. Incorporate the information from your notes, but make sure it's in your own words. And make your writing flow with good transitions and descriptive language.

4 **ADD VISUALS.** Include maps, diagrams, photos, and other visual aids.

5 **PROOFREAD AND REVISE.** Correct any mistakes, and polish your language. Do your best!

6 **CITE YOUR SOURCES.** Be sure to keep a record of your sources.

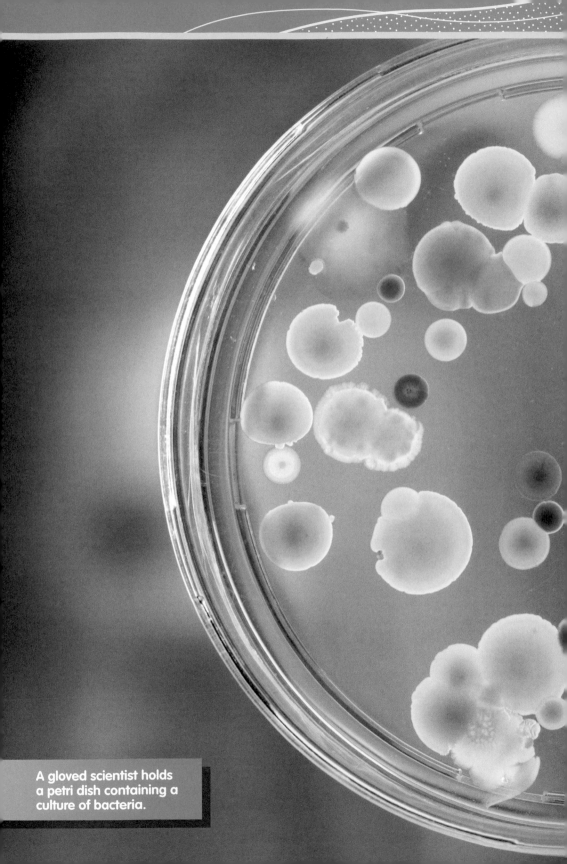

A gloved scientist holds a petri dish containing a culture of bacteria.

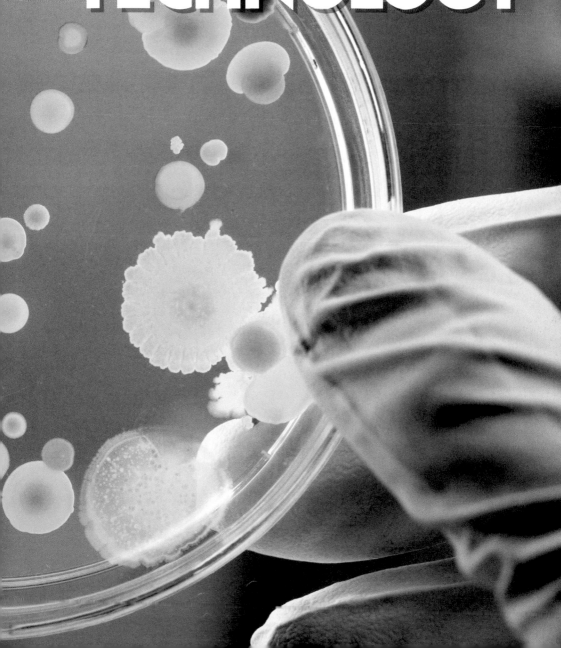

SCIENCE and
TECHNOLOGY

THIS
RACE CAR

HYPERCARS can **ACCELERATE** from **0** TO **60** **MILES AN HOUR** (0 to 97 km/h) in less than three seconds, about four seconds faster than a minivan.

CAN REACH TOP SPEEDS OF MORE THAN
200 MILES AN HOUR
(322 KM/H)—
MORE THAN THREE TIMES THE LEGAL LIMIT ON MOST HIGHWAYS.

Forget flying cars: This is the future of racing. Known as hypercars, these custom-built, super-lightweight vehicles have powerful engines with electric components that can rocket them to breakneck speeds. Top competitions, such as the Le Mans 24 Hours race in France, now have a special division for hypercars.

IN 2021, **TOYOTA'S GR010 HYBRID** raced into the **RECORD BOOKS,** becoming the **FIRST CAR TO WIN** in the new Hypercar category at Le Mans.

The **ELECTRIC MOTORS** used in **HYPERCARS** allow them to **SPEED UP FASTER** than cars powered by gas alone.

A hypercar's body is usually made of **CARBON FIBER**—a material that is up to **10 TIMES STRONGER THAN STEEL,** but five times lighter.

Toyota GR010 Hybrid

6 COOL INVENTIONS

SUPERSMART GADGETS, ACCESSORIES, AND VEHICLES THAT COULD CHANGE YOUR LIFE

1 BIKE TAKES FLIGHT

The Speeder has a seat and handlebars just like a motorcycle, but this contraption travels to a place you could never reach on a regular bike—**the sky!** Just press a button to take off. Four **turbojet engines** on the bike's front and back launch it off the ground. Steer the handlebars to move the craft **through the air.** Weighing about 230 pounds (104 kg), the bike won't require a pilot's license to fly. Although still being tested, the Speeder is expected to reach speeds of **60 miles an hour (97 km/h) and climb up to 15,000 feet (4,572 m).** Talk about getting a lift!

2 SMOKELESS FIREPLACE

Typically, where there's smoke, there's fire—and vice versa. But a **neat new gadget** called the **Le Feu** generates the heat and ambiance of a flickering fire ... and that's it. How? The burner inside this sleek, steel orb is **heated by bioethanol fuel,** which is **made from plants like corn and sugarcane,** and doesn't produce any smoke. And the Le Feu doesn't just keep you cozy: It's **better for the environment,** too, since **bioethanol emits no harmful or toxic gases,** either. Meaning it warms you up without contributing to global warming.

③ VIRTUAL KEYBOARD

Tap out an **email right on** your **kitchen table,** or type up a report on your bedroom floor. With the **Magic Cube,** you can turn any flat, opaque surface into a **keyboard.** Connect the small, cube-shaped device to a smartphone, tablet, or computer. The cube uses a laser beam to **project a keyboard** onto the surface. A **sensor** inside the cube **tracks** where your fingers are tapping and then translates the movements into letters and numbers. The cube even plays **tapping sounds** while you type, just in case you miss the **clickety-clack** of your old-fashioned keyboard.

④ BENDY BIKE

Here's one way to confuse a bike thief: Wrap your bike around a pole! Bendy bikes let you do just that, thanks to a frame that's **flexible enough to wrap around lampposts and street signs.** Hoping to decrease the number of bikes stolen each year, a design student came up with this **clever cycle** that looks like a regular bike when you're riding it. Once you're ready to lock it up, however, loosen a cable below the seat to **split the bike into two segments.** Then bend the frame up to 180 degrees. Next, secure it to a pole with a regular bike lock, leaving would-be thieves **scratching their heads.**

⑤ IN-EAR TRANSLATOR

So you're visiting Paris, **but you don't speak** French. No problem! Just pop in the **Pilot earpiece** and use the app to **understand every word another user says to you.** The earbud device **translates languages** like Spanish and Italian in real time. Simply select which language you want from an **app on your phone,** then let the Pilot do the translating. **Voilà!**

⑥ SMART RING

When the lights are too low for you to read on your couch, just tap your thumb to your ring finger three times. And while you're at it, **make a call,** too—all without ever touching your phone. That's what a smart ring called **ORII** can do. Simply slide the ring onto your finger, and a **Bluetooth chip** in the ring will control your smart devices wirelessly. **Sync it to your smart gadget,** then call a friend or **shoot off a text** just by speaking into a pair of microphones on the inside of the device. This ring's not quite the same as having a personal assistant—but it's the **next best thing.**

WHAT IS LIFE?

This seems like such an easy question to answer. Everybody knows that singing birds are alive and rocks are not. But when we start studying bacteria and other microscopic creatures, things get more complicated.

SO WHAT EXACTLY IS LIFE?
Most scientists agree that something is alive if it can reproduce, grow in size to become more complex in structure, take in nutrients to survive, give off waste products, and respond to external stimuli, such as increased sunlight or changes in temperature.

KINDS OF LIFE
Biologists classify living organisms by how they get their energy. Organisms such as algae, green plants, and some bacteria use sunlight as an energy source. Animals (like humans), fungi, and some single-celled microscopic organisms called Archaea use chemicals to provide energy. When we eat food, chemical reactions within our digestive system turn our food into fuel.

Living things inhabit land, sea, and air. In fact, life thrives deep beneath the oceans, embedded in rocks miles below Earth's crust, in ice, and in other extreme environments. The life-forms that thrive in these challenging environments are called extremophiles. Some of these draw directly upon the chemicals surrounding them for energy. Because these are very different forms of life than what we're used to, we may not think of them as alive, but they are.

HOW IT ALL WORKS
To understand how a living organism works, it helps to look at one example of its simplest form—the single-celled bacterium called *Streptococcus*. There are many kinds of these tiny organisms, and some are responsible for human illnesses. What makes us sick or uncomfortable are the toxins the bacteria give off in our bodies.

A single *Streptococcus* bacterium is so small that at least 500 of them could fit on the dot above this letter *i*. These bacteria are some of the simplest forms of life we know. They have no moving parts, no lungs, no brain, no heart, no liver, and no leaves or fruit. Yet this life-form reproduces. It grows in size by producing long-chain structures, takes in nutrients, and gives off waste products. This tiny life-form is alive, just as you are alive.

What makes something alive is a question scientists grapple with when they study viruses, such as the ones that cause the common cold and COVID-19. They can grow and reproduce within host cells, such as those that make up your body. Because viruses lack cells and cannot metabolize nutrients for energy or reproduce without a host, scientists ask if they are indeed alive. And don't go looking for them without a strong microscope—viruses are a hundred times smaller than bacteria.

Scientists think life began on Earth more than four billion years ago, but no fossils exist from that time. The earliest fossils ever found are from the primitive life that existed 3.5 billion years ago. Other life-forms, some of which are shown below, soon followed. Scientists continue to study how life evolved on Earth and whether it is possible that life exists on other planets.

MICROSCOPIC ORGANISMS

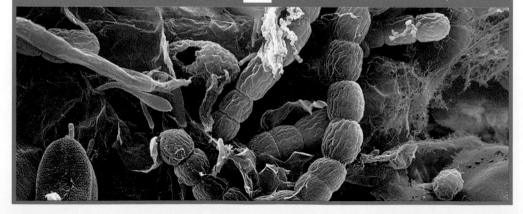

The Three Domains of Life

Biologists divide all living organisms into three domains, or groups: Bacteria, Archaea, and Eukarya. Archaea and Bacteria cells do not have nuclei—cellular parts that are essential to reproduction and other cell functions—but they are different from each other in many ways. Because human cells have a nucleus, we belong to the Eukarya domain.

1 BACTERIA

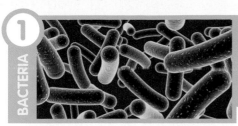

DOMAIN BACTERIA: These single-celled microorganisms are found almost everywhere in the world. Bacteria are small and do not have nuclei. They can be shaped like rods, spirals, or spheres. Some of them are helpful to humans, and some are harmful.

2 ARCHAEA

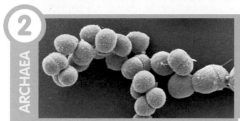

DOMAIN ARCHAEA: These single-celled micro-organisms are often found in extremely hostile environments. Like Bacteria, Archaea do not have nuclei, but they have some genes in common with Eukarya. For this reason, scientists think the Archaea living today most closely resemble the earliest forms of life on Earth.

3 EUKARYA

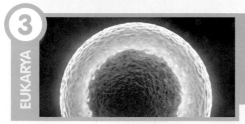

DOMAIN EUKARYA: This diverse group of life-forms is more complicated than Bacteria and Archaea, as Eukarya have one or more cells with nuclei. These are the tiny cells that make up your whole body. Eukarya are divided into four groups: fungi, protists, plants, and animals.

FYI

WHAT IS A DOMAIN? Scientifically speaking, a domain is a major taxonomic division into which natural objects are classified (see page 44 for "What Is Taxonomy?").

FUNGI

KINGDOM FUNGI Mainly multicellular organisms, fungi cannot make their own food. Mushrooms and yeast are fungi.

PROTISTS

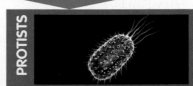

PROTISTS Once considered a kingdom, this group is a "grab bag" that includes unicellular and multicellular organisms of great variety.

PLANTS

KINGDOM PLANTAE Plants are multi-cellular, and many can make their own food using photosynthesis (see page 198 for "Photosynthesis").

ANIMALS

KINGDOM ANIMALIA Most animals, which are multicellular, have their own organ systems. Animals do not make their own food.

HOW DOES YOUR GARDEN GR🌻W?

The plant kingdom is about 400,000 species strong, growing all over the world: on top of mountains, in the sea, in frigid temperatures—everywhere. Without plants, life on Earth would not be able to survive. Plants provide food and oxygen for animals, including humans.

Plants have three distinct characteristics:

1. Most have chlorophyll (a green pigment that makes photosynthesis work and turns sunlight into energy), while some are parasitic. Parasitic plants don't make their own food—they take it from other plants.
2. Plants cannot change their location on their own.
3. Their cell walls are made from a stiff material called cellulose.

Photosynthesis

Plants are lucky—most don't have to hunt or shop for food. Most use the sun to produce their own food. In a process called photosynthesis, a plant's chloroplast (the part of the plant where the chemical chlorophyll is located) captures the sun's energy and combines it with carbon dioxide from the air and nutrient-rich water from the ground to produce a sugar called glucose.

Plants burn the glucose for energy to help them grow. As a waste product, plants emit oxygen, which humans and other animals need to breathe. When we breathe, we exhale carbon dioxide, which the plants then use for more photosynthesis—it's all a big, finely tuned system. So the next time you pass a lonely houseplant, give it thanks for helping you live.

Plants That STINK!

Not all plants smell like roses. Here are two of the STINKIEST members of the plant kingdom.

Giant Rafflesia

THE RAFFLESIA IS THE LARGEST FLOWER IN THE WORLD.

THE RAFFLESIA'S ODOR ATTRACTS FLIES.

Western Skunk Cabbage

EASTERN SKUNK CABBAGE

If you ever walk by a rafflesia flower or a skunk cabbage, you may be unpleasantly surprised by the not-so-sweet smell wafting from these peculiar plants. The giant rafflesia, which grows in the rainforests of Indonesia and is also the largest flower in the world, is called the "corpse flower" because of its offensive odor. Some people compare it to the smell of rotting meat or fish! And the skunk cabbage, a wildflower that grows in swampy, wet areas in North American forests, gets its name from the pungent scent that its leaves and flowers emit when they're crushed or bruised.

So what's up with these flowers' funky fragrances? The odor is actually the plants' superpower! The stink of the rafflesia attracts flies and beetles, which sometimes even lay their eggs inside the flower and help to pollinate it. And the skunk cabbage's stink does the same for flies, butterflies, wasps, and other pollinators. Both plants also generate heat—a very rare trait among plants—which creates an extra-cozy spot for bugs to hang out and lay eggs.

While humans may, uh, turn their noses up at the stench of stinky plants, insects experience just the opposite effect, and that's a good thing. Why? Pollination is super important. Without it, plants can't make seeds and reproduce. And because all plants play a role in maintaining a healthy ecosystem, we need them around—no matter how bad they smell.

Your Amazing Body!

About **10,000** of the **CELLS** in your body could fit on the head of a **PIN.**

The human body is a complicated mass of systems—nine systems, to be exact. Each has a unique and critical purpose in the body, and we wouldn't be able to survive without all of them.

The **NERVOUS** system controls the body.

The **MUSCULAR** system makes movement possible.

The **SKELETAL** system supports the body.

The **CIRCULATORY** system moves blood throughout the body.

The **RESPIRATORY** system provides the body with oxygen.

The **DIGESTIVE** system breaks down food into nutrients and gets rid of waste.

The **IMMUNE** system protects the body against disease and infection.

The **ENDOCRINE** system regulates the body's functions.

The **REPRODUCTIVE** system enables people to produce offspring.

weird but true!

If you **NEVER CUT YOUR HAIR,** it could grow more than **30 FEET** (9 M) in your lifetime.

MESSAGES FROM YOUR BRAIN TRAVEL ALONG YOUR **NERVES** at up to **200 MILES** AN HOUR (322 KM/H).

WHAT'S YOUR TYPE?

Everyone's blood is made of the same basic elements, but not all blood is alike. There are four main blood types. If a person needs to use donated blood, the donated blood can react with their body's immune system if it's not the right type. This diagram shows which types of blood are compatible with each other.

GROUP O can donate red blood cells to anybody. It's the universal donor.

GROUP A can donate red blood cells to A's and AB's.

GROUP B can donate red blood cells to B's and AB's.

GROUP AB can donate to other AB's, but can receive from all others.

O+ is the most common blood type: **38%** of people in the U.S. have this type.

Blood types can be positive or negative. Only **18%** of people in the U.S. have a negative blood type.

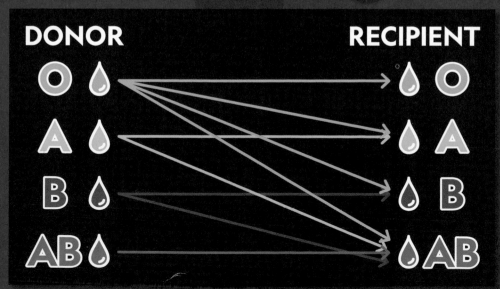

DONOR   RECIPIENT

O
A
B
AB

WHY can't
I eat peanuts or pet a fluffy dog without
FEELING ICKY?

Sounds like you have an allergy, and you're not alone! As many as 30 percent of grown-ups and 40 percent of kids suffer from allergies. Allergic reactions include itching, sneezing, coughing, a runny nose, vomiting, rashes, and shortness of breath. They happen when your body's immune system—which normally fights germs—treats something harmless, like food or a particular medicine, like it's a dangerous invader. Once it detects one of these intruders, called an allergen, your immune system goes into high alert. It creates antibodies to repel the intruder, causing the tissues around the allergen to become inflamed or swollen, which can make it hard for you to breathe. Extreme reactions can even result in a potentially deadly full-body response known as anaphylactic shock.

AWFUL allergens

PEANUTS

One of the most common food allergens, along with shellfish.

PET DANDER

Tiny flakes of shed fur and feathers can make your eyes water and your nose go *ahchoo!*

DUST MITES

Millions of these microscopic arachnids live in your house, feasting on your dead skin cells. Cleaning stirs up clouds of mite shells and their micro-poop.

PENICILLIN

Antibiotics like penicillin kill bacteria that make us sick, but they can do more harm than good for patients allergic to them.

POLLEN

Plants project this fine powdery substance into the breeze to fertilize other plants. It can irritate the nasal passages of allergy sufferers, causing sneezing and watery eyes—a condition commonly called hay fever.

Why do we have allergies?

Stories of allergies go back to ancient Egypt, yet their causes largely remain a mystery. Not everyone has allergies. Some form in childhood. Some happen later in life. And sometimes they go away as you get older. You may inherit a likelihood of having allergies from your parents but usually not their particular allergies.

Scientists suspect humans evolved with these extreme and mysterious immune reactions to combat genuinely deadly threats, such as parasitic worms or other toxins. And though doctors are doubtful they can ever cure allergies, they've come up with many ways to test for them and provide medications that treat the symptoms.

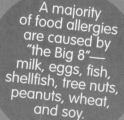

A majority of food allergies are caused by "the Big 8"— milk, eggs, fish, shellfish, tree nuts, peanuts, wheat, and soy.

WHY can't I USE my left hand as well as my right one
(or the other way around)?

About nine out of 10 of you reading this book will turn its pages with your right hand— the same hand you use to write a note or chuck a fastball. About 90 percent of humans are right-handed, meaning their right hand is their dominant hand. The other 10 percent are left-handed. Activities that feel natural with the dominant hand are awkward or difficult with the other one. Ever try to sign your name with your nondominant hand? Not so easy!

Cave paintings going back more than 5,000 years show humans favoring their right or left hand according to the same nine-to-one ratio we see today. And the same goes for the stone tools our evolutionary ancestors used 1.5 million years ago: Studies show a similar dominance of the right hand long before the human species, *Homo sapiens*, appeared in the fossil record.

So **why** is one hand dominant?

Scientists have discovered a sequence of genes linked to hand dominance, making it a trait that's passed along to children just like hair color or dimples. These traits determine how our brains are wired. How? The brain is split into two symmetrical halves known as hemispheres. In about 90 percent of people, the left side of the brain processes language skills. These people are typically right-handed. People born with genes for left-handedness—about 10 percent of the population—typically have brains that process speech on the right side.

So whichever side of the brain controls speech usually corresponds with a dominant hand on the opposite side. Because the left side of the brain controls the right side of the body and vice versa, scientists suspect that the evolution of our dominant hand is somehow connected to the development of our language capabilities. Humans can have a dominant eye, foot, and ear, too—but scientists aren't quite sure why. That's just one of many reasons the human brain is considered the most complex object in the universe.

$$NaOH + HCl \longrightarrow NaCl + H_2O$$

ARE YOU A "mixed-hander"?

What about people who can use their nondominant hand almost as well as their dominant? They're called mixed-handers. (Scientists don't like using the term "ambidextrous," which implies neither hand is dominant.) About one percent of people are elite lefties/righties. Are you? Grab a piece of scratch paper and find out!

15 COOL THINGS ABOUT SLEEP

Ancient Greeks believed that **LETTUCE JUICE** could help them sleep.

A hotel straddling the **border of France and Switzerland** lets you sleep with your **head in one country** and your **feet in the other.**

The position you sleep in may provide clues to **YOUR PERSONALITY.** If you sleep curled up, you might be shy.

Humans spend about **ONE-THIRD** of their lives **ASLEEP.**

ON AVERAGE, a person **PASSES GAS 14 times a day—** mostly while asleep.

People tend to **SLEEP LESS** during a **FULL MOON.**

The **LOUDEST SNORES** can reach more than **100 DECIBELS.** That's as loud as **highway traffic!**

Your brain is sometimes **MORE ACTIVE WHEN YOU SLEEP THAN WHEN YOU'RE AWAKE.**

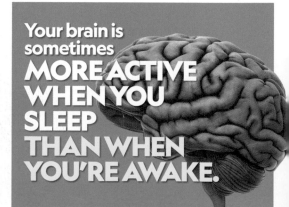

204

ASTRONAUTS on spaceships typically **sleep in sleeping bags** that **ARE STRAPPED TO THE WALL.**

You're **more likely to yawn** if **someone near you does,** especially if **you know them.**

PILLOWS have been found in **ANCIENT EGYPTIAN TOMBS.**

Your brain makes memories while you sleep.

To STAY AWAKE on the **FIRST EVER SOLO FLIGHT** over the Atlantic Ocean **in 1927, aviator Charles Lindbergh** held his eyes open with his fingers.

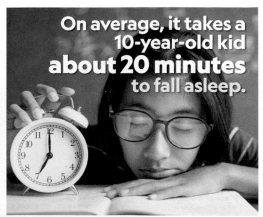

On average, it takes a 10-year-old kid **about 20 minutes** to fall asleep.

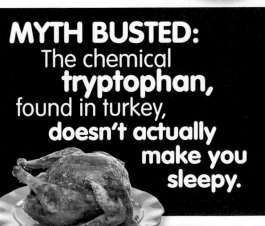

MYTH BUSTED: The chemical **tryptophan,** found in turkey, **doesn't actually make you sleepy.**

205

THE SCIENCE OF
SPOOKY

HOW THESE CREEPY THINGS AFFECT YOUR BRAIN

What's that strange noise in the night? Is it the wind? Or something else?

"When you encounter something scary, your brain releases chemicals," psychologist Martin Antony says. "These chemicals make our hearts race, so we breathe faster and sweat. Your nervous system is preparing your body to either fight a threat or run away from it." Scientists call this the "fight-or-flight" response.

So which so-called spookiness makes us feel this way—and why? Discover what puts the *eek!* in these five freaky things.

THE FEAR: SPIDERS

SCIENTIFIC NAME: Arachnophobia

SPOOKY SCIENCE: Humans have been afraid of spiders since our ancient human ancestors thought they carried deadly diseases. "Today, we know that's not true," psychologist Kyle Rexer says. "But a lot of people still have incorrect ideas about how dangerous spiders are." Although some spiders *can* be deadly, most are not. In fact, humans actually benefit from the existence of spiders. By eating disease-carrying critters such as mosquitoes and cockroaches, these arachnids act as a form of pest control. Plus, scientists are currently studying spider venom in the hope that it can one day be used in medicines to manage pain or cure illnesses.

THE FEAR: CLOWNS

SCIENTIFIC NAME: Coulrophobia

SPOOKY SCIENCE: One way we decide if a person is friend or foe is by evaluating their facial expressions. Clowns—with their makeup, wigs, and fake noses—are hard to read, which is what makes them scary to some people. "It's hard to tell how a clown is feeling," psychology professor Frank McAndrew says. "So we think, If clowns can hide their emotions, what else might they be hiding?"

FIGHT THE FRIGHT

It's natural to avoid things that scare us. "But to get over your fears—whether you're afraid of spiders, clowns, the dark, or, well, anything—you have to *focus* on them instead of avoid them," Rexer says.

THE FEAR: HEIGHTS
SCIENTIFIC NAME: Acrophobia
SPOOKY SCIENCE: When you're standing on solid ground, your eyes work with your inner ears to help you stay balanced. But if you're standing, say, at the edge of a cliff, your sense of balance can get out of whack. "Your inner ear is saying you're surrounded by solid ground, but your eyes are saying, 'Nope,'" inner-ear specialist Dennis Fitzgerald says. Your brain is getting mixed signals, which can cause vertigo, or dizziness that makes heights feel scary.

THE FEAR: DARKNESS
SCIENTIFIC NAME: Nyctophobia
SPOOKY SCIENCE: As with other phobias, humans developed a fear of the dark to avoid danger. Our ancestors had to be extra cautious at night to protect themselves against things like animal predators and human invaders. (This was before electric lighting!) "Many people still have that fear of the dark today," Antony says. "It's a fear of the unknown."

THE FEAR: SMALL SPACES
SCIENTIFIC NAME: Claustrophobia
SPOOKY SCIENCE: Maybe you've been stuck in an elevator before and thought it was no big deal. For some people, though, just the fear of being stuck can cause them to take the stairs. "Small spaces might cause some people to worry about running out of oxygen, or never being able to get out—no matter how unlikely that is," Antony says. "To increase our chances of survival, people have evolved to avoid being trapped. For some, that could be anywhere."

● Expose yourself to things that you're afraid of in a way that you feel safe. For example, if you fear public speaking, try practicing in front of a mirror first, and then give the speech to a small group of trusted friends.

● If you feel anxious, place one or both of your hands on your stomach and focus on breathing slowly and deeply. Regulating your breathing will help you feel calmer and can lessen your sense of panic.

● Don't be too hard on yourself! Everyone's afraid of *something*. Just make sure it doesn't stop you from living your life. Talk to an adult if it feels like too much to handle on your own.

FUTURE WORLD:

The year is 2070, and it's time to get dressed for school. You step in front of a large video mirror that projects different clothes on you. After you decide on your favorite T-shirt, a robot fetches your outfit. No time is lost trying to find matching socks! Chores? What chores? Get ready for a whole new homelife.

STAY CONNECTED

Whether your future home is an urban skyscraper or an underwater pod, all buildings will one day be connected via a central communications hub. Want to check out a *T. rex* skeleton at a faraway museum? You can virtually connect to it as though you were checking it out in person. But you're not just seeing something miles away. Connect to a beach house's balcony and smell the salty air and feel the breeze. Buildings might also share information about incoming weather and emergencies to keep you safe.

CUSTOM COMFORT

Soon, your house may give you a personal welcome home. No need for keys—sensors will scan your body and open the door. Walk into the living room, and the lighting adjusts to your preferred setting. Thirsty? A glass of water pops up on the counter. Before bed, you enter the bathroom and say, "Shower, please." The water starts flowing at exactly the temperature you want.

ON LOCATION

Your room has a spectacular view of the ocean ... because your house is suspended above it. New technologies will allow us to build our homes in unusual spots. In the future, "floating" structures elevated by supporting poles above water or other hard-to-access spots (think mountain peaks) will be more common as cities become more crowded. And this won't be limited to dry land on Earth. That means that one day your family could even live in space!

Homes

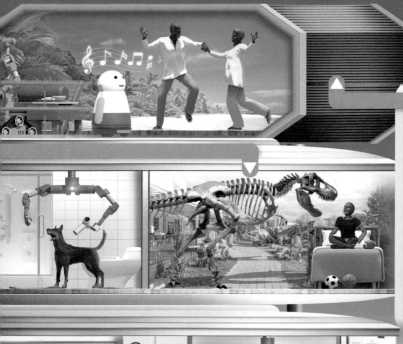

ON THE GO

Homes of the future will always be on the move. Walls will be capable of expanding and contracting, and houses will rotate with the sun's movements to conserve energy. Buildings will also be capable of changing size depending on who's inside. Grandparents could "move in" by attaching a modular section to the front, back, or top of the house.

BRING ON THE BOTS

While you were outside playing with your friends, your house robot did the laundry, vacuumed, and cleaned the bathroom. Meanwhile, a drone just delivered groceries for the home-bot to put away. Minutes later, lunch is ready. The service is great ... but how will you earn your allowance? Instead of taking out the garbage or setting the table, you'll earn money by helping clean and maintain the robots.

FUTURE WORLD:

What will restaurants be like decades from now? "You can expect a lot of changes in terms of using technology to grow and order our meals," says Paul Takhistov, a food scientist at Rutgers University in New Brunswick, New Jersey, U.S.A. "We'll also be able to personalize our food more." Check out what's cooking at this restaurant of the future.

HUNGRY? PRESS PRINT

A quick finger scan at your table shows that you're low on certain nutrients. Just press a button, and a 3D printer uses pureed food cartridges to "print" lasagna that's packed with specific vitamins that your body needs. "Healthy food isn't one size fits all," Takhistov says. "We have different bodies, so we need different nutrients." These printers will also increase efficiency, allowing chefs to quickly print personalized food for large crowds.

FOOD-IN-A-BOX

Some of the lettuce in this kitchen is sad. Or rather, one of the lettuce emojis on the giant computer screens is frowning. That's because the chef didn't use the right recipe of sunlight, water, and nutrients to get the real-life leafy plant inside a box behind the screen to grow. So she taps the touch screen to make the temperature cooler, and the lettuce's frown turns upside down on the fridge-shaped "box farm." Without planting seeds in soil, this restaurant can grow all the fruits and vegetables it needs. "Anybody can be a farmer," says Hildreth England, a senior strategist at the Massachusetts Institute of Technology. "If you live in Iceland, you can grow strawberries that taste as if they're from Mexico."

WASTE NOT

Researchers are currently working on ways to convert human waste into nutrients. Whether you're eating on Earth or during a space vacation, in the future some of your food will likely have recycled ingredients.

210

Food

GROW UP

What will happen to farms in the future? Some will be *much* taller. Cities will continue to expand as the human population climbs to nine billion people, leaving less land to farm. Agriculture will likely be housed in towering vertical skyscrapers situated in these cities. Luckily, indoor farms typically use less water, and plants seem to grow faster in these environments.

HUNTING FOR HOLOGRAMS

Let's go fishing ... in the kitchen? The catch of the day is a 3D hologram that the chef hooks in midair. One day people will stock their kitchens by gathering ingredients in a virtual world. Simply pick a berry from a digital bush or choose a cut of beef from a cow on a virtual farm. After you're done foraging, the hologram setup sends details to a local market that delivers your order. Scientists working on this program hope to connect people to their food sources and make shopping more fun.

GET SMART

To order with ease and keep germs from spreading at your favorite restaurant, you tap the table to open a digital menu and choose from freshly grown salads and 3D-printed creations. An alarm lets you know when your food is waiting in the cubby at one side of the table—just lift the door and take your meal. Forgot something? A robot server will stop by to see if you need anything else.

211

QUIZ WHIZ

Test your science and technology smarts by taking this quiz!

Write your answers on a piece of paper. Then check them below.

1 The giant rafflesia flower is called the "corpse flower" because it _____.
a. blooms on Halloween
b. has an offensive odor
c. grows only in graveyards
d. looks like a dead animal

2 **True or false?** Peanuts are one of the most common food allergens.

3 A fear of clowns is also called _____.
a. chionophobia
b. clownaphobia
c. claustrophobia
d. coulrophobia

4 In the near future, you may be able to _____.
a. project a keyboard onto any flat surface
b. make a phone call from a ring on your finger
c. warm yourself by a smokeless fire
d. all of the above

5 Ancient Greeks believed that lettuce juice could _____.
a. help them sleep
b. clean their teeth
c. build big muscles
d. give them more energy

Not **STUMPED** yet? Check out the *NATIONAL GEOGRAPHIC KIDS QUIZ WHIZ* collection for more crazy **SCIENCE AND TECHNOLOGY** questions!

ANSWERS: 1. b; 2. True; 3. d; 4. d; 5. a

This Is How It's Done!

Sometimes, the most complicated problems are solved with step-by-step directions. These "how-to" instructions are also known as a process analysis essay. Although scientists and engineers use this tool to program robots and write computer code, you also use process analysis every day, from following a recipe to putting together a new toy or gadget. Here's how to write a basic process analysis essay.

Step 1: Choose Your Topic Sentence
Pick a clear and concise topic sentence that describes what you're writing about. Be sure to explain to the readers why the task is important—and how many steps there are to complete it.

Step 2: List Materials
Do you need specific ingredients or equipment to complete your process? Mention these right away so the readers will have all they need to do the activity.

Step 3: Write Your Directions
Your directions should be clear and easy to follow. Assume that you are explaining the process for the first time, and define any unfamiliar terms. List your steps in the exact order the readers will need to follow to complete the activity. Try to keep your essay limited to no more than six steps.

Step 4: Restate Your Main Idea
Your closing idea should revisit your topic sentence, drawing a conclusion relating to the importance of the subject.

EXAMPLE OF A PROCESS ANALYSIS ESSAY

Downloading an app is a simple way to enhance your tablet. Today, I'd like to show you how to search for and add an app to your tablet. First, you will need a tablet with the ability to access the internet. You'll also want to ask a parent for permission before you download anything onto your tablet. Next, select the specific app you want by going to the app store on your tablet and entering the app's name into the search bar. Once you find the app you're seeking, select "download" and wait for the app to load. When you see that the app has fully loaded, tap on the icon and you will be able to access it. Now you can enjoy your app and have more fun with your tablet.

An aurora borealis glows brightly over Fairbanks, Alaska, U.S.A. This natural light show, also known as the northern lights, happens when solar wind interacts with Earth's magnetic field.

WONDERS of
NATURE

Biomes

A BIOME, OFTEN CALLED A MAJOR LIFE ZONE, is one of the natural world's major communities where plants and animals adapt to their specific surroundings. Biomes are classified depending on the predominant vegetation, climate, and geography of a region. They can be divided into six major types: forest, freshwater, marine, desert, grassland, and tundra. Each biome consists of many ecosystems.

Biomes are extremely important. Balanced ecological relationships among biomes help to maintain the environment and life on Earth as we know it. For example, an increase in one species of plant, such as an invasive one, can cause a ripple effect throughout a whole biome.

FOREST

Forests occupy about one-third of Earth's land area. There are three major types of forests: tropical, temperate, and boreal (taiga). Forests are home to a diversity of plants, some of which may hold medicinal qualities for humans, as well as thousands of animal species, some still undiscovered. Forests can also absorb carbon dioxide, a greenhouse gas, and give off oxygen.

In a tropical rainforest, less than 2 percent of the sunlight ever reaches the ground.

FRESHWATER

Most water on Earth is salty, but freshwater ecosystems—including lakes, ponds, wetlands, rivers, and streams—usually contain water with less than one percent salt concentration. The countless animal and plant species that live in freshwater biomes vary from continent to continent, but they include algae, frogs, turtles, fish, and the larvae of many insects.

Covering 1.5 million acres (607,000 ha), Everglades National Park in Florida, U.S.A., is one of the largest freshwater biomes in the world.

MARINE

The marine biome covers almost three-fourths of Earth's surface, making it the largest habitat on our planet. Oceans make up the majority of the saltwater marine biome. Coral reefs are considered to be the most biodiverse of any of the biome habitats. The marine biome is home to more than one million plant and animal species.

Scientists are almost certain that life originated in the ocean.

DESERT

Covering about one-fifth of Earth's surface, deserts are places where precipitation is less than 10 inches (25 cm) a year. Although most deserts are hot, there are other kinds as well. The four major kinds of deserts are hot, semiarid, coastal, and cold. Far from being barren wastelands, deserts are biologically rich habitats.

More than one billion people in the world live in deserts.

GRASSLAND

Biomes called grasslands are characterized by having grasses instead of large shrubs or trees. Grasslands generally have precipitation for only about half to three-fourths of the year. If it were more, they would become forests. Grasslands can be divided into two types: tropical (savannas) and temperate. Some of the world's largest land animals, such as elephants, live there.

Once thought to be extinct, the pygmy hog—the world's smallest pig (it's the size of a kitten)— recently made a return to the grasslands of the Himalayan foothills.

TUNDRA

The coldest of all biomes, a tundra is characterized by an extremely cold climate, simple vegetation, little precipitation, poor nutrients, and a short growing season. There are two types of tundra: Arctic and alpine. A tundra is home to few kinds of vegetation. Surprisingly, though, quite a few animal species can survive the tundra's extremes, such as wolves and caribou, and even mosquitoes.

The word "tundra" comes from the Finnish word *tunturia*, which means "treeless plain."

Sizing up

THE GREAT BARRIER REEF

The Great Barrier Reef is home to both huge whale sharks, which can reach 40 feet (12 m) in length, and tiny one-third-inch (8-mm)-long infantfish.

FISH SWIM AMONG ORANGE COMMON SEA FANS AND COLORFUL CORAL OF THE GREAT BARRIER REEF.

In June 1770, the ship *Endeavour* slammed into a razor-sharp reef somewhere in the middle of the Coral Sea, a part of the southwestern Pacific Ocean. At the helm of the ship? Captain James Cook, a British explorer who had been exploring the Pacific and ultimately mapped the east coast of Australia. What Cook soon realized was that the reef that nearly sank his ship wasn't just any coral formation: It was the Great Barrier Reef, the world's largest coral reef ecosystem. Covering 133,000 square miles (344,400 sq km), the Great Barrier Reef is bigger than the United Kingdom, Switzerland, and Holland combined! It's so big, in fact, that it can be spotted from space.

Experts believe the Great Barrier Reef first formed millions of years ago. Aboriginal Australians and the Torres Strait Islanders are considered the Traditional Owners of the Great Barrier Reef region, as their connection to the reef goes back 60,000 years.

A REEF AT RISK

Today the reef faces threats that are far worse than shipwrecks. Climate change, poor water quality due to pollution, overfishing, and other factors like an invasive, coral-eating starfish are huge threats to the future of the Great Barrier Reef and the marine life that call it home, like sharks, turtles, crocodiles, and thousands of

ANTHIAS FISH SWIM AROUND BRANCH CORAL.

Great Barrier Reef
By the Numbers

1,625: Species of fish that call the Great Barrier Reef home

3,000: Individual coral reef systems that compose the Great Barrier Reef as a whole

980: Approximate number of islands found along the Great Barrier Reef

1,000: Life span in years of boulder coral colonies—the longest-living coral on the Great Barrier Reef

2.4 million: Average number of visitors who travel to the Great Barrier Reef Marine Park in a typical year

A DIVER SCRUBS ALGAE FROM CORAL IN A CORAL NURSERY.

other species. Sadly, the reef has shrunk by more than 50 percent in recent years.

PROTECTING THE FUTURE

The good news? Conservationists are working hard to protect and preserve the Great Barrier Reef, which was declared a marine protected area. They hope that by educating people about global warming, making laws to prevent overfishing, and taking other steps, such as creating "coral nurseries" to rescue and rehabilitate unhealthy coral, the remaining reef may be saved.

NEW REEF DISCOVERED

Scientists in Australia recently discovered a giant coral reef off the coast of Queensland, Australia. The massive detached reef is more than a mile (1,609 m) wide and measures some 1,640 feet (500 m) high. That's taller than the Empire State Building! The reef, detached from the Great Barrier Reef, is the first discovery of its kind in 120 years. The find is a bright light for the marine world, as it means there may be more healthy ecosystems lurking beneath the ocean's surface.

THE OCEANS

PACIFIC OCEAN

STATS

Surface area
65,100,000 sq mi (168,600,000 sq km)

Percentage of all oceans
46 percent

Surface temperatures
Summer high:
90°F (32°C)
Winter low: 28°F (-2°C)

Tides
Highest: 30 ft (9 m)
near Korean Peninsula
Lowest: 1 ft (0.3 m) near Midway Islands

Cool creatures: giant Pacific octopus, bottlenose whale, clownfish, great white shark

Clownfish

ATLANTIC OCEAN

STATS

Surface area
33,100,000 sq mi (85,600,000 sq km)

Percentage of all oceans
24 percent

Surface temperatures
Summer high: 90°F (32°C)
Winter low: 28°F (-2°C)

Tides
Highest: 52 ft (16 m)
Bay of Fundy, Canada
Lowest: 1.5 ft (0.5 m)
Gulf of Mexico and Mediterranean Sea

Cool creatures: blue whale, Atlantic spotted dolphin, sea turtle, bottlenose dolphin

Bottlenose dolphin

INDIAN OCEAN

STATS

Surface area
27,500,000 sq mi (71,200,000 sq km)

Percentage of all oceans
20 percent

Surface temperatures
Summer high: 93°F (34°C)
Winter low: 28°F (-2°C)

Tides
Highest: 36 ft (11 m)
Lowest: 2 ft (0.6 m)
Both along Australia's west coast

Cool creatures: **humpback whale,**
Portuguese man-of-war, dugong
(sea cow), leatherback turtle

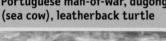

Leatherback turtle

ARCTIC OCEAN

STATS

Surface area
6,100,000 sq mi (15,700,000 sq km)

Percentage of all oceans
4 percent

Surface temperatures
Summer high:
41°F (5°C)
Winter low: 28°F (-2°C)

Tides
Less than 1 ft (0.3 m)
variation throughout the ocean

Cool creatures:
beluga whale, orca,
harp seal, narwhal

Narwhal

SOUTHERN OCEAN

STATS

Surface area
8,500,000 sq mi (21,900,000 sq km)

Percentage of all oceans
6 percent

Surface temperatures
Summer high: 50°F (10°C)
Winter low: 28°F (-2°C)

Tides
Less than 2 ft (0.6 m)
variation throughout the ocean

Cool creatures: **emperor**
penguin, colossal squid, mackerel
icefish, Antarctic toothfish

Emperor penguin

To see the major oceans and bays in relation to landmasses, look at the map on pages 272 and 273.

THE DEEP BLUE SEA

Oceans cover 71 percent of our planet's surface. Some areas in them are so deep that they'd cover the tallest mountains on Earth! Dive in and discover the deepest parts of our oceans.

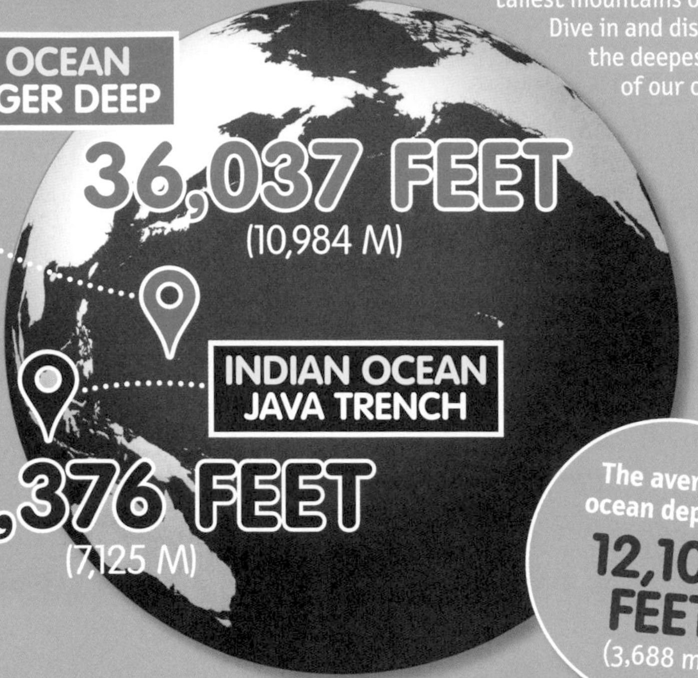

PACIFIC OCEAN CHALLENGER DEEP

36,037 FEET
(10,984 M)

INDIAN OCEAN JAVA TRENCH

23,376 FEET
(7,125 M)

The average ocean depth is
12,100 FEET
(3,688 m).

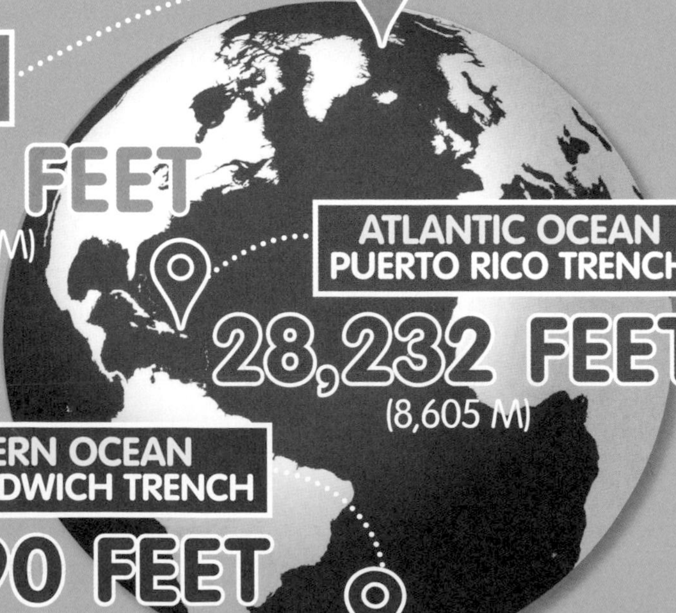

ARCTIC OCEAN MOLLOY DEEP

18,599 FEET
(5,669 M)

ATLANTIC OCEAN PUERTO RICO TRENCH

28,232 FEET
(8,605 M)

SOUTHERN OCEAN SOUTH SANDWICH TRENCH

24,390 FEET
(7,434 M)

WATER CYCLE

Precipitation falls

Water storage in ice and snow

Water vapor condenses in clouds

Water filters into the ground

Meltwater and surface runoff

Freshwater storage

Evaporation

Groundwater discharge

Water storage in ocean

The amount of water on Earth is more or less constant—

only the form changes. As the sun warms Earth's surface, liquid water is changed into water vapor in a process called **evaporation.** Water on the surface of plants' leaves turns into water vapor in a process called **transpiration.** As water vapor rises into the air, it cools and changes form again. This time, it becomes clouds in a process called **condensation.** Water droplets fall from the clouds as **precipitation,** which then travels as groundwater or runoff back to the lakes, rivers, and oceans, where the cycle (shown above) starts all over again.

To a meteorologist— a person who studies the weather—a "light rain" is less than 1/48 inch (0.5 mm). A "heavy rain" is more than 1/6 inch (4 mm).

You drink the same water as the dinosaurs! Earth has been recycling water for more than four billion years.

223

Weather and Climate

Weather is the condition of the atmosphere—temperature, wind, humidity, and precipitation—at a given place at a given time. Climate, however, is the average weather for a particular place over a long period of time. Different places on Earth have different climates, but climate is not a random occurrence. It is a pattern that is controlled by factors such as latitude, elevation, prevailing winds, the temperature of ocean currents, and location on land relative to water. Climate is generally constant, but evidence indicates that human activity is causing a change in its patterns.

WEATHER EXTREMES

MOST SNOW RECORDED IN ONE SEASON: 1,140 inches (29 m) in Mount Baker, Washington, U.S.A.

FASTEST TEMPERATURE RISE: 49 degrees Fahrenheit (27.2°C) in two minutes, in Rapid City, South Dakota, U.S.A.

HEAVIEST HAILSTONE: 2.25 pounds (1 kg) in Gopalganj, Bangladesh

GLOBAL CLIMATE ZONES

Climatologists, people who study climate, have created different systems for classifying climates. One that is often used is called the Köppen system, which classifies climate zones according to precipitation, temperature, and vegetation. It has five major categories—tropical, dry, temperate, cold, and polar—with a sixth category for locations where high elevations override other factors.

ARCTIC OCEAN
ARCTIC CIRCLE
TROPIC OF CANCER
ATLANTIC OCEAN
PACIFIC OCEAN
EQUATOR
PACIFIC OCEAN
TROPIC OF CAPRICORN
INDIAN OCEAN
ANTARCTIC CIRCLE
SOUTHERN OCEAN

Climate
■ Tropical ■ Dry ■ Temperate ■ Cold ■ Polar

Climate CHANGE

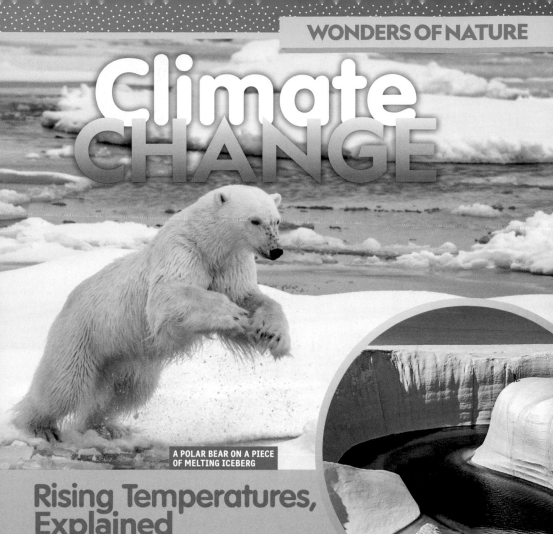

A POLAR BEAR ON A PIECE OF MELTING ICEBERG

SCIENTISTS ARE CONCERNED THAT GREENLAND'S ICE SHEET HAS BEGUN TO MELT IN SUMMER. BIRTHDAY CANYON, SHOWN HERE, WAS CARVED BY MELTWATER.

Rising Temperatures, Explained

Fact: The world is getting warmer.
Earth's surface temperature has been increasing. In the past 50 years, our planet has warmed twice as fast as in the 50 years before that. This is the direct effect of climate change, which refers not only to the increase in Earth's average temperature (known as global warming), but also to its long-term effects on winds, rain, and ocean currents. Global warming is the reason glaciers and polar ice sheets are melting—resulting in rising sea levels and shrinking habitats. This makes survival for some animals a big challenge. Warming also means more flooding along the coasts and drought for inland areas.

Why are temperatures climbing?
While some of the recent climate changes can be tied to natural causes—such as changes in the sun's intensity, the unusually warm ocean currents of El Niño, and volcanic activity— human activities are the greatest contributor.

Everyday activities that require burning fossil fuels, such as driving gasoline-powered cars, contribute to global warming. These activities produce greenhouse gases, which enter the atmosphere and trap heat. At the current rate, Earth's global average temperature is projected to rise some 5.4°F (3°C) by the year 2100, and it will get even warmer after that. And as the climate continues to warm, it will unfortunately continue to affect the environment and our society in many ways.

THERE ARE ABOUT 40 LIGHTNING FLASHES ON EARTH EVERY SECOND.

When you see **LIGHTNING,** it's **TRAVELING** at about **227 MILLION** (365 MILLION KM/H) miles an hour.

LIGHTNING can produce **HEAT** up to **FIVE TIMES HOTTER** than the sun.

Just how long can a lightning bolt be? Some of these giant electrical sparks can extend five miles (8 km) from top to bottom. One horizontal lightning bolt, spotted in South America, was a whopping 440 miles (708 km) long!

226

Lightning **STRIKES** the **EIFFEL TOWER** in Paris, France, about 10 TIMES A YEAR.

ONE LIGHTNING FLASH has enough energy to **LIGHT** a **100-WATT BULB** for three months.

THE SKY IS FALLING

"PRECIPITATION" IS A FANCY WORD
FOR THE WET STUFF THAT FALLS FROM THE SKY.

Precipitation is rain, freezing rain, sleet, snow, or hail. It forms when water vapor in the air condenses into clouds, gets heavier, and drops to the ground. Precipitation can ruin a picnic, but life on Earth couldn't exist without it.

Develops when ice crystals fall toward the ground, partly melt, and then refreeze. This happens mainly in winter when air near the ground is below freezing temperatures.

SLEET

RAIN

Formed when ice crystals in high, cold clouds get heavy and fall. Even in summer, falling ice crystals could remain frozen, but warm air near the ground melts them into raindrops.

FREEZING RAIN

Falls during winter, when rain freezes immediately as it hits a surface. Freezing rain creates layers of ice on roads and causes dangerous driving conditions.

Produced when ice crystals in clouds get heavy enough to fall. The air has to be cold enough all the way down for the crystals to stay frozen.

SNOW

HAIL

Formed inside thunderstorms when ice crystals covered in water pass through patches of freezing air in the tops of cumulonimbus clouds. The water on the ice crystals freezes. The crystals become heavy and fall to the ground.

Types of Clouds

If you want a clue about the weather, look up at the clouds. They'll tell a lot about the condition of the air and what weather might be on the way. Clouds are made of both air and water. On fair days, warm air currents rise up and push against the water in clouds, keeping it from falling. But as the raindrops in a cloud get bigger, it's time to set them free. The bigger raindrops become too heavy for the air currents to hold up, and they fall to the ground.

How Much Does a Cloud Weigh?

A light, fluffy cumulus cloud typically weighs about 216,000 pounds (98,000 kg). That's about the weight of 18 elephants. A rain-soaked cumulonimbus cloud typically weighs 105.8 million pounds (48 million kg), or about the same as 9,000 elephants.

1 STRATUS These clouds make the sky look like a bowl of thick gray porridge. They hang low in the sky, blanketing the day in dreary darkness. Stratus clouds form when cold, moist air close to the ground moves over a region.

2 CIRRUS These wispy tufts of clouds are thin and hang high up in the atmosphere where the air is extremely cold. Cirrus clouds are made of tiny ice crystals.

3 CUMULUS These white, fluffy clouds make people sing, "Oh, what a beautiful morning!" They form low in the atmosphere and look like marshmallows. They often mix with large patches of blue sky. Formed when hot air rises, cumulus clouds usually disappear when the air cools at night.

4 CUMULONIMBUS These are the monster clouds. Rising air currents force fluffy cumulus clouds to swell and shoot upward, as much as 70,000 feet (21,000 m). When these clouds bump against the top of the troposphere, known as the tropopause, they flatten out on top like tabletops.

HURRICANE
HAPPENINGS

A storm is brewing—but is this a tropical cyclone, a hurricane, or a typhoon? These weather events go by different names depending on where they form, how fast their winds get, or both. Strong tropical cyclones are called hurricanes in the Atlantic and parts of the Pacific Ocean; in the western Pacific, they are called typhoons. But any way you look at it, these storms pack a punch. And they all form when warm moist air rises from the ocean, causing air from surrounding areas to be "sucked" in. That air then becomes warm and moist, and rises, too, beginning a cycle that forms clouds, which rotate with the spin of Earth. If there is enough warm water to feed the storm, it will result in a hurricane. And the warmer the water, and the more moisture in the air, the more powerful the hurricane.

HURRICANE NAMES FOR 2023

Atlantic hurricane names come from six official international lists. The names alternate between male and female. When a storm becomes a hurricane, a name from the list is used, in alphabetical order. (If the hurricane season is especially active and the list runs out, the World Meteorological Organization will provide extra names to draw from.) Each list is reused every six years. A name is "retired" if that hurricane caused a lot of damage or many deaths.

Arlene	Franklin	Jose	Nigel	Sean
Bret	Gert	Katia	Ophelia	Tammy
Cindy	Harold	Lee	Philippe	Vince
Don	Idalia	Margot	Rina	Whitney
Emily				

SCALE OF HURRICANE INTENSITY

CATEGORY	ONE	TWO	THREE	FOUR	FIVE
DAMAGE	Minimal	Moderate	Extensive	Extreme	Catastrophic
WINDS	74–95 mph (119–153 km/h)	96–110 mph (154–177 km/h)	111–129 mph (178–208 km/h)	130–156 mph (209–251 km/h)	157 mph or higher (252+ km/h)
(DAMAGE refers to wind and water damage combined.)					

THE ENHANCED FUJITA SCALE

The Enhanced Fujita (EF) Scale, named after tornado expert T. Theodore Fujita, classifies tornadoes based on wind speed and the intensity of damage that they cause.

What Is a Tornado?

EF0
65–85 mph winds
(105–137 km/h)
Slight damage

EF1
86–110 mph winds
(138–177 km/h)
Moderate damage

EF2
111–135 mph winds
(178–217 km/h)
Substantial damage

EF3
136–165 mph winds
(218–266 km/h)
Severe damage

TORNADOES, ALSO KNOWN AS TWISTERS, are funnels of rapidly rotating air that are created during a thunderstorm. With wind speeds that can exceed 300 miles an hour (483 km/h), tornadoes have the power to pick up and destroy everything in their path.

EF4
166–200 mph winds
(267–322 km/h)
Massive damage

EF5
More than 200 mph winds
(322+ km/h)
Catastrophic damage

THIS ROTATING FUNNEL OF AIR, formed in a cumulus or cumulonimbus cloud, became a tornado when it touched the ground.

TORNADOES HAVE OCCURRED IN ALL 50 U.S. STATES AND ON EVERY CONTINENT EXCEPT ANTARCTICA.

FLOOD

For an entire week in July 2020, torrential rain battered the island of Kyushu, the southernmost of Japan's four main islands. The record-breaking band of storms brought rain that fell at times nearly four inches (10 cm) an hour on the island. That triggered rivers to burst past their banks, unleashing a watery torrent that washed over main streets, neighborhoods, bridges, and businesses. The entire island experienced widespread flooding, with the water level rising to eight feet (2.5 m) in some parts. There were also landslides that caused even more damage. All told, nearly 15,000 homes in Japan were damaged, and, sadly, more than 75 people perished.

To aid the ailing island, Japan's Prime Minister Shinzo Abe dispatched tens of thousands of Japanese troops. Along with firefighters and coast guard sailors, the rescue teams steered boats down the streets to save those stranded in the rising water and help others in need. And as the rains slowed and the water receded, Kyushu was slowly able to begin the recovery process.

FREEZE

When three severe winter storms swept across Texas, U.S.A., in February 2021, residents were hit with an unexpected double disaster. First, as people cranked up the heat in their homes and businesses to warm up in the unusually frigid temps, the sudden electricity spike caused a massive power grid failure that impacted some 4.5 million residences. This left Texans stuck in their homes with no heat as temperatures outside dipped to lows the state hadn't seen in some 70 years. Those who did leave their homes to travel to a safer spot faced icy roads and malfunctioning streetlights, causing car crashes and even more hardship. At least 111 Texans died as a result of the winter weather.

When power was restored days later, another catastrophe: flooded homes. Millions of homes faced water damage as pipes, which had frozen, burst under pressure while thawing. Water treatment plants were also impacted, resulting in a crisis in which millions had no running water or were under orders to boil it before use to kill harmful microorganisms and make it safe to drink.

While the Texas freeze was devastating, those impacted have been able to recover and rebuild. And, perhaps most important, the entire state will be better prepared to avoid a similar catastrophe in the future.

BOBCAT WILDFIRE RESCUE

An injured bobcat searches for prey among blackened tree stumps but finds nothing to eat. It's been three weeks since the Camp Fire destroyed the cat's habitat in northern California, U.S.A. The underweight juvenile won't survive much longer without food.

Luckily, a passerby spots the cat and calls Sallysue Stein, the founder of Gold Country Wildlife Rescue. Stein arranges to have the cat brought to her facility. "When he arrived, we could see that his paws were singed and he was obviously hungry," Stein says. "When we were able to examine him, we saw that the pads of his paws had been burned all the way to the bone."

HIGH-TECH TREATMENT

Medicine helps make the cat comfortable, but his paws need much more care. The cat's rescuers call in veterinarian Jamie Peyton, who specializes in animal burns.

Peyton suggests a new type of treatment to heal the animal's wounds: fish skin. By wrapping the cat's paws in bandages made from tilapia (a type of fish) skin, they can protect his paws from getting infected; plus, the collagen—a kind of protein—found in the tilapia might help the wounds heal faster.

After a week of treatments, the bobcat's appetite increases, and he switches from just gruel to having birds and mice added to his meals. "We knew he was ready to be released when he started trying to escape from his kennel," Stein says.

GOING HOME

After 11 weeks of treatment, the bobcat is taken to Big Chico Creek Ecological Reserve, which hasn't been impacted by the fires. The cage door is opened. The bobcat steps out, sprints up a tall tree, and disappears from view.

"Our goal was to give the bobcat a second chance in the wild," Stein says. "It's where he belongs."

Although bobcats are rarely seen, they're the most common wild cat in North America.

VETERINARIANS APPLY SKIN FROM TILAPIA (A TYPE OF FISH) TO THE BOBCAT'S PAWS TO KEEP THEM FROM GETTING INFECTED.

NEARLY FOUR MONTHS AFTER BEING INJURED IN A FIRE, THE HEALED BOBCAT IS ABLE TO CLIMB TREES AGAIN.

QUIZ WHIZ

Quiz yourself to find out if you're a natural when it comes to nature knowledge!

Write your answers on a piece of paper. Then check them below.

1 **True or false?** A rain-soaked cumulonimbus cloud weighs about the same as 9,000 pandas.

2 **Which is NOT an example of precipitation?**
a. rain
b. sleet
c. hail
d. thunder

3 In February 2021, _____ were an unexpected double disaster in parts of Texas, U.S.A.
a. a widespread power outage and flooded homes
b. a heat wave and wildfires
c. a hailstorm and dented cars
d. a rain deluge and flooded streets

4 **True or false?** The Great Barrier Reef is bigger than the United Kingdom, Switzerland, and Holland combined.

5 At the current rate, Earth's global average temperature is projected to rise some _____ by the year 2100.
a. .54°F (-17.5°C)
b. 5.4°F (3°C)
c. 54°F (12°C)
d. 540°F (282°C)

Not **STUMPED** yet? Check out the *NATIONAL GEOGRAPHIC KIDS QUIZ WHIZ* collection for more crazy **NATURE** questions!

ANSWERS: 1. False: It weighs the same as 9,000 elephants.; **2.** d; **3.** a; **4.** True; **5.** b

Oral Reports Made Easy

Does the thought of public speaking start your stomach churning like a tornado? Would you rather get caught in an avalanche than give a speech?

Giving an oral report does not have to be a natural disaster. The basic format is very similar to that of a written essay. There are two main elements that make up a good oral report—the writing and the presentation. As you write your oral report, remember that your audience will be hearing the information as opposed to reading it. Follow the guidelines below, and there will be clear skies ahead.

Writing Your Material

Follow the steps in the "How to Write a Perfect Essay" section on page 129, but prepare your report to be spoken rather than written. Try to keep your sentences short and simple. Long, complex sentences are harder to follow. Limit yourself to just a few key points. You don't want to overwhelm your audience with too much information. To be most effective, hit your key points in the introduction, elaborate on them in the body, and then repeat them once again in your conclusion.

AN ORAL REPORT HAS THREE BASIC PARTS:

- **Introduction**—This is your chance to engage your audience and really capture their interest in the subject you are presenting. Use a funny personal experience or a dramatic story, or start with an intriguing question.

- **Body**—This is the longest part of your report. Here you elaborate on the facts and ideas you want to convey. Give information that supports your main idea, and expand on it with specific examples or details. In other words, structure your oral report in the same way you would a written essay, so that your thoughts are presented in a clear and organized manner.

- **Conclusion**—This is the time to summarize the information and emphasize your most important points to the audience one last time.

Preparing Your Delivery

1 **Practice makes perfect.** Practice! Practice! Practice! Confidence, enthusiasm, and energy are key to delivering an effective oral report, and they can best be achieved through rehearsal. Ask family and friends to be your practice audience and give you feedback when you're done. Were they able to follow your ideas? Did you seem knowledgeable and confident? Did you speak too slowly or too fast, too softly or too loudly? The more times you practice giving your report, the more you'll master the material. Then you won't have to rely so heavily on your notes or papers, and you will be able to give your report in a relaxed and confident manner.

2 **Present with everything you've got.** Be as creative as you can. Incorporate videos, sound clips, slide presentations, charts, diagrams, and photos. Visual aids help stimulate your audience's senses and keep them intrigued and engaged. They can also help to reinforce your key points. And remember that when you're giving an oral report, you're a performer. Take charge of the spotlight and be as animated and entertaining as you can. Have fun with it.

3 **Keep your nerves under control.** Everyone gets a little nervous when speaking in front of a group. That's normal. But the more preparation you've done—meaning plenty of researching, organizing, and rehearsing—the more confident you'll be. Preparation is the key. And if you make a mistake or stumble over your words, just regroup and keep going. Nobody's perfect, and nobody expects you to be.

235

HISTORY HAPPENS

Archaeologists work on the mosaic floor of a 1,500-year-old church from the Byzantine Empire recently discovered during a three-year excavation in Beit Shemesh, Israel.

ANCIENT EGYPT

BY THE NUMBERS

1 Number of major organs left in the body after mummification. The heart was kept inside, but all other organs were removed.

9 Age that King Tut became pharaoh of Egypt, in 1332 B.C.

97 Percentage of ancient Egyptian land that was covered in desert.

130 Number of Egyptian pyramids discovered to date.

2.8 TONS (2.5 t) Weight of a single stone block used to build a pyramid.

1 MILE (1.6 km) The average length of the bandages used to wrap an Egyptian mummy.

Brainy Questions

HEY, SMARTY-PANTS!

GOT BIG, WEIRD QUESTIONS?

WE'VE GOT ANSWERS!

Why are ancient statues and buildings always white?

The paint has come off! Ancient Greeks and Romans painted their statues and temples in many different colors, but over the past few thousand years, the paint has worn away. Ancient artists mixed colorful minerals—like crushed-up malachite for green or azurite for blue—with beeswax or egg yolks to create paint. Today, archaeologists are using ultraviolet and infrared lamps, along with chemical analysis to discover the traces of colors and patterns left behind on the statues. We know ancient people would approve: A line in one Greek play implies that wiping color off a statue would make it uglier.

What's inside the Great Pyramid of Giza?

Not much, anymore! The Great Pyramid was built about 4,570 years ago as the final resting place of Khufu, an Egyptian pharaoh. It also stored all the stuff he'd need in the afterlife, like bread, fruit, furniture, clothes, and jewelry. The 481-foot (147-m)-tall stone structure was Khufu's way of telling people that he was super important. But it also screamed, "Hey, stuff to steal inside!" Today, you can walk through a passageway deep into the center of the pyramid until you reach the King's Chamber, which has a granite sarcophagus—but nothing else.

THE LOST CITY OF POMPEII

When will the volcano that buried this ancient civilization blow again?

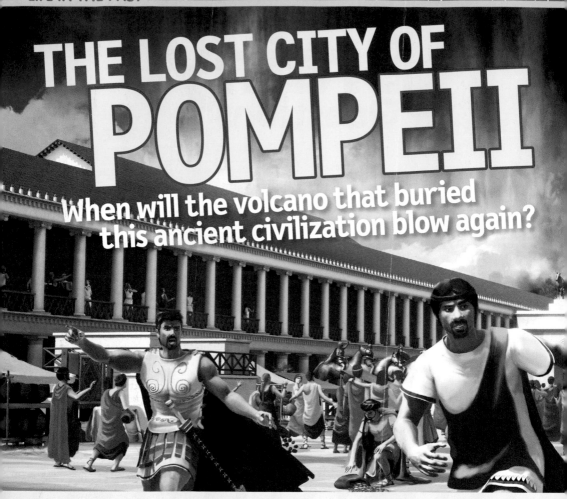

A deafening boom roars through Pompeii's crowded marketplace. The ground shakes violently, throwing the midday shoppers off balance and toppling stands of fish and meat. People start screaming and pointing toward Mount Vesuvius, a massive volcano that rises above the bustling city, located in what is now southern Italy.

Vesuvius has been silent for nearly 2,000 years, but it roars back to life, shooting ash and smoke into the air. Almost overnight, the city and most of its residents vanish under a blanket of ash and lava.

Now, almost 2,000 years later, scientists agree that Vesuvius is overdue for another major eruption—but no one knows when it will happen. Three million people live in the volcano's shadow, in the modern-day city of Naples, Italy. Correctly predicting when the eruption might take place will mean the difference between life and death for many.

THE SKY IS FALLING

Thanks to excavations that started in 1748 and continue to this day, scientists have been able to re-create almost exactly what happened in Pompeii on that terrible day in A.D. 79.

"The thick ash turned everything black," says Pompeii expert Andrew Wallace-Hadrill.

"People couldn't see the sun. All the landmarks disappeared. They didn't have the foggiest idea which way they were going."

Some people ran for their lives, clutching their valuable coins and jewelry. Other people took shelter in their homes. But the debris kept falling. Piles grew as deep as nine feet (2.7 m) in some places, blocking doorways and caving in roofs.

Around midnight, the first of four searing-hot clouds, or surges, of ash, pumice, rock, and toxic gas rushed down the mountainside. Traveling toward Pompeii at up to 180 miles an hour (290 km/h), it scorched everything in its path. Around 7 a.m., 18 hours after the

TODAY, MILLIONS OF TOURISTS VISIT THE RUINS OF POMPEII, INCLUDING THE FORUM, BELOW.

THIS ARTIST'S CONCEPT RE-CREATES THE FORUM AT POMPEII AS IT LOOKED THE DAY OF THE ERUPTION IN A.D. 79. THE FORUM WAS THE CENTER OF PUBLIC LIFE.

eruption, the last fiery surge buried the city.

LOST AND FOUND

Visiting the ruins of Pompeii today is like going back in time. The layers of ash actually helped preserve buildings, artwork, and even the forms of bodies. "It gives you the feeling you can reach out and touch the ancient world," Wallace-Hadrill says.

There are kitchens with pots on the stove and bakeries with loaves of bread—now turned to charcoal—still in the ovens. Narrow corridors lead to magnificent mansions with elaborate gardens and fountains. Mosaics, or designs made out of tiles, decorate the walls and floors.

WARNING SIGNS

Pompeii's destruction may be ancient history, but there's little doubt that disaster will strike again. Luckily, people living near Vesuvius today will likely receive evacuation warnings before the volcano blows.

Scientists are closely monitoring Vesuvius for shifts in the ground, earthquakes, and rising levels of certain gases, which could be signs of an upcoming eruption. The Italian government is also working on a plan to help people flee the area in the event of a natural disaster.

CREEPY CASTS

Volcanic ash settled around many of the victims at the moment of death. When the bodies decayed, holes remained inside the solid ash. Scientists poured plaster into the holes to preserve the shapes of the victims.

THE HAGIA SOPHIA
IN ISTANBUL, TURKEY, HAS BEEN A CATHEDRAL, A MOSQUE, AND A MUSEUM.

The **HAGIA SOPHIA** was once the **LARGEST CATHEDRAL** in the **WORLD** (it's now the fourth).

The **ORIGINAL DOME** was **DESTROYED** by an **EARTHQUAKE** around A.D. 550. It was soon **REBUILT** to its current height of **182 FEET** (55 m).

The Hagia Sophia (Greek for "holy wisdom") was built as a cathedral some 1,500 years ago. Later, it was transformed into a mosque under Ottoman rule, which is how it remained until 1934, when it opened as a museum. In 2020, Turkey's president declared the site a mosque once again.

There are **140 COLUMNS** in the Hagia Sophia, **INCLUDING** the partly bronze-covered **"SWEATING COLUMN,"** which is damp to the touch.

MOSAICS dating back some **700 YEARS** were recently **UNEARTHED** under layers of plaster beneath the dome.

ROYAL

Check out what some of history's most

FIT FOR A
QUEEN

Though militaries of the past were made up mostly of men, a few notable women—royal and otherwise—rode into battle, leading troops to victory. Not much is known about many of them. Check out what we *do* know about fierce females on the battlefield.

Armor for All

The few historical accounts of royal women in battle say that they likely donned the same gear as men. They're usually described as wearing hauberks: garments made of metal that covered the arms, torso, and upper legs.

Legendary Look

Many images of armor-clad women depict fictional figures like Minerva, the Roman goddess of women and warfare. According to legend, Minerva's father, Jupiter, swallowed her pregnant mother after a prophecy foretold that their unborn child would grow up to defeat him. When Minerva eventually escaped from inside Jupiter, she was wearing full battle armor and ready to fight her father.

MINERVA

Secret Suit

Though some historical paintings depict women in metal armor, no one knows for sure how accurate these illustrations are. That means the exact appearance of women's armor in the past is still a mystery, but historians think it looked similar to what men wore, like the suit above worn by English nobility during the 16th century.

Knight Me

In 1149, when invaders threatened to take over the town of Tortosa, Spain, local women threw on men's clothing and fought off the enemy. Spanish count Ramon Berenguer IV was so impressed that he created the Order of the Hatchet, granting the women rights similar to those of knights, such as not having to pay taxes.

CHECK OUT
THE BOOK!

Custom Fit

Joan of Arc is one of history's most famous warriors. During the 15th century, France's King Charles VII presented the military leader with armor tailored to fit her perfectly.

RUMBLE

fearsome fighters wore on the battlefield.

So Much Metal

Being a knight sounds exciting, but wearing armor was not. Mail armor, invented around the third century B.C., was made of interlocking metal circles layered over quilted fabric to protect against arrows. Plate armor, invented around the late 1300s, was heavy and hard to see out of. But because it was made of bands of steel over leather, it defended against heavy blows while allowing for movement. The best protection? Probably a combination of both.

MAIL ARMOR

PLATE ARMOR

FIT FOR A KING

On the battlefield, sturdy armor meant the difference between life and death. Good armor protected its wearers against a variety of weapons while still allowing them to move easily. Discover what kings and their soldiers wore throughout history.

Works of Art

Today, Japanese samurai are famous for their long blades known as katanas, but their armor during the Heian period (A.D. 794–1185) was just as well known. Samurai armor, called *o-yoroi* (pronounced oh-YO-roy, above), was made of metal and leather and was designed to deflect blades and arrows. It consisted of multiple pieces laced together, including the *kabuto* (helmet), the *menpo* (face mask), and extra leg and arm guards. Some pieces were decorated so beautifully that today they're regarded as works of art.

Cat Fight

The Aztec Empire, which reigned over central Mexico from 1345 to 1521, was known for a group of warriors called the *ocelotl* (pronounced oh-seh-LO-tl), meaning "jaguars." In addition to wearing regular armor in battle, these jaguar fighters donned symbols of their namesake. One example was a helmet shaped like a jaguar head, with room for the soldier to peek out from below the teeth. And they sometimes wore capes made from real jaguar pelts. These outfits were thought to transfer the fierceness of the jaguar to the wearer.

Animal Armor

Throughout history, some animals donned armor along with their soldiers, including battle horses and even elephants. War elephants, first used in what is now India during the 12th century, were sometimes dressed in fancy sets of metal armor weighing more than 350 pounds (159 kg). A few were also adorned with "tusk swords," which were metal weapons mounted on the elephants' tusks. Other elephants were saddled with carriages where archers could sit and fire on their enemies.

THE BOOK OF KINGS

CHECK OUT THE BOOK!

SIXTH-CENTURY STATUE OF A JAGUAR WARRIOR

TO HONOR A QUEEN

The Taj Mahal might be the world's grandest tomb.

The Taj Mahal in India might look like a fancy home for important kings and queens. After all, it was likely the inspiration for the palace in *Aladdin*. But no one ever lived here: It's actually a tomb. Who's buried inside? Read on to find out!

A PORTRAIT OF MUMTAZ MAHAL (LEFT) AND SHAH JAHAN

MEET THE MAKER

For more than 200 years, the Mughal Empire ruled over parts of what is today India, Pakistan, Afghanistan, and Nepal. To become emperor, a royal male had to prove himself to be the best choice before being named as heir—but the family could still change its mind.

That's what happened to Shah Jahan, a third-born son who had been named heir but later fell from favor. When his father died, he returned home in 1628 to reclaim the throne. And just in case, he put his rivals—including his brother and a few nephews—to death.

The new emperor loved architecture and art, and he adored his second wife, Mumtaz Mahal. (Shah Jahan had three wives; emperors at this time usually had many spouses to gain power through their families.) Mumtaz Mahal traveled with him everywhere, even on military campaigns. "They had a true partnership and a true love," Mughal art historian Mehreen Chida-Razvi says. The couple was married for nearly 20 years before Mumtaz Mahal died in 1631.

Legend says that after his wife's death, Shah Jahan's black hair turned white from grief. He decided her tomb would be a grand monument to his lost love. "Nothing had ever been built like this to honor a queen before," Chida-Razvi says.

BEST BUILDING

About 20,000 craftsmen baked bricks made of mud to form the building's structure. They then

Mumtaz Mahal means "chosen one of the palace."

In the Persian language, Shah Jahan means "king of the world."

Shah Jahan sat on a throne called the Peacock Throne, which was studded with gems from his treasury.

ASIA

INDIA

INDIAN OCEAN

PAKISTAN

CHINA

New Dehli

BHUTAN

NEPAL

Agra

MYANMAR (BURMA)

INDIA

BANGLADESH

Arabian Sea

Bay of Bengal

WORKERS CLEAN THE TAJ MAHAL WITH CLAY, THEN WASH IT OFF WITH DISTILLED WATER.

Solving a Mystery

Every few years, the Taj Mahal gets a mud bath to remove mysterious yellow-brown stains from the white marble. Environmental scientist Mike Bergin thought that if he could find the cause of the stains, people could better protect the tomb.

In 2012, he placed marble tiles on the monument for two months, then used a special high-powered microscope to look at the stained tiles. He found tiny particles of pollution from cars and the burning of wood, trash, and dung. The pollution absorbed light instead of reflecting it, which created the stains. As a result, the Indian government restricted burning trash and driving cars near the monument to help decrease the staining pollution.

"Once you know the problem," Bergin says, "you can make policies to fix it."

covered them in white marble for the tomb or red sandstone for nearby buildings. Artisans covered the tomb with designs made from more than 40 types of semiprecious gems. And calligraphers hand-carved poems and scripture all over walls and columns.

What looks like Mumtaz Mahal's sarcophagus was placed in the central room. But it's actually a cenotaph, a false tomb that allows visitors to pay their respects without disturbing her actual remains. Those were laid in a crypt directly underneath.

Nearly 20 years later, the massive, 42-acre (17-ha) complex was complete.

INLAID PIECES OF JADE AND CORAL CREATE ART THROUGHOUT THE TAJ MAHAL.

TOMB TRUTH

Shah Jahan likely would have built his own tomb nearby, Chida-Razvi says. But in 1657, he fell gravely ill. Seizing the chance to become ruler—just like Shah Jahan had done 30 years before—one of his sons imprisoned him in a fort. His only comfort: that he could see the Taj Mahal from a window.

The ex-emperor died eight years later, but his son didn't honor him with a majestic tomb. Instead, his body was brought to the Taj Mahal at night. His sarcophagus was plopped to the side of his wife's, even though the tomb was to honor Mumtaz Mahal—and no one else.

More than 350 years later, people still marvel at the Taj Mahal. Shah Jahan would probably be happy that people continue to honor his beloved wife.

PiRATES!

MEET THREE OF HISTORY'S MOST FEARSOME HIGH-SEAS BADDIES.

Yo-ho, yo-ho—*uh-oh!* A mysterious ship on the horizon flying a skull-and-crossbones flag wasn't a welcome sight to sailors in the 18th and 19th centuries. That flag meant one thing: pirates. Faced with faster, cannon-crammed vessels typically crewed by pirates, a ship captain was left with two choices: lower the sails and surrender—or turn and fight.

Life wasn't one big swashbuckling adventure for the pirates, however. Lousy food, cramped quarters, stinky crewmates, and hurricanes were all part of the job. Still, a handful of pirates managed to enjoy success at sea ... and inspired fear in those who were unfortunate enough to meet them face-to-face. Check out some of history's most famous pirates.

RACHEL WALL

REIGN OF TERROR New England coast, U.S.A., late 1700s

Rachel Wall and her husband, George, worked together as pirates, targeting small islands off the coast of present-day Maine in the Atlantic Ocean. After storms, they'd stop their sailboat and raise a distress flag. When passersby responded to Rachel's screams for help, they were robbed—or worse—for their trouble. After just two summers of piracy, Rachel and George killed at least 24 men and raked in about $6,000, plus an unknown amount of valuable goods. They later sold their loot, pretending they'd found it washed up on a beach.

CRIME DOESN'T PAY Eventually the law caught up with Rachel Wall. In 1789, she made history when she was the last woman to be hanged in the state of Massachusetts.

CHENG I SAO

REIGN OF TERROR South China Sea, 1801–1810

Cheng I Sao ruled a pirate fleet of nearly 2,000 ships. Sometimes called Madame Cheng, she turned to crime after she married a famous pirate. More than 80,000 buccaneers—men, women, and even children—reported to Madame Cheng. They seized loot in all sorts of ways: selling "protection" from pirate attacks, raiding ships, and kidnapping for ransom. Madame Cheng was best known for paying her pirates cash for each head they brought back from their assaults. (Yikes!)

CRIME DOESN'T PAY—USUALLY Every government attempt to stop Madame Cheng was a failure. Rumor has it that after she retired from piracy, she started a second career as a smuggler. She died peacefully at age 69.

BLACKBEARD

REIGN OF TERROR North America's East Coast and the Caribbean, 1713–1718

Nobody knows Blackbeard's real name—historians think it might've been Edward Teach—but he's arguably history's most famous pirate. He began his career as a privateer, or a kind of legal pirate, who was hired by the British government to attack enemy fleets and steal their goods.

Blackbeard abandoned privateering in 1713 and went full-pirate when he sailed to the Caribbean on a French ship that was gifted to him by another pirate, adding cannons to the vessel and renaming it *Queen Anne's Revenge*. He terrified his enemies by strapping pistols and knives across his chest and sticking smoking cannon fuses in his beard. According to legend, Blackbeard hid a treasure somewhere ... but it's never been found.

CRIME DOESN'T PAY A few years into Blackbeard's time as a pirate, he was nabbed by the British Navy. He was executed, and his head stuck on the front of a ship as a way to warn wannabe pirates to stay away from seafaring crime.

GOING TO WAR

Since the beginning of time, different countries, territories, and cultures have feuded with each other over land, power, and politics. Major military conflicts include the following wars:

1095–1291 THE CRUSADES
Starting late in the 11th century, these wars over religion were fought in the Middle East for nearly 200 years.

1337–1453 HUNDRED YEARS' WAR
France and England battled over rights to land for more than a century before the French eventually drove the English out in 1453.

1754–1763 FRENCH AND INDIAN WAR (part of Europe's Seven Years' War)
A nine-year war between the British and French for control of North America.

1775–1783 AMERICAN REVOLUTION
Thirteen British colonies in America united to reject the rule of the British government and to form the United States of America.

1861–1865 AMERICAN CIVIL WAR
This war occurred when the northern states (the Union) went to war with the southern states, which had seceded, or withdrawn, to form the Confederate States of America. Slavery was one of the key issues in the Civil War.

1910–1920 MEXICAN REVOLUTION
The people of Mexico revolted against the rule of dictator President Porfirio Díaz, leading to his eventual defeat and to a democratic government.

1914–1918 WORLD WAR I
The assassination of Austria's Archduke Ferdinand by a Serbian nationalist sparked this wide-spreading war. The U.S. entered after Germany sank the British ship *Lusitania,* killing more than 120 Americans.

1918–1920 RUSSIAN CIVIL WAR
Following the 1917 Russian Revolution, this conflict pitted the Communist Red Army against the foreign-backed White Army. The Red Army won, leading to the establishment of the Union of Soviet Socialist Republics (U.S.S.R.) in 1922.

1936–1939 SPANISH CIVIL WAR
Aid from Italy and Germany helped Spain's Nationalists gain victory over the Communist-supported Republicans. The war resulted in the loss of more than 300,000 lives and increased tension in Europe leading up to World War II.

1939–1945 WORLD WAR II
This massive conflict in Europe, Asia, and North Africa involved many countries that aligned with the two sides: the Allies and the Axis. After the bombing of Pearl Harbor in Hawaii in 1941, the U.S. entered the war on the side of the Allies. More than 50 million people died during the war.

1946–1949
CHINESE CIVIL WAR
Also known as the "War of Liberation," this war pitted the Communist and Nationalist Parties in China against each other. The Communists won.

1950–1953 KOREAN WAR
Kicked off when the Communist forces of North Korea, with backing from the Soviet Union, invaded their democratic neighbor to the south. A coalition of 16 countries from the United Nations stepped in to support South Korea. An armistice, or temporary truce, ended active fighting in 1953.

1950s–1975 VIETNAM WAR
This war was fought between the Communist North, supported by allies including China, and the government of South Vietnam, supported by the United States and other anticommunist nations.

1967 SIX-DAY WAR
This was a battle for land between Israel and the states of Egypt, Jordan, and Syria. The outcome resulted in Israel's gaining control of coveted territory, including the Gaza Strip and the West Bank.

1991–PRESENT
SOMALI CIVIL WAR
The war began when Somalia's last president, a dictator named Mohamed Siad Barre, was overthrown. This has led to years of fighting and anarchy.

2001–2014
WAR IN AFGHANISTAN
After attacks in the U.S. by the terrorist group al Qaeda, a coalition that eventually included more than 40 countries invaded Afghanistan to find Osama bin Laden and other al Qaeda members and to dismantle the Taliban. Bin Laden was killed in a U.S. covert operation in 2011. The North Atlantic Treaty Organization (NATO) took control of the coalition's combat mission in 2003. That combat mission officially ended in 2014.

2003–2011 WAR IN IRAQ
A coalition led by the U.S., and including Britain, Australia, and Spain, invaded Iraq over suspicions that Iraq had weapons of mass destruction.

WARTIME INVENTIONS

It's said that necessity is the mother of invention. And in wartime, necessity—or at least the need for making life easier—is especially key. So it's not too surprising that some of the more useful things in our world today were created during times of conflict—in particular, during World War I, when industrialization led to innovations across the board.

Take, for example, Kleenex tissues. What we use today to blow our noses was born out of what was first meant to be a thin, cottony liner used in a gas mask. In 1924, the company Kimberly-Clark started selling the same tissue liners as a disposable makeup remover for women. But when an employee with hay fever started blowing his nose in the wipes, Kimberly-Clark saw an opportunity—and sold the Kleenex as an alternative to cloth handkerchiefs.

Then there are zippers: Originally known as "hookless fasteners," they first widely appeared on the flying suits of aviators during World War I. Before then, buttons were the fashionable way to fasten shirts, pants, and boots, but the new invention was much more, well, zippy. In 1923, the B.F. Goodrich Company coined the term zipper, and the name stuck.

And whenever you check the time on your wristwatch, you can thank World War I soldiers for making this type of timepiece trendy. At the time of the war, wristwatches were popular with women, while men mostly kept the time on pocket watches, which they'd have tucked away on a chain. But during the war, male soldiers switched to wristwatches for easier access to the time (and to keep both hands free in the trenches). After the war, the wristwatch became a common look for all genders—and remains so today.

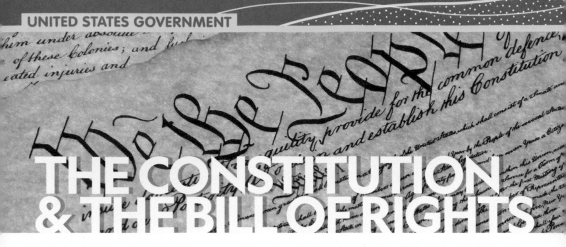

THE CONSTITUTION & THE BILL OF RIGHTS

The United States Constitution was written in 1787 by a group of political leaders from the 13 states that made up the United States at the time. Thirty-nine men, including Benjamin Franklin and James Madison, signed the document to create a national government. While some feared the creation of a strong federal government, all 13 states eventually ratified, or approved, the Constitution, making it the law of the land. The Constitution has three major parts: the preamble, the articles, and the amendments.

Here's a summary of what topics are covered in each part of the Constitution. The Constitution can be found online or at your local library for the full text.

THE PREAMBLE outlines the basic purposes of the government: *We the People of the United States, in order to form a more perfect Union, establish justice, insure domestic tranquility, provide for the common defense, promote the general welfare, and secure the blessings of liberty to ourselves and our posterity, do ordain and establish this Constitution for the United States of America.*

SEVEN ARTICLES outline the powers of Congress, the president, and the court system:

Article I outlines the legislative branch—the Senate and the House of Representatives—and its powers and responsibilities.

Article II outlines the executive branch—the presidency—and its powers and responsibilities.

Article III outlines the judicial branch—the court system—and its powers and responsibilities.

Article IV describes the individual states' rights and powers.

Article V outlines the amendment process.

Article VI establishes the Constitution as the law of the land.

Article VII gives the requirements for the Constitution to be approved.

THE AMENDMENTS, or additions to the Constitution, were put in later as needed. In 1791, the first 10 amendments, known as the **Bill of Rights,** were added. Since then, another 17 amendments have been added. This is the Bill of Rights:

1st Amendment: guarantees freedom of religion, speech, and the press, and the right to assemble and petition. The U.S. may not have a national religion.

2nd Amendment: discusses the militia and the right of people to bear arms

3rd Amendment: prohibits the military or troops from using private homes without consent

4th Amendment: protects people and their homes from search, arrest, or seizure without probable cause or a warrant

5th Amendment: grants people the right to have a trial and prevents punishment before prosecution; protects private property from being taken without compensation

6th Amendment: guarantees the right to a speedy and public trial

7th Amendment: guarantees a trial by jury in certain cases

8th Amendment: forbids "cruel and unusual punishments"

9th Amendment: states that the Constitution is not all-encompassing and does not deny people other, unspecified rights

10th Amendment: grants the powers not covered by the Constitution to the states and the people

Read the full text version of the United States Constitution at constitutioncenter.org/constitution/full-text

White House

BRANCHES OF GOVERNMENT

The **UNITED STATES GOVERNMENT** is divided into three branches: executive, legislative, and judicial. The system of checks and balances is a way to control power and to make sure one branch can't take the reins of government. For example, most of the president's actions require the approval of Congress. Likewise, the laws passed in Congress must be signed by the president before they can take effect.

Executive Branch

The Constitution lists the central powers of the president: to serve as commander in chief of the armed forces; make treaties with other nations; grant pardons; inform Congress on the state of the union; and appoint ambassadors, officials, and judges. The executive branch includes the president and the 15 governmental departments.

Legislative Branch

This branch is made up of Congress—the Senate and the House of Representatives. The Constitution grants Congress the power to make laws. Congress is made up of elected representatives from each state. Each state has two representatives in the Senate, while the number of representatives in the House is determined by the size of the state's population. Washington, D.C., and the territories elect nonvoting representatives to the House of Representatives. The Founding Fathers set up this system as a compromise between big states—which wanted representation based on population—and small states—which wanted all states to have equal representation rights.

The U.S. Capitol in Washington, D.C.

Judicial Branch

The U.S. Supreme Court Building in Washington, D.C.

The judicial branch is composed of the federal court system—the U.S. Supreme Court, the courts of appeals, and the district courts. The Supreme Court is the most powerful court. Its motto is "Equal Justice Under Law." This influential court is responsible for interpreting the Constitution and applying it to the cases that it hears. The decisions of the Supreme Court are absolute—they are the final word on any legal question.

There are nine justices on the Supreme Court. They are appointed by the president of the United States and confirmed by the Senate.

253

The Native American Experience

Native Americans are Indigenous

to North and South America—they are the people who were here before Columbus and other European explorers came to these lands. They live in nations, tribes, and bands across both continents. For decades following the arrival of Europeans in 1492, Native Americans clashed with the newcomers who had ruptured the Indigenous people's ways of living.

Tribal Land

During the 19th century, both United States legislation and military action restricted the movement of Native Americans, forcing them to live on reservations and attempting to dismantle tribal structures. For centuries, Native Americans were displaced or killed, or became assimilated into the general U.S. population. In 1924, the Indian Citizenship Act granted citizenship to all Native Americans. Unfortunately, this was not enough to end the social discrimination and mistreatment that many Indigenous people have faced. Today, Native Americans living in the United States still face many challenges.

Healing the Past

Many members of the 560-plus recognized tribes in the United States live primarily on reservations. Some tribes have more than one reservation, while others have none. Together these reservations make up less than 3 percent of the nation's land area. The tribal governments on reservations have the right to form their own governments and to enforce laws, similar to individual states. Many feel that this sovereignty is still not enough to right the wrongs of the past: They hope for a change in the U.S. government's relationship with Native Americans.

An annual powwow in New Mexico features more than 3,000 dancers from more than 500 North American tribes.

Navajo is the most commonly spoken Native American language in the United States.

Top: A Navajo teenager holds her pet lamb.

Middle: A Monacan girl dances in a traditional jingle dress.

Bottom: Navajo siblings on their horses

The president of the United States is the chief of the executive branch, the commander in chief of the U.S. armed forces, and head of the federal government. Elected every four years, the president is the highest policy-maker in the nation. The 22nd Amendment (1951) says that no person may be elected to the office of president more than twice. There have been 46 presidencies and 45 presidents.

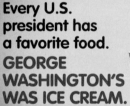

GEORGE WASHINGTON
1st President of the United States ★ *1789–1797*
BORN Feb. 22, 1732, in Pope's Creek, Westmoreland County, VA
POLITICAL PARTY Federalist
NO. OF TERMS two
VICE PRESIDENT John Adams
DIED Dec. 14, 1799, at Mount Vernon, VA

Every U.S. president has a favorite food. **GEORGE WASHINGTON'S WAS ICE CREAM.**

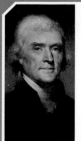

JOHN ADAMS
2nd President of the United States ★ *1797–1801*
BORN Oct. 30, 1735, in Braintree (now Quincy), MA
POLITICAL PARTY Federalist
NO. OF TERMS one
VICE PRESIDENT Thomas Jefferson
DIED July 4, 1826, in Quincy, MA

THOMAS JEFFERSON
3rd President of the United States ★ *1801–1809*
BORN April 13, 1743, at Shadwell, Goochland (now Albemarle) County, VA
POLITICAL PARTY Democratic-Republican
NO. OF TERMS two
VICE PRESIDENTS 1st term: Aaron Burr
2nd term: George Clinton
DIED July 4, 1826, at Monticello, Charlottesville, VA

JAMES MADISON
4th President of the United States ★ *1809–1817*
BORN March 16, 1751, at Belle Grove, Port Conway, VA
POLITICAL PARTY Democratic-Republican
NO. OF TERMS two
VICE PRESIDENTS 1st term: George Clinton
2nd term: Elbridge Gerry
DIED June 28, 1836, at Montpelier, Orange County, VA

JAMES MONROE
5th President of the United States ★ *1817–1825*
BORN April 28, 1758, in Westmoreland County, VA
POLITICAL PARTY Democratic-Republican
NO. OF TERMS two
VICE PRESIDENT Daniel D. Tompkins
DIED July 4, 1831, in New York, NY

JOHN QUINCY ADAMS
6th President of the United States ★ *1825–1829*
BORN July 11, 1767, in Braintree (now Quincy), MA
POLITICAL PARTY Democratic-Republican
NO. OF TERMS one
VICE PRESIDENT John Caldwell Calhoun
DIED Feb. 23, 1848, at the U.S. Capitol, Washington, D.C.

ANDREW JACKSON
7th President of the United States ★ *1829–1837*
BORN March 15, 1767, in the Waxhaw region, NC and SC
POLITICAL PARTY Democrat
NO. OF TERMS two
VICE PRESIDENTS 1st term: John Caldwell Calhoun
2nd term: Martin Van Buren
DIED June 8, 1845, in Nashville, TN

MARTIN VAN BUREN
8th President of the United States ★ *1837–1841*
BORN Dec. 5, 1782, in Kinderhook, NY
POLITICAL PARTY Democrat
NO. OF TERMS one
VICE PRESIDENT Richard M. Johnson
DIED July 24, 1862, in Kinderhook, NY

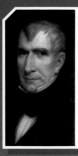

WILLIAM HENRY HARRISON

9th President of the United States ★ 1841

BORN Feb. 9, 1773, in Charles City County, VA

POLITICAL PARTY Whig

NO. OF TERMS one (died while in office)

VICE PRESIDENT John Tyler

DIED April 4, 1841, in the White House, Washington, D.C.

JOHN TYLER

10th President of the United States ★ 1841–1845

BORN March 29, 1790, in Charles City County, VA

POLITICAL PARTY Whig

NO. OF TERMS one (partial)

VICE PRESIDENT none

DIED Jan. 18, 1862, in Richmond, VA

JOHN TYLER HAD 15 KIDS— THE MOST OF ANY PRESIDENT!

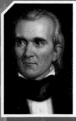

JAMES K. POLK

11th President of the United States ★ 1845–1849

BORN Nov. 2, 1795, near Pineville, Mecklenburg County, NC

POLITICAL PARTY Democrat

NO. OF TERMS one

VICE PRESIDENT George Mifflin Dallas

DIED June 15, 1849, in Nashville, TN

ZACHARY TAYLOR

12th President of the United States ★ 1849–1850

BORN Nov. 24, 1784, in Orange County, VA

POLITICAL PARTY Whig

NO. OF TERMS one (died while in office)

VICE PRESIDENT Millard Fillmore

DIED July 9, 1850, in the White House, Washington, D.C.

MILLARD FILLMORE

13th President of the United States ★ 1850–1853

BORN Jan. 7, 1800, in Cayuga County, NY

POLITICAL PARTY Whig

NO. OF TERMS one (partial)

VICE PRESIDENT none

DIED March 8, 1874, in Buffalo, NY

FRANKLIN PIERCE

14th President of the United States ★ 1853–1857

BORN Nov. 23, 1804, in Hillsborough (now Hillsboro), NH

POLITICAL PARTY Democrat

NO. OF TERMS one

VICE PRESIDENT William Rufus De Vane King

DIED Oct. 8, 1869, in Concord, NH

JAMES BUCHANAN

15th President of the United States ★ 1857–1861

BORN April 23, 1791, in Cove Gap, PA

POLITICAL PARTY Democrat

NO. OF TERMS one

VICE PRESIDENT John Cabell Breckinridge

DIED June 1, 1868, in Lancaster, PA

ABRAHAM LINCOLN

16th President of the United States ★ 1861–1865

BORN Feb. 12, 1809, near Hodgenville, KY

POLITICAL PARTY Republican (formerly Whig)

NO. OF TERMS two (assassinated)

VICE PRESIDENTS 1st term: Hannibal Hamlin
2nd term: Andrew Johnson

DIED April 15, 1865, in Washington, D.C.

ANDREW JOHNSON

17th President of the United States ★ 1865–1869

BORN Dec. 29, 1808, in Raleigh, NC

POLITICAL PARTY Democrat

NO. OF TERMS one (partial)

VICE PRESIDENT none

DIED July 31, 1875, in Carter's Station, TN

ULYSSES S. GRANT
18th President of the United States ★ 1869–1877
BORN April 27, 1822, in Point Pleasant, OH
POLITICAL PARTY Republican
NO. OF TERMS two
VICE PRESIDENTS 1st term: Schuyler Colfax
2nd term: Henry Wilson
DIED July 23, 1885, in Mount McGregor, NY

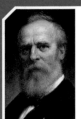

RUTHERFORD B. HAYES
19th President of the United States ★ 1877–1881
BORN Oct. 4, 1822, in Delaware, OH
POLITICAL PARTY Republican
NO. OF TERMS one
VICE PRESIDENT William Almon Wheeler
DIED Jan. 17, 1893, in Fremont, OH

JAMES A. GARFIELD
20th President of the United States ★ 1881
BORN Nov. 19, 1831, near Orange, OH
POLITICAL PARTY Republican
NO. OF TERMS one (assassinated)
VICE PRESIDENT Chester A. Arthur
DIED Sept. 19, 1881, in Elberon, NJ

CHESTER A. ARTHUR
21st President of the United States ★ 1881–1885
BORN Oct. 5, 1829, in Fairfield, VT
POLITICAL PARTY Republican
NO. OF TERMS one (partial)
VICE PRESIDENT none
DIED Nov. 18, 1886, in New York, NY

GROVER CLEVELAND
22nd and 24th President of the United States
1885–1889 ★ 1893–1897
BORN March 18, 1837, in Caldwell, NJ
POLITICAL PARTY Democrat
NO. OF TERMS two (nonconsecutive)
VICE PRESIDENTS 1st administration:
Thomas Andrews Hendricks
2nd administration:
Adlai Ewing Stevenson
DIED June 24, 1908, in Princeton, NJ

BENJAMIN HARRISON
23rd President of the United States ★ 1889–1893
BORN Aug. 20, 1833, in North Bend, OH
POLITICAL PARTY Republican
NO. OF TERMS one
VICE PRESIDENT Levi Parsons Morton
DIED March 13, 1901, in Indianapolis, IN

WILLIAM MCKINLEY
25th President of the United States ★ 1897–1901
BORN Jan. 29, 1843, in Niles, OH
POLITICAL PARTY Republican
NO. OF TERMS two (assassinated)
VICE PRESIDENTS 1st term:
Garret Augustus Hobart
2nd term:
Theodore Roosevelt
DIED Sept. 14, 1901, in Buffalo, NY

THEODORE ROOSEVELT
26th President of the United States ★ 1901–1909
BORN Oct. 27, 1858, in New York, NY
POLITICAL PARTY Republican
NO. OF TERMS one, plus balance of McKinley's term
VICE PRESIDENTS 1st term: none
2nd term: Charles Warren Fairbanks
DIED Jan. 6, 1919, in Oyster Bay, NY

WILLIAM HOWARD TAFT
27th President of the United States ★ 1909–1913
BORN Sept. 15, 1857, in Cincinnati, OH
POLITICAL PARTY Republican
NO. OF TERMS one
VICE PRESIDENT James Schoolcraft Sherman
DIED March 8, 1930, in Washington, D.C.

WOODROW WILSON
28th President of the United States ★ 1913–1921
BORN Dec. 29, 1856, in Staunton, VA
POLITICAL PARTY Democrat
NO. OF TERMS two
VICE PRESIDENT Thomas Riley Marshall
DIED Feb. 3, 1924, in Washington, D.C.

WARREN G. HARDING
29th President of the United States ★ 1921–1923
BORN Nov. 2, 1865, in Caledonia
(now Blooming Grove), OH
POLITICAL PARTY Republican
NO. OF TERMS one (died while in office)
VICE PRESIDENT Calvin Coolidge
DIED Aug. 2, 1923, in San Francisco, CA

DWIGHT D. EISENHOWER
34th President of the United States ★ 1953–1961
BORN Oct. 14, 1890, in Denison, TX
POLITICAL PARTY Republican
NO. OF TERMS two
VICE PRESIDENT Richard Nixon
DIED March 28, 1969,
in Washington, D.C.

CALVIN COOLIDGE
30th President of the United States ★ 1923–1929
BORN July 4, 1872, in Plymouth, VT
POLITICAL PARTY Republican
NO. OF TERMS one, plus balance of
Harding's term
VICE PRESIDENTS 1st term: none
2nd term:
Charles Gates Dawes
DIED Jan. 5, 1933, in Northampton, MA

JOHN F. KENNEDY
35th President of the United States ★ 1961–1963
BORN May 29, 1917, in Brookline, MA
POLITICAL PARTY Democrat
NO. OF TERMS one (assassinated)
VICE PRESIDENT Lyndon B. Johnson
DIED Nov. 22, 1963, in Dallas, TX

HERBERT HOOVER
31st President of the United States ★ 1929–1933
BORN Aug. 10, 1874,
in West Branch, IA
POLITICAL PARTY Republican
NO. OF TERMS one
VICE PRESIDENT Charles Curtis
DIED Oct. 20, 1964, in New York, NY

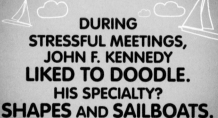

DURING STRESSFUL MEETINGS, JOHN F. KENNEDY LIKED TO DOODLE. HIS SPECIALTY? SHAPES AND SAILBOATS.

FRANKLIN D. ROOSEVELT
32nd President of the United States ★ 1933–1945
BORN Jan. 30, 1882, in Hyde Park, NY
POLITICAL PARTY Democrat
NO. OF TERMS four (died while in office)
VICE PRESIDENTS 1st & 2nd terms: John
Nance Garner; 3rd term:
Henry Agard Wallace;
4th term: Harry S. Truman
DIED April 12, 1945,
in Warm Springs, GA

LYNDON B. JOHNSON
36th President of the United States ★ 1963–1969
BORN Aug. 27, 1908, near Stonewall, TX
POLITICAL PARTY Democrat
NO. OF TERMS one, plus balance of
Kennedy's term
VICE PRESIDENTS 1st term: none
2nd term: Hubert
Horatio Humphrey
DIED Jan. 22, 1973, near San Antonio, TX

HARRY S. TRUMAN
33rd President of the United States ★ 1945–1953
BORN May 8, 1884, in Lamar, MO
POLITICAL PARTY Democrat
NO. OF TERMS one, plus balance of
Franklin D. Roosevelt's term
VICE PRESIDENTS 1st term: none
2nd term:
Alben William Barkley
DIED Dec. 26, 1972, in Independence, MO

RICHARD NIXON
37th President of the United States ★ 1969–1974
BORN Jan. 9, 1913, in Yorba Linda, CA
POLITICAL PARTY Republican
NO. OF TERMS two (resigned)
VICE PRESIDENTS 1st term & 2nd term
(partial): Spiro Theodore
Agnew; 2nd term
(balance): Gerald R. Ford
DIED April 22, 1994, in New York, NY

GERALD R. FORD
38th President of the United States ★ 1974–1977
BORN July 14, 1913, in Omaha, NE
POLITICAL PARTY Republican
NO. OF TERMS one (partial)
VICE PRESIDENT Nelson Aldrich Rockefeller
DIED Dec. 26, 2006, in Rancho Mirage, CA

JIMMY CARTER
39th President of the United States ★ 1977–1981
BORN Oct. 1, 1924, in Plains, GA
POLITICAL PARTY Democrat
NO. OF TERMS one
VICE PRESIDENT Walter Frederick (Fritz) Mondale

RONALD REAGAN
40th President of the United States ★ 1981–1989
BORN Feb. 6, 1911, in Tampico, IL
POLITICAL PARTY Republican
NO. OF TERMS two
VICE PRESIDENT George H. W. Bush
DIED June 5, 2004, in Los Angeles, CA

GEORGE H. W. BUSH
41st President of the United States ★ 1989–1993
BORN June 12, 1924, in Milton, MA
POLITICAL PARTY Republican
NO. OF TERMS one
VICE PRESIDENT James Danforth (Dan) Quayle III
DIED Nov. 30, 2018, in Houston, TX

BILL CLINTON
42nd President of the United States ★ 1993–2001
BORN Aug. 19, 1946, in Hope, AR
POLITICAL PARTY Democrat
NO. OF TERMS two
VICE PRESIDENT Albert Arnold Gore, Jr.

GEORGE W. BUSH
43rd President of the United States ★ 2001–2009
BORN July 6, 1946, in New Haven, CT
POLITICAL PARTY Republican
NO. OF TERMS two
VICE PRESIDENT Richard Bruce Cheney

BARACK OBAMA
44th President of the United States ★ 2009–2017
BORN Aug. 4, 1961, in Honolulu, HI
POLITICAL PARTY Democrat
NO. OF TERMS two
VICE PRESIDENT Joe Biden

DONALD TRUMP
45th President of the United States ★ 2017–2021
BORN June 14, 1946, in Queens, NY
POLITICAL PARTY Republican
NO. OF TERMS one
VICE PRESIDENT Mike Pence

JOE BIDEN
46th President of the United States ★ 2021–
BORN November 20, 1942, in Scranton, PA
POLITICAL PARTY Democrat
VICE PRESIDENT Kamala Harris

Check out this book!

OUR COUNTRY'S PRESIDENTS

AS A LAWYER IN DELAWARE, JOE BIDEN ONCE **DEFENDED** A **FISHERMAN** WHO **STOLE** A **PRIZE-WINNING COW.**

AMAZING ANIMALS

PRESIDENTIAL Pets

BO

U.S. presidents might lead the country, but their pets rule the White House.

COMMANDER PLAYS ON THE SOUTH LAWN OF THE WHITE HOUSE.

The President: Joe Biden
Years in office: 2021 to present
The pet: In December 2021, the Bidens welcomed a **German shepherd** puppy to the White House. The new puppy's name is **Commander.**

FIRST LADY GRACE COOLIDGE HOLDS REBECCA AT THE WHITE HOUSE EASTER EGG ROLL IN 1927.

The president: Calvin Coolidge
Years in office: 1923 to 1929
The pet: A raccoon named **Rebecca** was a gift to President Coolidge. She spent hours splashing around in a partly filled bathtub and even walked on a leash.

The president: Abraham Lincoln
Years in office: 1861 to 1865
The pet: A citizen sent the Lincoln family **a turkey** as a gift for their Christmas feast. The president's youngest son, Tad, quickly bonded with the bird—named **Jack**—and convinced his father to let him keep it as a pet. (Earlier that year, in 1863, President Lincoln had proclaimed the first national Thanksgiving holiday.)

PAULINE WAYNE WALKS ON THE LAWN OF WHAT'S NOW THE EISENHOWER EXECUTIVE OFFICE BUILDING NEXT TO THE WHITE HOUSE.

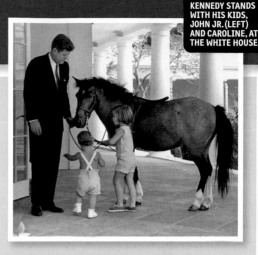

PRESIDENT KENNEDY STANDS WITH HIS KIDS, JOHN JR. (LEFT) AND CAROLINE, AT THE WHITE HOUSE.

The president: William Howard Taft
Years in office: 1909 to 1913
The pet: President Taft kept **a dairy cow** named **Pauline Wayne** that grazed on the White House lawn.

The president: John F. Kennedy
Years in office: 1961 to 1963
The pet: President Kennedy's daughter, Caroline, had **a pony** called **Macaroni** that she rode around the White House gardens.

BO (LEFT) AND SUNNY SIT AT A TABLE IN THE STATE DINING ROOM OF THE WHITE HOUSE.

PRESIDENT JOHNSON PLAYS WITH YUKI.

The president: Barack Obama
Years in office: 2009 to 2017
The pets: President Obama promised his daughters, Sasha and Malia, that they could adopt a dog after the 2008 election. Eventually the family adopted not one but **two Portuguese water dogs, Bo** and **Sunny.** The pups had a few official duties, such as cheering up patients at hospitals and greeting visiting world leaders. But that didn't stop them from occasionally being naughty: Bo once chewed on the commander in chief's gym shoes.

The president:
Lyndon B. Johnson
Years in office: 1963 to 1969
The pet: President Johnson enjoyed having howling duets in the Oval Office with **Yuki the mutt,** one of his six dogs.

CIVIL RIGHTS

Although the Constitution protects the civil rights of American citizens, it has not always been able to protect all Americans from persecution or discrimination. During the first half of the 20th century, many Americans, particularly Black Americans, were subjected to widespread discrimination and racism. By the mid-1950s, many people were eager to end the barriers caused by racism and bring freedom to all men and women.

The civil rights movement of the 1950s and 1960s sought to end racial discrimination against Black people, especially in the southern states. The movement wanted to give the fundamentals of economic and social equality to those who had been oppressed.

Woolworth Counter Sit-in

On February 1, 1960, four Black college students walked into a Woolworth's "five-and-dime" store in Greensboro, North Carolina. They planned to have lunch there, but were refused service as soon as they sat down at the counter. In a time of heightened racial tension, the Woolworth's manager had a strict whites-only policy. But the students wouldn't take no for an answer. The men—later dubbed the "Greensboro Four"—stayed seated, peacefully and quietly, at the lunch counter until closing. The next day, they returned with 15 additional college students. The following day, even more. By February 5, some 300 students gathered at Woolworth's, forming one of the most famous sit-ins of the civil rights movement. The protest—which sparked similar sit-ins throughout the country—worked: Just six months later, restaurants across the South began to integrate.

Key Events in the Civil Rights Movement

1954	The Supreme Court case *Brown v. Board of Education* declares school segregation illegal.
1955	Rosa Parks refuses to give up her bus seat to a white passenger and spurs a bus boycott.
1957	The Little Rock Nine help to integrate schools.
1960	Four Black college students begin sit-ins at a restaurant in Greensboro, North Carolina.
1961	Freedom Rides to southern states begin as a way to protest segregation in transportation.
1963	Martin Luther King, Jr., leads the famous March on Washington.
1964	The Civil Rights Act, signed by President Lyndon B. Johnson, prohibits discrimination based on race, color, religion, sex, and national origin.
1967	Thurgood Marshall becomes the first Black American to be named to the Supreme Court.
1968	President Lyndon B. Johnson signs the Civil Rights Act of 1968, which prohibits discrimination in the sale, rental, and financing of housing.

STONE OF HOPE:
THE LEGACY OF MARTIN LUTHER KING, JR.

On April 4, 1968, Dr. Martin Luther King, Jr., was shot by James Earl Ray while standing on a hotel balcony in Memphis, Tennessee, U.S.A. The news of his death sent shock waves throughout the world: Dr. King, a Baptist minister and founder of the Southern Christian Leadership Conference, was the most prominent civil rights leader of his time. His nonviolent protests and marches against segregation, as well as his powerful speeches—including his famous "I Have a Dream" speech—motivated people to fight for justice for all.

More than 50 years after his death, Dr. King's dream lives on through a memorial on the National Mall in Washington, D.C. Built in 2011, the memorial features a 30-foot (9-m) statue of Dr. King carved into a granite boulder named the "Stone of Hope."

Today, Dr. King continues to inspire people around the world with his words and his vision for a peaceful world without racism. He will forever be remembered as one of the most prominent leaders of the civil rights movement.

"The time is always right to do what is right."

Martin Luther King, Jr., Memorial in Washington, D.C.

JOHN LEWIS: GETTING IN GOOD TROUBLE

On March 7, 1965, a 25-year-old man linked arms with five other people, including Dr. Martin Luther King, Jr., as they led hundreds in a march across the Edmund Pettus Bridge in Selma, Alabama, U.S.A. It was a simple act, but it carried a very loud message: Those marching along the bridge were marching for racial justice and equality during a time when Black people were treated unjustly by many and were denied the same basic rights as white people, including the right to vote.

That young man was John Lewis. And, after crossing the bridge, Lewis was attacked by state troopers and beaten badly. The scene was so shocking that it made national news and created a public outcry. An act that prevented Black people from being denied the right to vote was passed just five months later. From then on, Lewis, who survived the attack, became a legend in the civil rights movement for his quiet yet powerful ability to create change. He called it getting in "good trouble": Standing up for what you believe is right and just, even if it means ruffling feathers along the way.

Lewis went on to serve in the U.S. House of Representatives for 33 years until his death in 2020. Before he passed, he was able to speak about the Black Lives Matter movement, once again encouraging people to fight for justice. "We must use our time and our space on this little planet that we call Earth to make a lasting contribution, to leave it a little better than we found it," said Lewis. "And now that need is greater than ever before."

John Lewis joins hands with President Barack Obama as they lead a commemorative march across the Edmund Pettus Bridge in Selma, Alabama, in 2015.

WOMEN

FIGHTING FOR EQUALITY

Women in New York City cast their votes for the first time in November 1920.

Today, women make up about half of the workforce in the United States. But a little over a century ago, less than 20 percent worked outside the home. In fact, they didn't even have the right to vote!

That began to change in the mid-1800s when women, led by pioneers like Elizabeth Cady Stanton and Susan B. Anthony, started speaking up about inequality. They organized public demonstrations, gave speeches, published documents, and wrote newspaper articles to express their ideas. In 1848, about 300 people attended the Seneca Falls Convention in New York State to address the need for equal rights. By the late 1800s, the National American Woman Suffrage Association had made great strides toward giving women the freedom to vote. One by one, states began allowing women to vote. By 1920, the U.S. Constitution was amended, giving women across the country the ability to cast a vote during any election.

But the fight for equality did not end there. In the 1960s and 1970s, the women's rights movement experienced a rebirth, as feminists protested against injustices in areas such as the workplace and in education.

While these efforts enabled women to make great strides in our society, the efforts to even the playing field among men and women continue today.

New Zealand gave women the right to vote in 1893, becoming the world's first country to do so.

In 2020, Katie Sowers became the first female football coach in Super Bowl history.

KAMALA HARRIS IS SWORN IN AS VICE PRESIDENT ON JANUARY 20, 2021.

Key Events in U.S. Women's History

1848: **Elizabeth Cady Stanton** and **Lucretia Mott** organize the Seneca Falls Convention in New York. Attendees rally for equitable laws, equal educational and job opportunities, and the right to vote.

1920: **The 19th Amendment,** guaranteeing women the right to vote, is ratified.

1964: **Title VII of the Civil Rights Act of 1964,** which prohibits employment discrimination on the basis of sex, is successfully amended.

1971: **Gloria Steinem** heads up the National Women's Political Caucus, which encourages women to be active in government. She also launches *Ms.,* a magazine about women's issues.

1972: Congress approves **the Equal Rights Amendment** (ERA), proposing that women and men have equal rights under the law. It is ratified by 35 of the necessary 38 states, and is still not part of the U.S. Constitution.

1981: President Ronald Reagan appoints **Sandra Day O'Connor** as the first female Supreme Court justice.

2009: President Obama signs **the Lilly Ledbetter Fair Pay Act** to protect against pay discrimination among men and women.

2013: The **ban against women in military combat positions** is removed, overturning a 1994 Pentagon decision restricting women from combat roles.

2016: Democratic presidential nominee **Hillary Rodham Clinton** becomes the first woman to lead the ticket of a major U.S. party.

2021: **Kamala Harris** is sworn in as vice president of the United States, becoming the first woman to hold that office.

Ava DuVernay
Lived: 1972–

WHY SHE'S MEMORABLE: A history-making director, writer, and producer, DuVernay is the first Black woman to win Best Director at the Sundance Film Festival, be nominated as Best Director at the Golden Globes, and to direct a film nominated for Best Picture at the Academy Awards. Getting her start as a director at the age of 32 after a career in marketing and publicity, DuVernay went on to become an innovator behind the camera—and the highest-grossing Black female director in American box office history. Through her films, which include *Selma* and *A Wrinkle in Time,* DuVernay is known for telling powerful stories that focus on the lives and times of Black Americans.

Patsy Takemoto Mink
Lived: 1927–2002

WHY SHE'S MEMORABLE: Not only was Mink the first woman of color in Congress, but she played an important role in the passing of Title IX, which guaranteed equal opportunity in education for all students regardless of their gender. An Asian-American, Mink was born in Hawaii and faced both gender and racial discrimination herself as a student, even being rejected from medical school, likely because she was a woman. This sparked her desire to advocate for equal rights for future generations, and she worked tirelessly to earn the nickname of "The Mother of Title IX." Mink is also known for becoming the first Asian-American woman to run for president, which she did unsuccessfully in 1972.

QUIZ WHIZ

Go back in time to seek the answers to this history quiz!

Write your answers on a piece of paper. Then check them below.

1 **True or false?** Kleenex tissues were first used as liners in gas masks during World War I.

2 At the ruins of Pompeii, layers of ash have helped to preserve what kinds of artifacts?

a. artwork
b. loaves of bread
c. kitchen pots
d. all of the above

3 The Taj Mahal was originally built for which purpose?

a. a place of worship
b. an event space for grand parties
c. a shopping mall
d. an elaborate tomb for a queen

4 **True or false?** Japanese Samurai armor was made of metal and leather to deflect blades and arrows.

5 What was the name of Blackbeard's famous pirate ship?

a. *The Caribbean Conqueror*
b. *Queen Anne's Revenge*
c. *Blackbeard's Boat*
d. *The Treasure Hunter*

Not **STUMPED** yet? Check out the
NATIONAL GEOGRAPHIC KIDS QUIZ WHIZ collection
for more crazy **HISTORY** questions!

ANSWERS: 1. True; 2. d; 3. d; 4. True; 5. b

HOMEWORK HELP

Brilliant Biographies

Malala Yousafzai

A biography is the story of a person's life. It can be a brief summary or a long book. Biographers—those who write biographies—use many different sources to learn about their subjects. You can write your own biography of a famous person you find inspiring.

How to Get Started

Choose a subject you find interesting. If you think Cleopatra is cool, you have a good chance of getting your readers interested, too. If you're bored by ancient Egypt, your readers will be snoring after your first paragraph.

Your subject can be almost anyone: an author, an inventor, a celebrity, a politician, or a member of your family. To find someone to write about, ask yourself these simple questions:

1. Who do I want to know more about?
2. What did this person do that was special?
3. How did this person change the world?

Do Your Research

• Find out as much about your subject as possible. Read books, news articles, and encyclopedia entries. Watch video clips and movies. Conduct interviews, if possible.

• Take notes, writing down important facts and interesting stories about your subject.

Write the Biography

• Come up with a title. Include the person's name.

• Write an introduction. Consider asking a probing question about your subject.

• Include information about the person's childhood. When was this person born? Where did he or she grow up? Who did he or she admire?

• Highlight the person's talents, accomplishments, and personal attributes.

• Describe the specific events that helped to shape this person's life. Did this person ever have a problem and overcome it?

• Write a conclusion. Include your thoughts about why it is important to learn about this person.

• Once you have finished your first draft, revise and then proofread your work.

Here's a SAMPLE BIOGRAPHY of Malala Yousafzai, a human rights advocate and the youngest ever recipient of the Nobel Peace Prize. Of course, there is so much more for you to discover and write about on your own!

Malala Yousafzai

Malala Yousafzai was born in Pakistan on July 12, 1997. Malala's father, Ziauddin, a teacher, made it a priority for his daughter to receive a proper education. Malala loved school. She learned to speak three languages and even wrote a blog about her experiences as a student.

Around the time Malala turned 10, the Taliban—a group of strict Muslims who believe women should stay at home—took over the region where she lived. The Taliban did not approve of Malala's outspoken love of learning. One day, on her way home from school, Malala was shot in the head by a Taliban gunman. Very badly injured, she was sent to a hospital in England.

Not only did Malala survive the shooting—she thrived. She used her experience as a platform to fight for girls' education worldwide. She began speaking out about educational opportunities for all. Her efforts gained worldwide attention, and she was eventually awarded the Nobel Peace Prize in 2014 at the age of 17. She is the youngest person to earn the prestigious prize.

Each year on July 12, World Malala Day honors her heroic efforts to bring attention to human rights issues.

GEOGRAPHY
ROCKS

Acid ponds and hot springs create an alien-looking landscape in the Danakil Depression in Ethiopia—one of the hottest and driest places on Earth.

THE POLITICAL WORLD

Earth's land area is made up of seven continents, but people have divided much of the land into smaller political units called countries. Australia is a continent made up of a single country, and Antarctica is used for scientific research. But the other five continents include almost 200 independent countries. The political map shown here depicts boundaries—imaginary lines created by treaties—that separate countries. Some boundaries, such as the one between the United States and Canada, are very stable and have been recognized for many years.

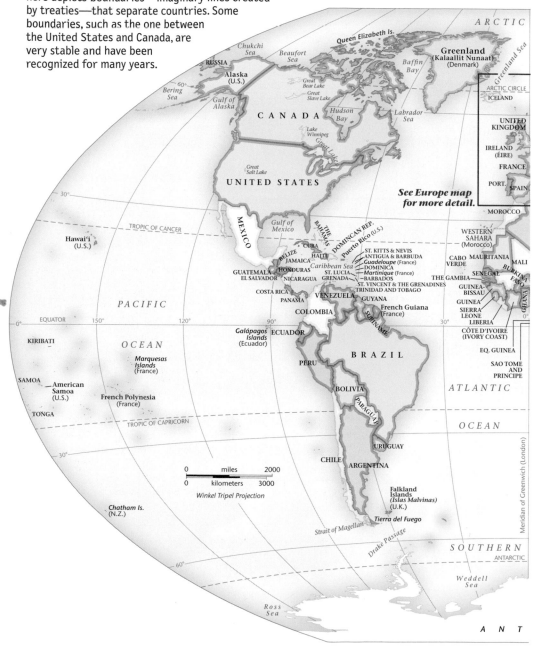

ARCTIC

Queen Elizabeth Is.

Chukchi Sea
Beaufort Sea
Baffin Bay

Greenland
(Kalaallit Nunaat)
(Denmark)

Greenland Sea

RUSSIA

Alaska (U.S.)

60°

Bering Sea

Gulf of Alaska

Great Bear Lake

Great Slave Lake

CANADA

Hudson Bay

Labrador Sea

ARCTIC CIRCLE

ICELAND

UNITED KINGDOM

IRELAND (ÉIRE)

FRANCE

Lake Winnipeg

Great Lakes

Great Salt Lake

UNITED STATES

See Europe map
for more detail.

PORT. SPAIN

30°

MOROCCO

TROPIC OF CANCER

Hawai'i (U.S.)

Gulf of Mexico

MEXICO

THE BAHAMAS

CUBA

DOMINICAN REP.

Puerto Rico (U.S.)

WESTERN SAHARA
(Morocco)

ST. KITTS & NEVIS

BELIZE

HAITI

ANTIGUA & BARBUDA

CABO VERDE

MAURITANIA

MALI

JAMAICA

Guadeloupe (France)

DOMINICA

GUATEMALA

HONDURAS

Caribbean Sea

ST. LUCIA

Martinique (France)

SENEGAL

BURKINA FASO

EL SALVADOR

NICARAGUA

GRENADA

BARBADOS

ST. VINCENT & THE GRENADINES

THE GAMBIA

GUINEA-BISSAU

COSTA RICA

VENEZUELA

TRINIDAD AND TOBAGO

GUINEA

GHANA

PANAMA

GUYANA

SIERRA LEONE

COLOMBIA

French Guiana
(France)

LIBERIA

CÔTE D'IVOIRE
(IVORY COAST)

PACIFIC

Galápagos Islands
(Ecuador)

ECUADOR

SURINAME

EQ. GUINEA

EQUATOR

150°

120°

90°

30°

KIRIBATI

OCEAN

PERU

BRAZIL

SAO TOME AND PRINCIPE

Marquesas Islands
(France)

BOLIVIA

ATLANTIC

SAMOA

American Samoa (U.S.)

French Polynesia
(France)

PARAGUAY

TONGA

TROPIC OF CAPRICORN

OCEAN

30°

URUGUAY

CHILE

ARGENTINA

0 miles 2000

0 kilometers 3000

Winkel Tripel Projection

Chatham Is.
(N.Z.)

Falkland Islands
(Islas Malvinas)
(U.K.)

Tierra del Fuego

Strait of Magellan

Drake Passage

SOUTHERN

ANTARCTIC

Meridian of Greenwich (London)

60°

Weddell Sea

Ross Sea

A N T

Other boundaries, such as the one between Sudan and South Sudan in northeast Africa, are relatively new and still disputed. Countries come in all shapes and sizes. Russia and Canada are giants; others, such as El Salvador and Qatar, are small. Some countries are long and skinny—look at Chile in South America! Still other countries—such as Indonesia and Japan in Asia—are made up of groups of islands. The political map is a clue to the diversity that makes Earth so fascinating.

OCEAN

North Land
New Siberian Islands
East Siberian Sea
Barents Sea
Kara Sea
Laptev Sea
Svalbard (Norway)
Novaya Zemlya

60° Bering Sea
Sea of Okhotsk

R U S S I A

NORWAY
SWEDEN
FINLAND
DEN.
GERMANY
EST.
LATV.
LITH.
BELARUS
POLAND
UKRAINE
MOLD.
ROMANIA
GEORGIA
BULGARIA
ITALY
ALBANIA
GREECE
TURKEY
TUNISIA
CYPRUS SYRIA
LEBANON
ISRAEL
JORDAN
IRAQ
IRAN
KUWAIT
BAHRAIN QATAR
SAUDI ARABIA
U.A.E.
OMAN
YEMEN

KAZAKHSTAN

MONGOLIA

Lake Baikal

UZBEK.
TURKMEN.
KYRGYZSTAN
TAJIKISTAN
ARM.
AZERB.
Caspian Sea
AFGHAN.
PAKISTAN
NEPAL BHUTAN
BANGLADESH

C H I N A

NORTH KOREA
SOUTH KOREA
JAPAN

TAIWAN
The People's Republic of China claims Taiwan as its 23rd province. Taiwan's government (Republic of China) maintains that there are two political entities.

TAIWAN

30°

ALGERIA
LIBYA
EGYPT
Red Sea

INDIA
MYANMAR (BURMA)
LAOS
VIETNAM
THAILAND
CAMBODIA

Bay of Bengal

South China Sea

Philippine Sea
PHILIPPINES

Northern Mariana Islands (U.S.)
Guam (U.S.)

PACIFIC

MARSHALL ISLANDS

OCEAN

NIGER
CHAD
SUDAN
ERITREA
DJIBOUTI
Arabian Sea
SRI LANKA
MALDIVES

PALAU
FEDERATED STATES OF MICRONESIA

KIRIBATI

BENIN
NIGERIA
CAMEROON
CEN. AF. REP.
SOUTH SUDAN
ETHIOPIA
SOMALILAND
SOMALIA

BRUNEI
MALAYSIA
SINGAPORE

TOGO
GABON
CONGO
DEM. REP. OF THE CONGO
RWANDA
UGANDA
KENYA
BURUNDI
TANZANIA
SEYCHELLES

60°
90°

150°
EQUATOR
0°

NAURU

I N D O N E S I A

New Guinea
PAPUA NEW GUINEA
SOLOMON ISLANDS

ANGOLA
ZAMBIA
ZIMBABWE
NAMIBIA
BOTSWANA
MALAWI
MOZAMBIQUE
MADAGASCAR
COMOROS

I N D I A N

TIMOR-LESTE

TUVALU

Coral Sea
VANUATU
FIJI

O C E A N

MAURITIUS
Réunion (France)

ESWATINI (SWAZILAND)
SOUTH AFRICA
LESOTHO

A U S T R A L I A

New Caledonia (France)

30°

Great Australian Bight

Tasman Sea
North Island

NEW ZEALAND

Kerguelen Islands (France)

Tasmania

South Island

OCEAN
CIRCLE

60°

Ross Sea

A R C T I C A

THE PHYSICAL WORLD

Earth is dominated by large landmasses called continents—seven in all—and by an interconnected global ocean that is divided into five parts by the continents. More than 70 percent of Earth's surface is covered by oceans, and the rest is made up of land areas.

Different landforms give variety to the surface of the continents. The Rocky Mountains divide North America, the Andes mark the western edge of South America, and the Himalaya tower above South Asia. The Plateau of Tibet forms the rugged core of Asia,

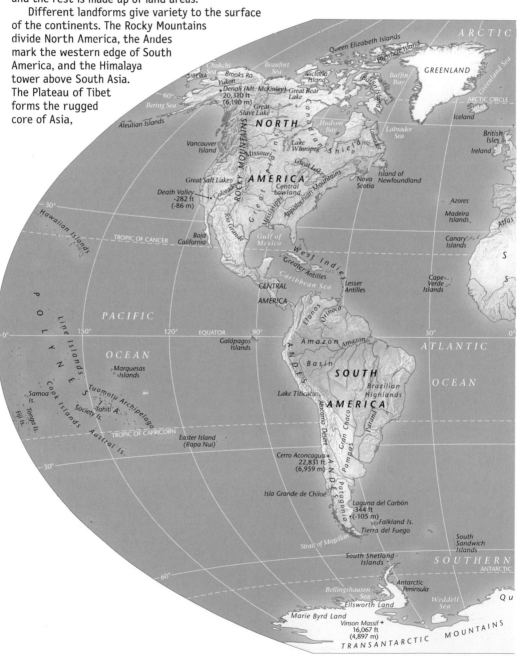

while the Northern European Plain extends from the North Sea to the Ural Mountains. Much of Africa is a plateau, and dry plains cover large areas of Australia. Mountains rise more than 16,000 feet (4,877 m) above Antarctica's massive ice sheets. Mountains and trenches make the ocean floors as varied as any continent. A mountain chain called the Mid-Atlantic Ridge runs the length of the Atlantic Ocean. In the western Pacific, trenches drop deep into the ocean floor.

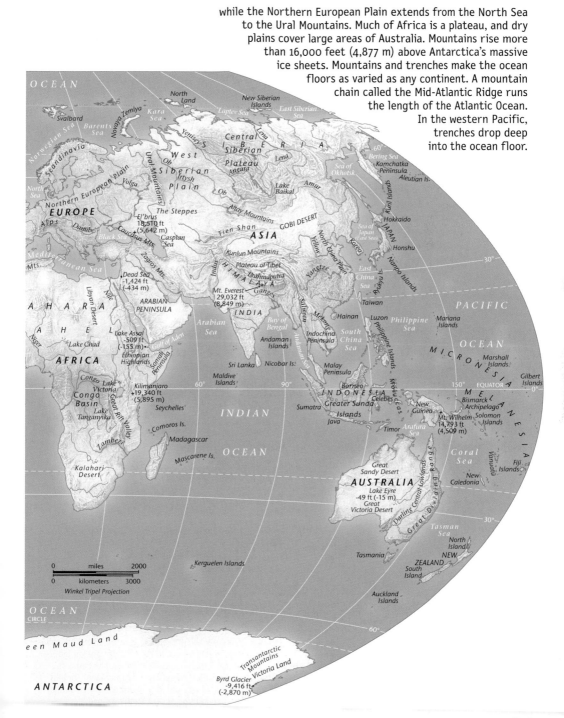

KINDS OF MAPS

Maps are special tools that geographers use to tell a story about Earth. Maps can be used to show just about anything related to places. Some maps show physical features, such as mountains or vegetation. Maps can also show climates or natural hazards and other things we cannot easily see. Other maps illustrate different features on Earth—political boundaries, urban centers, and economic systems.

AN IMPERFECT TOOL

Maps are not perfect. A globe is a scale model of Earth with accurate relative sizes and locations. Because maps are flat, they involve distortions of size, shape, and direction. Also, cartographers—people who create maps—make choices about what information to include. Because of this, it is important to study many different types of maps to learn the complete story of Earth. Three commonly found kinds of maps are shown on this page.

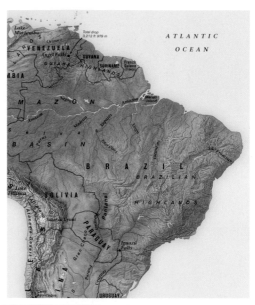

PHYSICAL MAPS. Earth's natural features—landforms, water bodies, and vegetation—are shown on physical maps. The map above uses color and shading to illustrate mountains, lakes, rivers, and deserts of central South America. Country names and borders are added for reference, but they are not natural features.

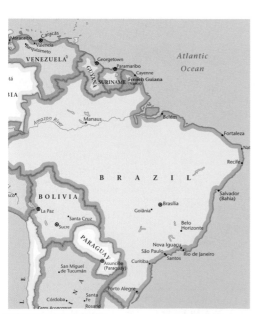

POLITICAL MAPS. These maps represent characteristics of the landscape created by humans, such as boundaries, cities, and place-names. Natural features are added only for reference. On the map above, capital cities are represented with a star inside a circle, while other cities are shown with black dots.

THEMATIC MAPS. Patterns related to a particular topic or theme, such as population distribution, appear on these maps. The map above displays the region's climate zones, which range from tropical wet (bright green) to tropical wet and dry (light green) to semiarid (dark yellow) to arid or desert (light yellow).

MAKING MAPS

Meet a Cartographer!

As a National Geographic cartographer, **Mike McNey** works with maps every day. Here, he shares more about his cool career.

National Geographic staff cartographers Mike McNey and Rosemary Wardley review a map of Africa for the *National Geographic Kids World Atlas.*

What exactly does a cartographer do?

I create maps specifically for books and atlases to help the text tell the story on the page. The maps need to fit into the size and the style of the book, with the final goal being that it's accurate and appealing for the reader.

What kinds of stories have you told with your maps?

Once, I created a map that showed the spread of the Burmese python population in Florida around the Everglades National Park. I've also made maps that show data like farmland, food production, cattle density, and fish catch in a particular location, like the United States.

How do you rely on technology in your job?

All aspects of mapmaking are on the computer. This makes it much quicker to make a map. It also makes it easier to change anything on the map. If you want to change the color of the rivers on the map, you just have to hit one button on the mouse.

How do you create your maps?

I work with geographic information systems (GIS), a computer software that allows us to represent any data on a specific location of the world, or even the entire world. Data can be anything from endangered species, animal ranges, and population of a particular place. We also use remote systems, like satellites and aerial imagery, to analyze Earth's surface.

Satellites in orbit around Earth act as eyes in the sky, recording data about the planet's land and ocean areas. The data are converted to numbers transmitted back to computers that are specially programmed to interpret the data. They record the information in a form that cartographers can use to create maps.

What will maps of the future look like?

In the future, you'll see more and more data on maps. I also think more online maps are going to be made in a way that you can switch from a world view to a local view to see data at any scale.

What's the best part of your job?

I love the combination of science and design involved in it. It's also fun to make maps interesting for kids.

UNDERSTANDING
MAPS

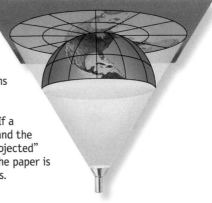

MAKING A PROJECTION

Globes present a model of Earth as it is—a sphere—but they are bulky and can be difficult to use and store. Flat maps are much more convenient, but certain problems can result from transferring Earth's curved surface to a flat piece of paper, a process called projection. Imagine a globe that has been cut in half, like the one to the right. If a light is shined into it, the lines of latitude and longitude and the shapes of the continent will cast shadows that can be "projected" onto a piece of paper, as shown here. Depending on how the paper is positioned, the shadows will be distorted in different ways.

KNOW THE CODE

Every map has a story to tell, but first you have to know how to read one. Maps represent information by using a language of symbols. When you know how to read these symbols, you can access a wide range of information. Look at the scale and compass rose or arrow to understand distance and direction (see box below).

To find out what each symbol on a map means, you must use the key. It's your secret decoder—identifying information by each symbol on the map.

There are three main types of map symbols: points, lines, and areas. Points, which can be either dots or small icons, represent the location or the number of things, such as schools, cities, or landmarks. Lines are used to show boundaries, roads, or rivers and can vary in color or thickness. Area symbols use pattern or color to show regions, such as a sandy area or a neighborhood.

SCALE AND DIRECTION

The scale on a map can be shown as a fraction, as words, or as a line or bar. It relates distance on the map to distance in the real world. Sometimes the scale identifies the type of map projection. Maps may include an arrow to indicate north on the map or a compass rose to show all principal directions.

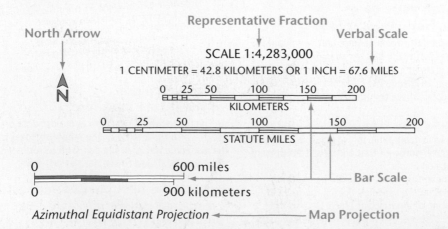

North Arrow

Representative Fraction

Verbal Scale

SCALE 1:4,283,000

1 CENTIMETER = 42.8 KILOMETERS OR 1 INCH = 67.6 MILES

0   25   50   100   150   200
KILOMETERS

0   25   50   100   150   200
STATUTE MILES

N

0   600 miles
0   900 kilometers

Bar Scale

Azimuthal Equidistant Projection ◄——————— Map Projection

GEOGRAPHIC FEATURES

From roaring rivers to parched deserts, from underwater canyons to jagged mountains, Earth is covered with beautiful and diverse environments. Here are examples of the most common types of geographic features found around the world.

WATERFALL

Waterfalls form when a river reaches an abrupt change in elevation. At left, the Iguazú waterfall system—on the border of Brazil and Argentina—is made up of 275 falls.

VALLEY

Valleys, cut by running water or moving ice, may be broad and flat or narrow and steep, such as the Indus River Valley (above)in Ladakh, India.

RIVER

As a river moves through flatlands, it twists and turns. Above, the Rio Los Amigos winds through a rainforest in Peru.

MOUNTAIN

Mountains are Earth's tallest landforms, and Mount Everest (above) rises highest of all, at 29,031.69 feet (8,848.86 m) above sea level.

GLACIER

Glaciers—"rivers" of ice—such as Hubbard Glacier (above) in Alaska, U.S.A., move slowly from mountains to the sea. Global warming is shrinking them.

CANYON

Steep-sided valleys called canyons are created mainly by running water. Buckskin Gulch (above) in Utah, U.S.A., is the deepest "slot" canyon in the American Southwest.

DESERT

Deserts are land features created by climate, specifically by a lack of water. Here, a camel caravan crosses the Sahara in North Africa.

MOUNT EVEREST,

THE WORLD'S TALLEST MOUNTAIN,

NOW MEASURES

2.8 FEET (.86 M) HIGHER

THAN NEPALI OFFICIALS PREVIOUSLY CALCULATED.

Experts used high-tech **GPS SATELLITES** and **LASER-EQUIPPED TOOLS** to get an **ACCURATE MEASUREMENT** of Mount Everest.

What's up with the mega mountain's growth spurt? It happened when Nepal and China, which both share the mountain, agreed to measure the snowcap on top, a point under debate until recently. Their new official measurement is 29,031.69 feet (8,848.86 m).

During the project, **NEPALI SURVEYORS SUMMITED EVEREST AT 3 A.M.** to avoid crowds to get a reading from the top.

The **DOME OF SNOW** atop Mount Everest is about the **SIZE OF A DINING ROOM TABLE,** with room for six people to stand.

EVEREST may rise as much as **A QUARTER OF AN INCH** (0.6 CM) **EACH YEAR** due to Earth's geological activity.

AFRICA

In 1979, 2016, 2018, and 2021, snow fell on parts of the Sahara.

Leopards are able to hear five times as many sounds as humans can hear.

A leopard in South Africa

The massive continent of Africa, where humankind began millions of years ago, is second only to Asia in size. Stretching nearly as far from west to east as it does from north to south, Africa is home to both the longest river in the world (the Nile) and the largest hot desert on Earth (the Sahara).

Luanda, Angola

NANO-CHAMELEON

Talk about a little lizard! What may be the world's smallest chameleon was recently discovered in the mountains of Madagascar. Male nano-chameleons are less than an inch long (25 mm), tiny enough to fit on the fingertip of an adult human.

COOL CANYON

Local legend says that Namibia's Fish River Canyon—the largest canyon in Africa—was carved by a giant serpent when it burrowed deep into the ground while hiding from hunters.

Great Pyramid, Great Numbers
How do the numbers for Earth's biggest pyramid stack up?

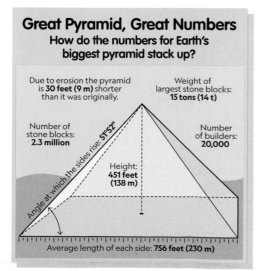

Due to erosion the pyramid is **30 feet (9 m)** shorter than it was originally.

Weight of largest stone blocks: **15 tons (14 t)**

Number of stone blocks: **2.3 million**

Number of builders: **20,000**

Angle at which the sides rise: **51°52'**

Height: **451 feet (138 m)**

Average length of each side: **756 feet (230 m)**

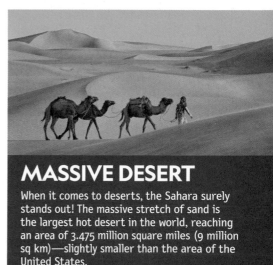

MASSIVE DESERT

When it comes to deserts, the Sahara surely stands out! The massive stretch of sand is the largest hot desert in the world, reaching an area of 3.475 million square miles (9 million sq km)—slightly smaller than the area of the United States.

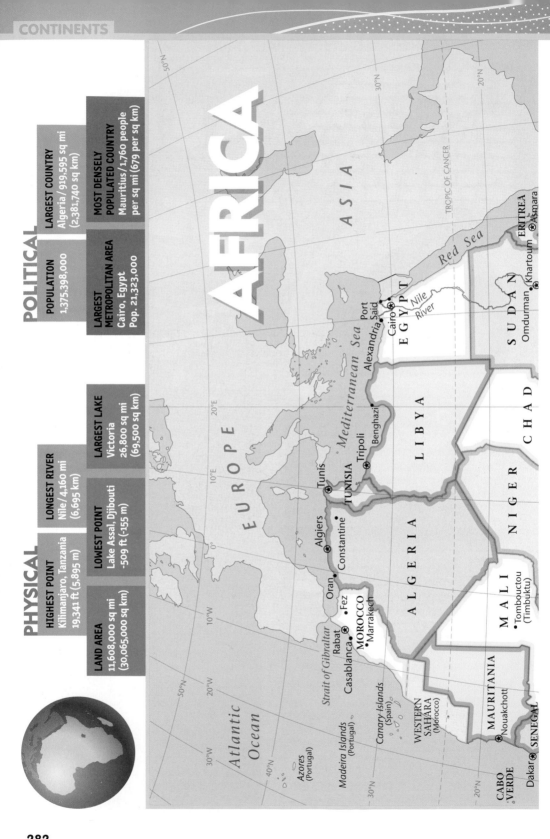

AFRICA

PHYSICAL

HIGHEST POINT	LOWEST POINT	LONGEST RIVER	LARGEST LAKE
Kilimanjaro, Tanzania 19,341 ft (5,895 m)	Lake Assal, Djibouti -509 ft (-155 m)	Nile / 4,160 mi (6,695 km)	Victoria 26,800 sq mi (69,500 sq km)

LAND AREA
11,608,000 sq mi (30,065,000 sq km)

POLITICAL

POPULATION	LARGEST COUNTRY
1,375,398,000	Algeria / 919,595 sq mi (2,381,740 sq km)

LARGEST METROPOLITAN AREA	MOST DENSELY POPULATED COUNTRY
Cairo, Egypt Pop. 21,323,000	Mauritius / 1,760 people per sq mi (679 per sq km)

EUROPE

ASIA

Atlantic Ocean

Mediterranean Sea

Red Sea

Strait of Gibraltar

Azores (Portugal)

Madeira Islands (Portugal)

Canary Islands (Spain)

TROPIC OF CANCER

Oran
Fez
Rabat
Casablanca
MOROCCO
Marrakech

Algiers
Constantine

Tunis
TUNISIA

Tripoli
Benghazi

Alexandria
Port Said
Cairo
EGYPT

Nile River

WESTERN SAHARA (Morocco)

ALGERIA

LIBYA

SUDAN

Omdurman (Khartoum)

ERITREA
Asmara

MAURITANIA
Nouakchott

MALI
Tombouctou (Timbuktu)

NIGER

CHAD

CABO VERDE

SENEGAL
Dakar

SOMALIA
Mogadishu

Gulf of Aden

SOMALILAND Djibouti
DJIBOUTI
Lake Assal
(-155 m) -509 ft▼

ETHIOPIA
Addis Ababa

SOUTH SUDAN

Juba

UGANDA
Kampala
Lake Victoria

KENYA
Nairobi
Mombasa

Kilimanjaro
19,340 ft▲
(5,895 m)
Dar es Salaam

RWANDA
Kigali

BURUNDI
Gitega
Bujumbura

TANZANIA
Dodoma

MALAWI
Lilongwe

COMOROS
Moroni

SEYCHELLES
Victoria ✳

MAURITIUS ✳
Port Louis ◌
Réunion
(France)

MADAGASCAR
Antananarivo

DARFUR

CENTRAL AFRICAN REPUBLIC
Bangui

DEMOCRATIC REPUBLIC OF THE CONGO
Kisangani
Kinshasa
Kananga
Mbuji-Mayi
Lubumbashi
Kolwezi

CONGO
Brazzaville

GABON
Libreville

CAMEROON
Yaoundé
Douala
Malabo

EQUATORIAL GUINEA

SAO TOME & PRINCIPE
São Tomé

NIGERIA
Kano
Abuja
Ogbomosho
Lagos

N'Djamena

BENIN
Porto-Novo
Cotonou

TOGO
Lomé

GHANA
Accra
Yamoussoukro

CÔTE D'IVOIRE (IVORY COAST)
Abidjan

BURKINA FASO
Ouagadougou
Niamey

THE GAMBIA
Banjul
GUINEA-BISSAU
Bissau
Bamako

GUINEA
Conakry

SIERRA LEONE
Freetown

LIBERIA
Monrovia

ANGOLA
Luanda
Cabinda (Angola)
Pointe-Noire

ZAMBIA
Lusaka
Kitwe

ZIMBABWE
Harare

MOZAMBIQUE
Maputo
Mozambique Channel

ESWATINI (SWAZILAND)
Lobamba
Mbabane

LESOTHO
Maseru

BOTSWANA
Gaborone

NAMIBIA
Windhoek

SOUTH AFRICA
Pretoria (Tshwane)
Johannesburg
Bloemfontein
Durban
Port Elizabeth
Cape Town

Indian Ocean

Atlantic Ocean

St. Helena (U.K.)

Ascension (U.K.)

TROPIC OF CAPRICORN

EQUATOR

Map Key
✳ National capital
• Other city
▲ Highest point (above sea level)
▼ Lowest point (below sea level)

800 Miles
800 Kilometers

Azimuthal Equal-Area Projection

10°N   0°   10°S   30°S   60°E

ANTARCTICA

Chinstrap penguin

No dogs are allowed in Antarctica.

Some penguins can spend up to 75 percent of their lives in the water.

This frozen continent may be a cool place to visit, but unless you're a penguin, you probably wouldn't want to hang out in Antarctica for long. The fact that it's the coldest, windiest, and driest continent helps explain why humans never colonized this ice-covered land surrounding the South Pole.

Weddell seal

GOING THE DISTANCE

Each year, a few dozen runners from around the world compete in the Antarctic Ice Marathon, during which participants face an average temperature with windchill of minus 4°F (-20°C).

WARMER THAN EVER

With Antarctica experiencing record-breaking high temperatures, the continent as a whole is getting warmer. Temperatures reached a record high of nearly 70°F (21°C) in February 2020, making the area one of the fastest warming regions on Earth.

Annual Average Snowfall

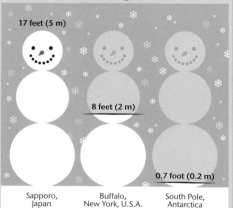

17 feet (5 m)

8 feet (2 m)

0.7 foot (0.2 m)

| Sapporo, Japan | Buffalo, New York, U.S.A. | South Pole, Antarctica |

SEEING GREEN

Green snow? Yes, it's in Antarctica! Swaths of the colorful snow can be seen spreading across the continent. Scientists say that the snow gets its odd hue from a type of algae that, because of climate change, is now growing faster than ever.

PHYSICAL

LAND AREA
5,100,000 sq mi
(13,209,000 sq km)

HIGHEST POINT
Vinson Massif
16,067 ft (4,897 m)

LOWEST POINT
Byrd Glacier
-9,416 ft (-2,870 m)

COLDEST PLACE
Ridge A, annual
average temperature
-94°F (-70°C)

**AVERAGE
PRECIPITATION ON
THE POLAR PLATEAU**
Less than 2 in (5 cm)

POLITICAL

POPULATION
There are no
indigenous inhabitants,
but there are both
permanent and
summer-only staffed
research stations.

**NUMBER OF
INDEPENDENT
COUNTRIES** 0

**NUMBER OF
COUNTRIES
CLAIMING LAND** 7

**NUMBER OF
COUNTRIES
OPERATING YEAR-
ROUND RESEARCH
STATIONS** 20

**NUMBER OF YEAR-
ROUND RESEARCH
STATIONS** 40

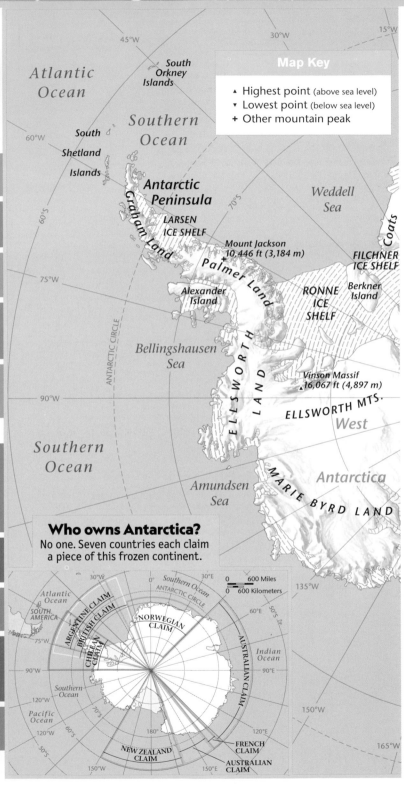

Map Key

▲ Highest point (above sea level)
▼ Lowest point (below sea level)
+ Other mountain peak

Atlantic
Ocean

South
Orkney
Islands

Southern
Ocean

South
Shetland
Islands

Antarctic
Peninsula

Weddell
Sea

Graham Land

LARSEN
ICE SHELF

Mount Jackson
10,446 ft (3,184 m)

Palmer Land

FILCHNER
ICE SHELF

Coats

Alexander
Island

RONNE
ICE
SHELF

Berkner
Island

ANTARCTIC CIRCLE

Bellingshausen
Sea

E L L S W O R T H   L A N D

Vinson Massif
▲16,067 ft (4,897 m)

ELLSWORTH MTS.

West

Southern
Ocean

Amundsen
Sea

M A R I E   B Y R D   L A N D

Antarctica

Who owns Antarctica?
No one. Seven countries each claim
a piece of this frozen continent.

Atlantic
Ocean

SOUTH
AMERICA

ARGENTINE CLAIM

BRITISH CLAIM

CHILEAN
CLAIM

NORWEGIAN
CLAIM

Southern Ocean
ANTARCTIC CIRCLE

AUSTRALIAN CLAIM

Indian
Ocean

Southern
Ocean

Pacific
Ocean

NEW ZEALAND
CLAIM

FRENCH
CLAIM

AUSTRALIAN
CLAIM

0   600 Miles
0   600 Kilometers

ANTARCTICA

FIMBUL
ICE SHELF

Southern
Ocean

RIISER-LARSEN
ICE SHELF

60°E

Land

ENDERBY
LAND

Q U E E N   M A U D   L A N D

Valkyrie
Dome

MacKenzie Bay

75°E

Lambert
Glacier

AMERY ICE SHELF

AMERICAN

T
R
A
N
S
A
N
T
A
R
C
T
I
C

HIGHLAND

WEST
ICE SHELF

Ridge A

POLAR PLATEAU

East

90°E

South Pole

SHACKLETON
ICE SHELF

M
O
U
N
T
A
I
N
S

Antarctica

105°E

80°S

ROSS
ICE
SHELF

Byrd Glacier
-9,416 ft (-2,870 m)

W
I
L
K
E
S

L
A
N
D

Roosevelt
Island

Taylor
Glacier

Ross Island

70°S

Mount Erebus
12,448 ft
(3,794 m)

V
I
C
T
O
R
I
A

L
A
N
D

Southern
Ocean

120°E

Ross
Sea

Talos
Dome

60°S

180°

0   600 Miles

150°E

135°E

0   600 Kilometers

Indian
Ocean

Azimuthal Equidistant Projection

ASIA

A whirling dervish performs in Istanbul, Turkey.

You can cross from Asia to Europe on an underwater railway in Turkey.

In Japan you can buy octopus-flavored ice cream.

Made up of 46 countries, Asia is the world's largest continent. Just how big is it? From western Turkey to the eastern tip of Russia, Asia spans nearly half the globe! Home to more than four billion citizens—that's three out of five people on the planet—Asia's population is bigger than that of all the other continents combined.

Women bicycling in Jakarta, Indonesia

CITY SCENTS

The name Hong Kong translates to "fragrant harbor" in Cantonese, the main language of the bustling city. Researchers think the name comes from Hong Kong's past as a trading post for oil and incense.

TREES, PLEASE

Plans are underway for one million trees to be planted throughout Singapore by 2030. The hope? To improve air quality and add more parks, so that everyone in the city will one day be within a 10-minute walk to a green space.

SAVING THE SNOW LEOPARDS

Countries with political tensions in Central and South Asia have found something to agree upon. "Peace parks"—protected stretches of the snow leopard's native habitat—will soon appear in border areas shared by countries that have a history of disputes.

World's Deepest Lakes

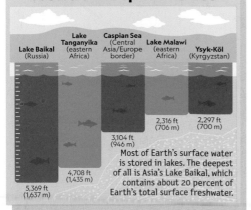

Lake Baikal (Russia)	Lake Tanganyika (eastern Africa)	Caspian Sea (Central Asia/Europe border)	Lake Malawi (eastern Africa)	Ysyk-Köl (Kyrgyzstan)
5,369 ft (1,637 m)	4,708 ft (1,435 m)	3,104 ft (946 m)	2,316 ft (706 m)	2,297 ft (700 m)

Most of Earth's surface water is stored in lakes. The deepest of all is Asia's Lake Baikal, which contains about 20 percent of Earth's total surface freshwater.

PHYSICAL

LAND AREA
17,208,000 sq mi
(44,570,000 sq km)

HIGHEST POINT
Mount Everest,
China–Nepal
29,032 ft (8,849 m)

LOWEST POINT
Dead Sea,
Israel–Jordan
-1,424 ft (-434 m)

LONGEST RIVER
Yangtze, China
3,880 mi (6,244 km)

**LARGEST LAKE
ENTIRELY IN ASIA**
Lake Baikal, Russia
12,200 sq mi
(31,500 sq km)

POLITICAL

POPULATION
4,582,970,000

**LARGEST
METROPOLITAN AREA**
Tokyo, Japan
Pop. 37,340,000

**LARGEST COUNTRY
ENTIRELY IN ASIA**
China
3,705,405 sq mi
(9,596,960 sq km)

**MOST DENSELY
POPULATED COUNTRY**
Singapore
21,101 people
per sq mi
(8,159 per sq km)

A commonly accepted division between Asia and Europe—marked here by a maroon dashed line—is formed by the Ural Mountains, Ural River, Caspian Sea, Caucasus Mountains, and the Black Sea with its outlets, the Bosporus and Dardanelles.

EUROPE

Line of Russian control

Dardanelles Bosporus

Mediterranean Sea

İzmir

TURKEY
Ankara

ARMENIA
Yerevan
GEORGIA
Tbilisi

Nizhniy Tagil
Tyumen'
Yekaterinburg
Magnitogorsk Chelyabinsk
Omsk

Nur-Sultan
(Astana)

TURKMENISTAN
Qaraghandy

KAZAKHSTAN

LEBANON
Beirut
Jerusalem
Amman
Damascus
SYRIA
EGYPT
ISRAEL
JORDAN
Dead Sea
-1,424 ft
(-434 m)
Baghdad
IRAQ
Basra
AZERBAIJAN
Baku

Bishkek
UZBEKISTAN
Ashgabat Tashkent
Almaty
Tehran
Samarqand
Mashhad Dushanbe
KYRGYZSTAN
TAJIKISTAN

Medina KUWAIT
Jeddah SAUDI ARABIA
Mecca
Riyadh
BAHRAIN
QATAR
Kuwait City
Manama
Doha
Dubai
Abu Dhabi
Muscat
IRAN
AFGHANISTAN
Kabul
Hotan
Islamabad
Rawalpindi
Faisalabad Lahore
PAKISTAN
Delhi
New Delhi NEPAL
Jaipur
Kanpur

Sanaa
YEMEN
Aden
OMAN
UNITED ARAB
EMIRATES
Karachi
Indore Bhopal
Surat
Mumbai INDIA
Pune
Hyderabad

AFRICA

Arabian
Sea

Bengaluru
Chennai

EQUATOR

SRI
Colombo LANKA
Sri Jayewardenepura Kotte
Male
MALDIVES

0   800 Miles
0   800 Kilometers
Two-point Equidistant Projection

Indian Ocean

ASIA

★ North Pole

Arctic Ocean

ARCTIC CIRCLE

60°N

Map Key

⊗ National capital
◉ Other capital
• Other city
▲ Highest point
(above sea level)
▼ Lowest point
(below sea level)

180°

170°E

160°E

150°E

S S I A

Magadan•

Sea of Okhotsk

40°N

•Tomsk
•Novosibirsk

Lake Baikal
Irkutsk• •Ulan-Ude

Khabarovsk•

•Sapporo

30°N

Qiqihar•

Harbin•

Vladivostok•

Sendai•

•Changchun
•Jilin
Fushun
Shenyang•

NORTH KOREA

JAPAN

Kyōto• •Tokyo

ULAANBAATAR ⊗

M O N G O L I A

Anshan•

Pyongyang ⊗

•Nagoya
•Ōsaka

•Ürümqi

Shijiazhuang•

Beijing ⊗

Dalian•

⊗Seoul

SOUTH KOREA

•Hiroshima
•Fukuoka

20°N

Taiyuan•

Qingdao•

Zhengzhou•
Xuzhou•

East China Sea

TROPIC OF CANCER

Lanzhou•
Luoyang•
Nanjing•

C H I N A

•Xi'an

Yangtze River

Shanghai•

Mount Everest
29,032 ft
(8,849 m)

Chengdu•

Nanchang•

BHUTAN
Chongqing•

Fuzhou•

150°E

•Lhasa

Guiyang•

Changsha•

•Taipei

TAIWAN

⊗Kathmandu ⊗Thimphu
BANGLADESH

Kunming•

Shantou•
Guangzhou•

Kaohsiung•

10°N

•Dhaka ⊗Chattogram
Kolkāta•

MYANMAR
(BURMA)

Nanning•

Macau• Hong Kong•

The People's Republic of China claims Taiwan as its 23rd province. Taiwan's government (Republic of China) maintains that there are two political entities.

Hanoi◉

LAOS

Naypyi
Taw

Haiphong•

South China Sea

Quezon City•

Pacific Ocean

⊗Vientiane

THAILAND

VIETNAM

Da Nang•

Manila ⊗

PHILIPPINES

Bangkok ⊗ CAMBODIA

Phnom ◉
Penh

•Ho Chi Minh City
(Saigon)

•Cagayan de Oro

EQUATOR 0°

Banda Aceh•

Bandar Seri
Begawan ⊗

BRUNEI

Manado•

•Jayapura

Medan•

M A L A Y S I A

Balikpapan•

⊗Kuala Lumpur

⊗SINGAPORE

I N D O N E S I A

10°S

Jambi•
Palembang•

Bandung

Semarang•

•Dili
TIMOR-LESTE

Jakarta ⊗

Surabaya•

AUSTRALIA

90°E   100°E   110°E   120°E   130°E

AUSTRALIA,
NEW ZEALAND, AND OCEANIA

It is considered rude to wear a hat in villages in Fiji.

Koalas eat so much eucalyptus, they often smell like it.

A koala munches on a eucalyptus leaf in Australia.

G'day, mate! This vast region, covering almost 3.3 million square miles (8.5 million sq km), includes Australia—the world's smallest and flattest continent—and New Zealand, as well as a fleet of mostly tiny islands scattered across the Pacific Ocean. Also known as "down under," most of the countries in this region are in the Southern Hemisphere, below the Equator.

Maori children of New Zealand in ceremonial clothing

WANGARRUS BOUNCE BACK

Good news for the wangarru: After a deluge of rain in Australia's outback, the species—also known as the yellow-footed rock wallaby—saw some growth in its dwindling numbers. It's a promising sign for the wild wangarru population, which had been shrinking due to drought.

ROCK ON

Western Australia's Mount Augustus—also called Burringurrah by the local Aboriginal people—is the world's largest rock. Actually made up of several different types of rocks, the reddish brown formation stands out against its barren desert surroundings, rising 2,346 feet (715 m) above the plain and stretching for five miles (8 km).

RAD RUINS

On a tiny island in the middle of the Pacific Ocean, you'll find Nan Madol, the only ancient city ever built atop a coral reef. What's left today—stone walls and columns—are the ruins of a once thriving civilization known as the Saudeleur, a dynasty that ruled the island of Pohnpei.

More Animals Than People

Figures in millions

	Sheep	Cattle	People
Australia	72	26	23.5
New Zealand	27	10	4.5

■ Australia ■ New Zealand

PHYSICAL

LAND AREA
3,297,000 sq mi
(8,538,000 sq km)

HIGHEST POINT*
Mount Wilhelm,
Papua New Guinea
14,793 ft (4,509 m)
*Includes Oceania

LOWEST POINT
Lake Eyre, Australia
-49 ft (-15 m)

LONGEST RIVER
Murray,
Australia
1,558 mi (2,508 km)

LARGEST LAKE
Lake Eyre, Australia
3,741 sq mi
(9,690 sq km)

POLITICAL

POPULATION
41,668,000

**LARGEST
METROPOLITAN AREA**
Melbourne, Australia
Pop. 5,061,000

LARGEST COUNTRY
Australia
2,988,902 sq mi
(7,741,220 sq km)

**MOST DENSELY
POPULATED COUNTRY**
Nauru
1,221 people per sq mi
(465 per sq km)

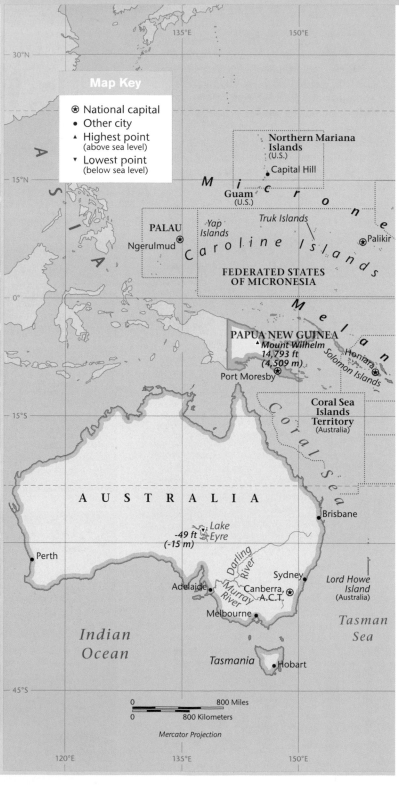

Map Key

⊛ National capital
● Other city
▲ Highest point
(above sea level)
▼ Lowest point
(below sea level)

Northern Mariana
Islands
(U.S.)
● Capital Hill

Guam
(U.S.)

A S I A

M i c r o n e
s i a

PALAU
Ngerulmud ⊛

Yap
Islands

Truk Islands

● Palikir

C a r o l i n e   I s l a n d s

FEDERATED STATES
OF MICRONESIA

M e l a
n e
s i a

PAPUA NEW GUINEA
▲ Mount Wilhelm
14,793 ft
(4,509 m)
Port Moresby

● Honiara
Solomon Islands

Coral Sea
Islands
Territory
(Australia)

C o r a l   S e a

AUSTRALIA

● Brisbane

● Perth

▼ Lake
-49 ft Eyre
(-15 m)

Darling
River

Murray
River

● Sydney
Canberra ⊛
A.C.T.

Adelaide ●

Lord Howe
Island
(Australia)

● Melbourne

Tasman
Sea

Indian
Ocean

Tasmania
● Hobart

0   800 Miles
0   800 Kilometers

Mercator Projection

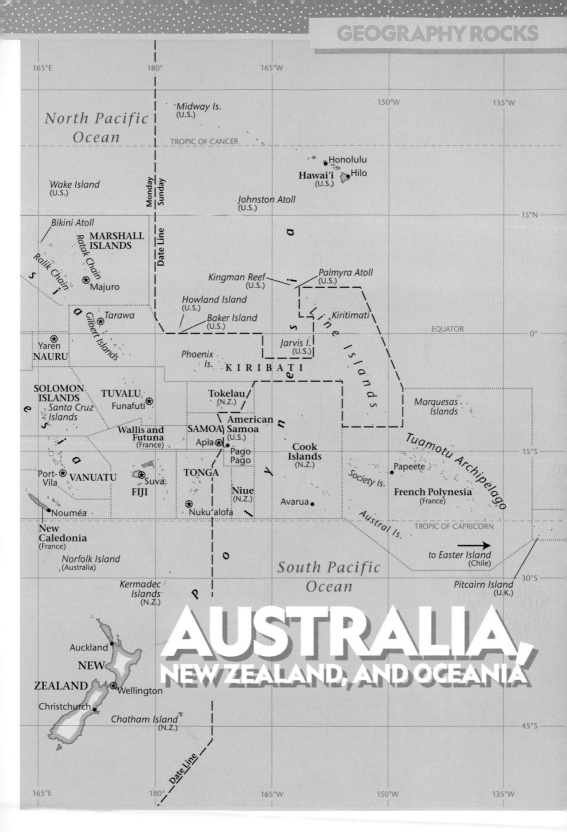

165°E   180°   165°W   150°W   135°W

North Pacific Ocean

Midway Is.
(U.S.)

TROPIC OF CANCER

Wake Island
(U.S.)

Monday / Sunday

a

● Honolulu
Hawai'i ●Hilo
(U.S.)

15°N

Bikini Atoll

MARSHALL ISLANDS

Ratak Chain

Ralik Chain

Date Line

Johnston Atoll
(U.S.)

s

⊛ Majuro

Gilbert Islands

● Tarawa

Kingman Reef
(U.S.)

Howland Island
(U.S.)

Baker Island
(U.S.)

Palmyra Atoll
(U.S.)

i

Kiritimati

Line Islands

EQUATOR   0°

⊛ Yaren
NAURU

Phoenix Is.

K I R I B A T I

Jarvis I.
(U.S.)

e

Marquesas Islands

SOLOMON ISLANDS
Santa Cruz Islands

TUVALU
Funafuti ⊛

Tokelau /
(N.Z.)

American
SAMOA **Samoa**
(U.S.)

Apia ⊛
● Pago Pago

n

s

l

Wallis and Futuna
(France)

Cook Islands
(N.Z.)

● Papeete

Tuamotu Archipelago

15°S

a

Port- ⊛ **VANUATU**
Vila

● Suva
FIJI

TONGA

Niue
(N.Z.)

● Avarua

Society Is.

French Polynesia
(France)

● Nouméa

⊛ Nuku'alofa

y

Austral Is.

TROPIC OF CAPRICORN

New Caledonia
(France)

Norfolk Island
(Australia)

o

South Pacific Ocean

to Easter Island
(Chile)

Pitcairn Island
(U.K.)

30°S

Kermadec Islands
(N.Z.)

P

Auckland ●

NEW

ZEALAND ⊛Wellington

Christchurch ●

Chatham Island
(N.Z.)

AUSTRALIA,
NEW ZEALAND, AND OCEANIA

Date Line

165°E   180°   165°W   150°W   135°W

45°S

EUROPE

A dachshund parade is held each September in Kraków, Poland.

There are no snakes in Ireland—except for those kept as pets.

Wawel Castle overlooks the Vistula River in Kraków, Poland.

A cluster of peninsulas and islands jutting west from Asia, Europe is bordered by the Atlantic and Arctic Oceans and more than a dozen seas. Here you'll find a variety of scenery, from mountains to countryside to coastlines. Europe is also known for its rich culture and fascinating history, which make it one of the most visited continents on Earth.

Traditional dance performed in Greece

BUG OFF

One place you'll never have to worry about mosquito bites? Iceland! The country is totally mosquito free, likely because of its unique weather patterns that disrupt the life cycle from egg to pesky bug.

COOL COMEBACK

Bring back the bison! The European bison's numbers are increasing across the continent, thanks to recent conservation efforts. At one point, the animals' population was about 50, but now it is up to around 7,000 in the wild and in captivity.

CHOCOLATE, CHOCOLATE EVERYWHERE

Attention chocolate lovers! Switzerland is now home to a museum all about the sweet stuff. The Lindt Home of Chocolate offers a deep dive into the rich history of chocolate and features what may be the world's tallest chocolate fountain at a soaring three stories high.

Europe's Longest Rivers

Volga	2,290 mi (3,685 km)
Danube	1,770 mi (2,848 km)
Dnieper	1,420 mi (2,285 km)
Rhine	765 mi (1,230 km)
Elbe	724 mi (1,165 km)

PHYSICAL

LAND AREA
3,841,000 sq mi
(9,947,000 sq km)

HIGHEST POINT
El'brus, Russia
18,510 ft (5,642 m)

LOWEST POINT
Caspian Sea
-92 ft (-28 m)

LONGEST RIVER
Volga, Russia
2,294 mi
(3,692 km)

**LARGEST LAKE
ENTIRELY IN EUROPE**
Ladoga, Russia
6,900 sq mi
(17,872 sq km)

POLITICAL

POPULATION
746,318,000

**LARGEST
METROPOLITAN AREA**
Moscow, Russia
Pop. 12,593,000

**LARGEST COUNTRY
ENTIRELY IN EUROPE**
France
248,573 sq mi
(643,801 sq km)

**MOST DENSELY
POPULATED COUNTRY**
Monaco
31,223 people per sq
mi (15,612 per sq km)

Map Key

⊛ National capital
⊛ Capital of Northern Ireland, Scotland, or Wales
◉ Other capital
• Other city
▫ Small country
▲ Highest point (above sea level)
▼ Lowest point (below sea level)

0   400 Miles
0   400 Kilometers
Azimuthal Equidistant Projection

10°E 20°E 30°E 40°E 50°E 60°E

Barents Sea

A commonly accepted division between Asia and Europe—marked here by a maroon dashed line—is formed by the Ural Mountains, Ural River, Caspian Sea, Caucasus Mountains, and the Black Sea with its outlets, the Bosporus and Dardanelles.

Asia
Europe

60°N

Murmansk

Arkhangel'sk

R U S S I A

EUROPE

Lake Ladoga

St. Petersburg

Volga River Kazan' •Ufa

Yaroslavl'
Tver' Nizhniy Novgorod

⊗ Moscow Samara Orenburg

Ryazan' •Penza

Smolensk 50°N

Bryansk Saratov•

Kursk K A Z A K H S T A N

Volgograd•

Astrakhan'

SWEDEN
NORWAY
FINLAND
Helsinki ⊗
Tallinn ⊗
⊗Stockholm ESTONIA
Baltic Sea
Rīga •
LATVIA
LITHUANIA
Vitsyebsk•
Russia Vilnius ⊗
Gdańsk• Kaunas⊗
⊗Minsk
POLAND BELARUS
⊗Warsaw Homyel'•
Bydgoszcz
•Łódź
•Wrocław •Kraków
CZECHIA
(CZECH REP.) •L'viv U K R A I N E
Vienna Poltava• Donets'k
⊗ SLOVAKIA Vinnytsya •Dnipro
⊗Bratislava MOLDOVA
⊗Budapest ⊗Chisinau
HUNGARY Line of Russian control
⊗Zagreb ROMANIA
CROATIA
BOSNIA & Belgrade Bucharest
HERZEGOVINA ⊗
Sarajevo ⊗SERBIA Varna
MONTENEGRO KOSOVO
Podgorica ⊗Prishtinë ⊗BULGARIA
Tirana ⊗Skopje Sofia
ALBANIA N. MAC.
Thessaloniki•
Dardanelles
GREECE
⊗Athens

Kyiv ⊗ Kharkiv

Rostov na Donu

Boundary claimed by Ukraine

El'brus Groznyy•
(5,642 m) 18,510 ft ▲

Odessa
Simferopol' CRIMEA
Sevastopol'

B l a c k   S e a

Sochi GEORGIA

Bosporus

Istanbul

T U R K E Y

Caspian Sea

-92 ft ▼
(-28 m)

Baku ⊗
AZERBAIJAN
40°N

CRIMEA
Russia invaded Crimea in 2014 and, after secession from Ukraine was approved in a disputed and boycotted referendum held in Crimea, the Russian parliament voted to annex Crimea into the Russian Federation. The United Nations General Assembly subsequently adopted a nonbinding resolution declaring the annexation invalid and affirming Ukraine's territorial jurisdiction. Russia administers and controls the peninsula, while Ukraine continues to maintain that Crimea is its sovereign territory.

Sea

Crete NORTHERN CYPRUS
Nicosia ⊗
CYPRUS

20°E 30°E 40°E

NORTH AMERICA

Flamingos are the national bird of the Bahamas.

Canada has more doughnut shops per person than any other country.

American flamingos

From the Great Plains of the United States and Canada to the rainforests of Panama, North America stretches 5,500 miles (8,850 km) from north to south. The third largest continent, North America can be divided into five regions: the mountainous west (including parts of Mexico and Central America's western coast), the Great Plains, the Canadian Shield, the varied eastern region (including Central America's lowlands and coastal plains), and the Caribbean.

A Day of the Dead (Día de los Muertos) parade in Mexico City, Mexico

BIG BONES

Canada was once a hotbed of activity for dinosaurs. In fact, the skeleton of the largest *Tyrannosaurus rex* found to date was recently uncovered by researchers at a site in Saskatchewan, Canada. Estimated to weigh more than an elephant, the giant dino—nicknamed "Scotty"—stomped around some 68 million years ago.

BRING BACK THE BEES

Efforts to boost honeybee numbers in the United States appear to be working. A recent study showed an increase in colonies across the country, which is good news for the buzzing pollinators, which have been threatened by climate change, habitat loss, and the use of harmful pesticides.

BLOW ON

For the first time in history, wind recently surpassed hydroelectricity as the top source of renewable energy in the United States. Currently, more than 60,000 wind turbines in the country can power at least 32 million homes across more than 40 states.

World's Longest Coastlines

Country	Coastline
Canada	151,023 miles (243,048 km)
Indonesia	33,998 miles (54,716 km)
Russia	23,397 miles (37,653 km)
Philippines	22,549 miles (36,289 km)
Japan	18,486 miles (29,751 km)

PHYSICAL

LAND AREA
9,449,000 sq mi
(24,474,000 sq km)

LONGEST RIVER
Mississippi–Missouri,
United States
3,710 mi (5,971 km)

HIGHEST POINT
Denali, Alaska, U.S.A.
20,310 ft (6,190 m)

LOWEST POINT
Death Valley,
California, U.S.A.
-282 ft (-86 m)

LARGEST LAKE
Lake Superior, U.S.–
Canada / 31,700 sq mi
(82,100 sq km)

POLITICAL

POPULATION
594,228,000

LARGEST COUNTRY
Canada
3,855,101 sq mi
(9,984,670 sq km)

LARGEST METROPOLITAN AREA
Mexico City, Mexico
Pop. 21,919,000

MOST DENSELY POPULATED COUNTRY
Barbados / 1,818 people
per sq mi (702 per sq km)

Map Key
⊛ National capital
• Other city
▲ Highest point
(above sea level)
▼ Lowest point
(below sea level)

EUROPE

ARCTIC CIRCLE

Greenland
(Kalaallit Nunaat)
(Denmark)

Arctic Ocean

80°N

ASIA

60°N

180°

160°W

Alaska
(U.S.)

(Mount McKinley) Denali ▲
(6,190 m) 20,310 ft

• Anchorage

C A N A D A

• Edmonton
• Calgary

Winnipeg •

Thunder
Bay •

Montréal •

Seattle •
Vancouver •
Victoria •

40°N

0°
20°W
40°W
40°N

800 Miles
0
800 Kilometers
0

Azimuthal Equidistant Projection

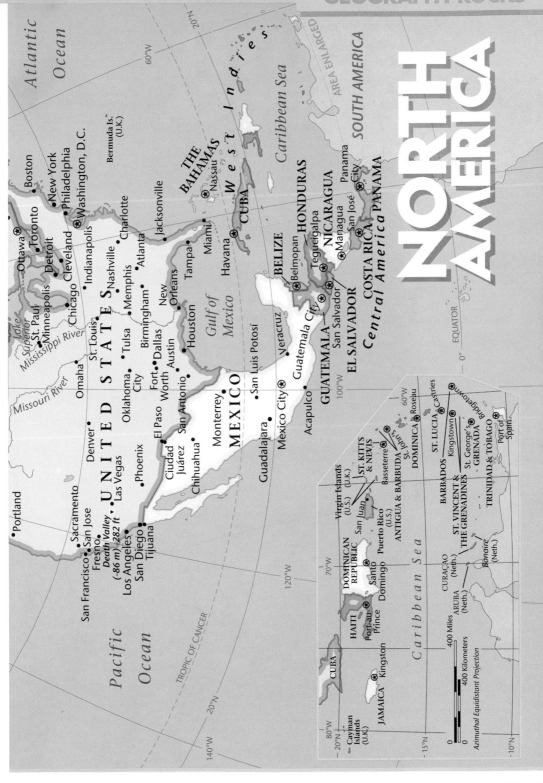

NORTH AMERICA

AREA ENLARGED

SOUTH AMERICA

Atlantic Ocean

Bermuda Is. (U.K.)

THE BAHAMAS
Nassau

West Indies

CUBA
Havana

Caribbean Sea

Boston
New York
Philadelphia
Washington, D.C.

Ottawa
Toronto
Detroit
Cleveland
Indianapolis
Charlotte
Jacksonville

Chicago
Nashville
Memphis
Atlanta

St. Paul
Minneapolis
Milwaukee

Tampa
Miami

Lake Superior

Mississippi River

Missouri River

Omaha
St. Louis
Tulsa
Birmingham
New Orleans
Houston

UNITED STATES

Oklahoma City
Dallas
Fort Worth
Austin
San Antonio

Denver
Las Vegas
Phoenix

Sacramento
San Jose
Fresno
Death Valley -282 ft (-86 m)
Los Angeles
San Diego
Tijuana

Portland
San Francisco

El Paso
Ciudad Juárez
Chihuahua

Pacific Ocean

Monterrey
Guadalajara

MEXICO

San Luis Potosí
Mexico City
Veracruz
Acapulco

Gulf of Mexico

BELIZE
Belmopan
GUATEMALA
Guatemala City
San Salvador
EL SALVADOR

HONDURAS
Tegucigalpa
NICARAGUA
Managua
San José
COSTA RICA
PANAMA
Panama City

Central America

EQUATOR

0°

TROPIC OF CANCER

20°N
20°N
20°N
15°N
10°N

0°
60°W
60°W
70°W
80°W
100°W
120°W
140°W

[Caribbean inset]

Caribbean Sea

CUBA

JAMAICA
Kingston

Cayman Islands (U.K.)

HAITI
Port-au-Prince
DOMINICAN REPUBLIC
Santo Domingo
Puerto Rico (U.S.)
San Juan

Virgin Islands (U.S.)
ST. KITTS & NEVIS
Basseterre
ANTIGUA & BARBUDA
St. John's

Roseau
DOMINICA
Castries
ST. LUCIA
BARBADOS
Bridgetown

St. Vincent
ST. VINCENT & THE GRENADINES
Kingstown
St. George's
GRENADA

CURAÇAO (Neth.)
ARUBA (Neth.)
Bonaire (Neth.)

TRINIDAD & TOBAGO
Port of Spain

400 Miles
400 Kilometers
0
Azimuthal Equidistant Projection

303

SOUTH AMERICA

Cuy, or guinea pig, is a traditional dish in Peru.

Argentina's name comes from *argentum*—the Latin word for "silver."

A woman sells fruit in Chivay, Peru.

South America is bordered by three major bodies of water—the Caribbean Sea, Atlantic Ocean, and Pacific Ocean. The world's fourth largest continent extends over a range of climates, from tropical in the north to subarctic in the south. South America produces a rich diversity of natural resources, including nuts, fruits, sugar, grains, coffee, and chocolate.

Santiago Cathedral in Santiago, Chile

CHECKMATE

Chess has a long history in Montevideo, Uruguay. The game has been part of the cultural heritage for decades, and the capital city even hosted the World Youth Chess Championship in 2017. Today, you can usually spot people playing in parks or on the sidewalks of Montevideo.

RUNNING WILD

Guanacos, wild relatives of camels that look like small llamas with longer necks, are native to the grasslands of the Andes. Super-speedy animals that can run as fast as 35 miles an hour (56 km/h), guanacos are a protected species in Chile and Peru.

Vast Watershed

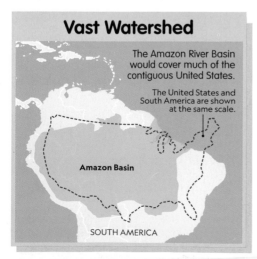

The Amazon River Basin would cover much of the contiguous United States.

The United States and South America are shown at the same scale.

Amazon Basin

SOUTH AMERICA

ANCIENT BRIDGE

Deep in the Peruvian Andes, a suspension bridge made of handwoven grass stretches more than 100 feet (30 m) over a rushing river. Once used to connect two villages on either side of the river, the bridge, which dates back more than 500 years, is now more of a symbolic nod to the past. Each June, the suspension bridge is rebuilt and replaced by the local Indigenous community.

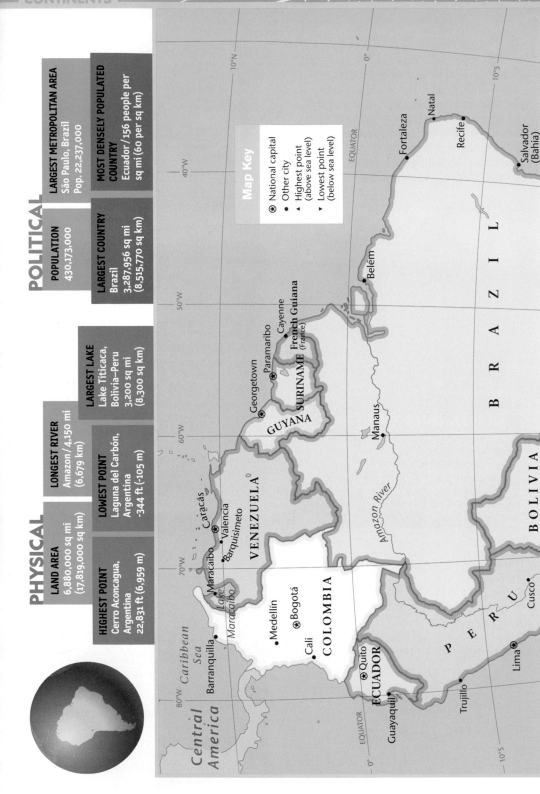

PHYSICAL

LAND AREA
6,880,000 sq mi
(17,819,000 sq km)

HIGHEST POINT
Cerro Aconcagua,
Argentina
22,831 ft (6,959 m)

LONGEST RIVER
Amazon / 4,150 mi
(6,679 km)

LOWEST POINT
Laguna del Carbón,
Argentina
-344 ft (-105 m)

LARGEST LAKE
Lake Titicaca,
Bolivia–Peru
3,200 sq mi
(8,300 sq km)

POLITICAL

POPULATION
430,173,000

LARGEST COUNTRY
Brazil
3,287,956 sq mi
(8,515,770 sq km)

LARGEST METROPOLITAN AREA
São Paulo, Brazil
Pop. 22,237,000

MOST DENSELY POPULATED COUNTRY
Ecuador / 156 people per
sq mi (60 per sq km)

Map Key

⊛ National capital
● Other city
▲ Highest point
  (above sea level)
▶ Lowest point
  (below sea level)

Central
America

Caribbean
Sea

Barranquilla
Maracaibo
Lake
Maracaibo

Caracás
Valencia
Barquisimeto

VENEZUELA

Medellín
●Bogotá

Cali

COLOMBIA

⊛Quito
ECUADOR
Guayaquil

Trujillo

Lima⊛

Cusco

P E R U

B O L I V I A

Georgetown
Paramaribo
Cayenne
French Guiana
(France)

GUYANA
SURINAME

Manaus

Amazon River

B R A Z I L

Belém

Fortaleza
Natal
Recife
Salvador
(Bahia)

EQUATOR

10°N
40°W
50°W
60°W
70°W
80°W
0°
10°S

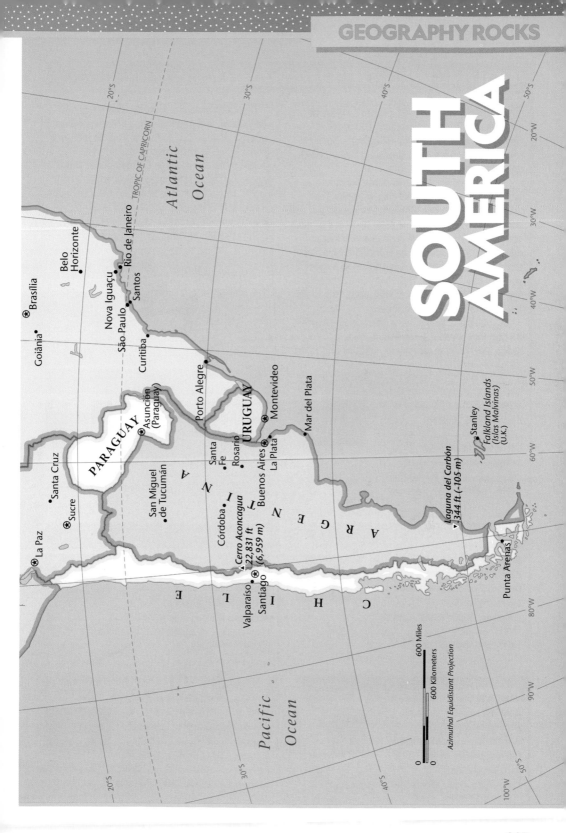

SOUTH AMERICA

Atlantic Ocean

Pacific Ocean

TROPIC OF CAPRICORN

Brasília

Goiânia

Belo Horizonte

Rio de Janeiro

Nova Iguaçu

São Paulo

Santos

Curitiba

Porto Alegre

Sucre

Santa Cruz

La Paz

PARAGUAY

Asunción (Paraguay)

San Miguel de Tucumán

Córdoba

Cerro Aconcagua 22,831 ft (6,959 m)

Valparaíso

Santiago

C H I L E

A R G E N T I N A

Santa Fe

Rosario

Buenos Aires

La Plata

URUGUAY

Montevideo

Mar del Plata

Laguna del Carbón 344 ft (-105 m)

Stanley

Falkland Islands (Islas Malvinas) (U.K.)

Punta Arenas

600 Miles

600 Kilometers

Azimuthal Equidistant Projection

20°S

30°S

40°S

50°S

50°W

40°W

30°W

20°W

20°S

30°S

40°S

60°W

50°W

80°W

90°W

100°W

COUNTRIES OF THE WORLD

The following pages present a general overview of all 195 independent countries recognized by the National Geographic Society, including the newest nation, South Sudan, which gained independence in 2011.

The flags of each independent country symbolize diverse cultures and histories. The statistical data cover highlights of geography and demography and provide a brief overview of each country. They present general characteristics and are not intended to be comprehensive. For example, not every language spoken in a specific country can be listed. Thus, languages shown are the most representative of that area. This is also true of the religions mentioned.

A country is defined as a political body with its own independent government, geographical space, and, in most cases, laws, military, and taxes.

Disputed areas such as Northern Cyprus and Taiwan, and dependencies of independent nations, such as Bermuda and Puerto Rico, are not included in this listing.

Note the color key at the bottom of the pages and the locator map below, which assign a color to each country based on the continent on which it is located. Some capital city populations include that city's metro area. All information is accurate as of press time.

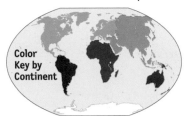

Color Key by Continent

Afghanistan

Area: 251,827 sq mi (652,230 sq km)
Population: 37,466,000
Capital: Kabul, pop. 4,336,000
Currency: afghani (AFN)
Religion: Muslim
Languages: Afghan Persian (Dari), Pashto, Uzbek, English

Andorra

Area: 181 sq mi (468 sq km)
Population: 86,000
Capital: Andorra la Vella, pop. 23,000
Currency: euro (EUR)
Religion: Roman Catholic
Languages: Catalan, French, Castilian, Portuguese

Albania

Area: 11,100 sq mi (28,748 sq km)
Population: 3,088,000
Capital: Tirana, pop. 503,000
Currency: lek (ALL)
Religions: Muslim, Roman Catholic, Eastern Orthodox
Language: Albanian

Angola

Area: 481,353 sq mi (1,246,700 sq km)
Population: 33,643,000
Capital: Luanda, pop. 8,632,000
Currency: kwanza (AOA)
Religions: Roman Catholic, Protestant
Languages: Portuguese, Umbundu, other African languages

Algeria

Area: 919,595 sq mi (2,381,740 sq km)
Population: 43,577,000
Capital: Algiers, pop. 2,809,000
Currency: Algerian dinar (DZD)
Religion: Muslim
Languages: Arabic, French, Berber (Tamazight)

Antigua and Barbuda

Area: 171 sq mi (443 sq km)
Population: 99,000
Capital: St. John's, pop. 21,000
Currency: East Caribbean dollar (XCD)
Religions: Protestant, Roman Catholic, other Christian
Languages: English, Antiguan creole

Argentina

Area: 1,073,518 sq mi
(2,780,400 sq km)
Population: 45,865,000
Capital: Buenos Aires,
pop. 15,258,000
Currency: Argentine peso (ARS)
Religion: Roman Catholic
Languages: Spanish, Italian, English, German, French

Austria

Area: 32,383 sq mi (83,871 sq km)
Population: 8,885,000
Capital: Vienna, pop. 1,945,000
Currency: euro (EUR)
Religions: Roman Catholic, Eastern Orthodox, Muslim
Languages: German, Croatian

Armenia

Area: 11,484 sq mi
(29,743 sq km)
Population: 3,012,000
Capital: Yerevan,
pop. 1,089,000
Currency: dram (AMD)
Religion: Oriental Orthodox
Languages: Armenian, Russian

Azerbaijan

Area: 33,436 sq mi
(86,600 sq km)
Population: 10,282,000
Capital: Baku, pop. 2,371,000
Currency: Azerbaijani manat (AZN)
Religion: Muslim
Languages: Azerbaijani (Azeri), Russian

Australia

Area: 2,988,902 sq mi
(7,741,220 sq km)
Population: 25,810,000
Capital: Canberra, A.C.T.,
pop. 462,000
Currency: Australian dollar (AUD)
Religions: Protestant, Roman Catholic
Language: English

Bahamas, The

Area: 5,359 sq mi
(13,880 sq km)
Population: 353,000
Capital: Nassau, pop. 280,000
Currency: Bahamian dollar (BSD)
Religions: Protestant, Roman Catholic, other Christian
Languages: English, Creole

3 cool things about AUSTRALIA

1. Australia is the only continent without an active volcano.

2. Australia was called New Holland by early Dutch settlers. It got its current name, which means "southern" in Latin, in 1803.

3. The main island of Australia is surrounded by some 8,000 smaller and secluded islands—all of which are part of the continent.

Bahrain

Area: 293 sq mi (760 sq km)
Population: 1,527,000
Capital: Manama, pop. 664,000
Currency: Bahraini dinar (BHD)
Religions: Muslim, Christian
Languages: Arabic, English, Farsi, Urdu

Bangladesh

Area: 57,321 sq mi
(148,460 sq km)
Population: 164,099,000
Capital: Dhaka, pop. 21,741,000
Currency: taka (BDT)
Religions: Muslim, Hindu
Language: Bangla (Bengali)

Barbados

Area: 166 sq mi (430 sq km)
Population: 302,000
Capital: Bridgetown, pop. 89,000
Currency: Barbadian dollar (BBD)
Religions: Protestant, other Christian
Languages: English, Bajan

Belgium

Area: 11,787 sq mi (30,528 sq km)
Population: 11,779,000
Capital: Brussels, pop. 2,096,000
Currency: euro (EUR)
Religions: Roman Catholic, Muslim
Languages: Dutch, French, German

Belarus

Area: 80,155 sq mi (207,600 sq km)
Population: 9,442,000
Capital: Minsk, pop. 2,039,000
Currency: Belarusian ruble (BYN)
Religions: Eastern Orthodox, Roman Catholic
Languages: Russian, Belarusian

Belize

Area: 8,867 sq mi (22,966 sq km)
Population: 406,000
Capital: Belmopan, pop. 23,000
Currency: Belizean dollar (BZD)
Religions: Roman Catholic, Protestant
Languages: English, Spanish, Creole, Maya

SNAPSHOT
Botswana

A male African elephant faces the camera in Botswana, home to more elephants than any other country in the world.

COLOR KEY ● Africa ● Australia, New Zealand, and Oceania

Benin

Area: 43,484 sq mi (112,622 sq km)
Population: 13,302,000
Capitals: Porto-Novo, pop. 285,000; Cotonou, pop. 699,000
Currency: CFA franc BCEAO (XOF)
Religions: Muslim, Roman Catholic, Protestant, Vodoun, other Christian
Languages: French, Fon, Yoruba, tribal languages

Bhutan

Area: 14,824 sq mi (38,394 sq km)
Population: 857,000
Capital: Thimphu, pop. 203,000
Currency: ngultrum (BTN)
Religions: Buddhist, Hindu
Languages: Sharchhopka, Dzongkha, Lhotshamkha

Bolivia

Area: 424,164 sq mi (1,098,581 sq km)
Population: 11,759,000
Capitals: La Paz, pop. 1,882,000; Sucre, pop. 278,000
Currency: boliviano (BOB)
Religions: Roman Catholic, Protestant
Languages: Spanish, Quechua, Aymara, Guarani

Bosnia and Herzegovina

Area: 19,767 sq mi (51,197 sq km)
Population: 3,825,000
Capital: Sarajevo, pop. 344,000
Currency: convertible mark (BAM)
Religions: Muslim, Eastern Orthodox, Roman Catholic
Languages: Bosnian, Serbian, Croatian

Botswana

Area: 224,607 sq mi (581,730 sq km)
Population: 2,351,000
Capital: Gaborone, pop. 269,000
Currency: pula (BWP)
Religion: Christian
Languages: Setswana, Sekalanga, Shekgalagadi, English

Brazil

Area: 3,287,956 sq mi (8,515,770 sq km)
Population: 213,445,000
Capital: Brasília, pop. 4,728,000
Currency: real (BRL)
Religions: Roman Catholic, Protestant
Language: Portuguese

Brunei

Area: 2,226 sq mi (5,765 sq km)
Population: 471,000
Capital: Bandar Seri Begawan, pop. 241,000
Currency: Bruneian dollar (BND)
Religions: Muslim, Christian, Buddhist, Indigenous beliefs
Languages: Malay, English, Chinese

Bulgaria

Area: 42,811 sq mi (110,879 sq km)
Population: 6,919,000
Capital: Sofia, pop. 1,284,000
Currency: lev (BGN)
Religions: Eastern Orthodox, Muslim
Language: Bulgarian

Burkina Faso

Area: 105,869 sq mi (274,200 sq km)
Population: 21,383,000
Capital: Ouagadougou, pop. 2,915,000
Currency: CFA franc BCEAO (XOF)
Religions: Muslim, Roman Catholic, traditional or animist, Protestant
Languages: French, African languages

Burundi

Area: 10,745 sq mi (27,830 sq km)
Population: 12,241,000
Capitals: Bujumbura, pop. 1,075,000; Gitega, pop. 135,000
Currency: Burundi franc (BIF)
Religions: Roman Catholic, Protestant
Languages: Kirundi, French, English, Swahili

Cabo Verde

Area: 1,557 sq mi (4,033 sq km)
Population: 589,000
Capital: Praia, pop. 168,000
Currency: Cabo Verdean escudo (CVE)
Religions: Roman Catholic, Protestant
Languages: Portuguese, Krioulo

Cambodia

Area: 69,898 sq mi (181,035 sq km)
Population: 17,304,000
Capital: Phnom Penh, pop. 2,144,000
Currency: riel (KHR)
Religion: Buddhist
Language: Khmer

Cameroon

Area: 183,568 sq mi (475,440 sq km)
Population: 28,524,000
Capital: Yaoundé, pop. 4,164,000
Currency: CFA franc BEAC (XAF)
Religions: Roman Catholic, Protestant, other Christian, Muslim
Languages: African languages, English, French

Canada

Area: 3,855,101 sq mi (9,984,670 sq km)
Population: 37,943,000
Capital: Ottawa, pop. 1,408,000
Currency: Canadian dollar (CAD)
Religions: Roman Catholic, Protestant, other Christian
Languages: English, French

Central African Republic

Area: 240,535 sq mi (622,984 sq km)
Population: 5,358,000
Capital: Bangui, pop. 910,000
Currency: CFA franc BEAC (XAF)
Religions: Christian, Muslim
Languages: French, Sangho, tribal languages

Chad

Area: 495,755 sq mi (1,284,000 sq km)
Population: 17,414,000
Capital: N'Djamena, pop. 1,476,000
Currency: CFA franc BEAC (XAF)
Religions: Muslim, Protestant, Roman Catholic
Languages: French, Arabic, Sara, Indigenous languages

Chile

Area: 291,932 sq mi (756,102 sq km)
Population: 18,308,000
Capital: Santiago, pop. 6,812,000
Currency: Chilean peso (CLP)
Religions: Roman Catholic, Protestant
Languages: Spanish, English

China

Area: 3,705,405 sq mi (9,596,960 sq km)
Population: 1,397,898,000
Capital: Beijing, pop. 20,897,000
Currency: Renminbi yuan (RMB)
Religions: folk religion, Buddhist, Christian
Languages: Standard Chinese (Mandarin), Yue (Cantonese), Wu, Minbei, Minnan, Xiang, Gan, regional official languages

Colombia

Area: 439,735 sq mi (1,138,910 sq km)
Population: 50,356,000
Capital: Bogotá, pop. 11,167,000
Currency: Colombian peso (COP)
Religions: Roman Catholic, Protestant
Language: Spanish

Comoros

Area: 863 sq mi (2,235 sq km)
Population: 864,000
Capital: Moroni, pop. 62,000
Currency: Comoran franc (KMF)
Religion: Muslim
Languages: Arabic, French, Shikomoro (Comorian)

Congo

Area: 132,047 sq mi (342,000 sq km)
Population: 5,417,000
Capital: Brazzaville,
pop. 2,470,000
Currency: CFA franc BEAC (XAF)
Religions: Roman Catholic, other Christian, Protestant
Languages: French, Lingala, Monokutuba, Kikongo, local languages

Côte d'Ivoire (Ivory Coast)

Area: 124,504 sq mi
(322,463 sq km)
Population: 28,088,000
Capitals: Abidjan, pop. 5,355,000;
Yamoussoukro, pop. 231,000
Currency: CFA franc BCEAO (XOF)
Religions: Muslim, Roman Catholic, Protestant
Languages: French, Diola, native dialects

Costa Rica

Area: 19,730 sq mi
(51,100 sq km)
Population: 5,151,000
Capital: San José, pop. 1,421,000
Currency: Costa Rican colón (CRC)
Religions: Roman Catholic, Protestant
Languages: Spanish, English

Croatia

Area: 21,851 sq mi
(56,594 sq km)
Population: 4,209,000
Capital: Zagreb, pop. 685,000
Currency: kuna (HRK)
Religion: Roman Catholic
Languages: Croatian, Serbian

SNAPSHOT
Chile

A visitor gazes at the massive "Mano del Desierto" ("Hand of the Desert") sculpture in Antofagasta, Chile.

● Asia ● Europe ● North America ● **South America**

Cuba

Area: 42,803 sq mi (110,860 sq km)
Population: 11,032,000
Capital: Havana, pop. 2,143,000
Currency: Cuban peso (CUP)
Religions: Christian, folk religion
Language: Spanish

Democratic Republic of the Congo

Area: 905,354 sq mi (2,344,858 sq km)
Population: 105,045,000
Capital: Kinshasa, pop. 14,970,000
Currency: Congolese franc (CDF)
Religions: Roman Catholic, Protestant, other Christian
Languages: French, Lingala, Kingwana, Kikongo, Tshiluba

Cyprus

Area: 3,572 sq mi (9,251 sq km)
Population: 1,282,000
Capital: Nicosia, pop. 269,000
Currency: euro (EUR)
Religion: Eastern Orthodox
Languages: Greek, Turkish, English

Denmark

Area: 16,639 sq mi (43,094 sq km)
Population: 5,895,000
Capital: Copenhagen, pop. 1,359,000
Currency: Danish krone (DKK)
Religions: Protestant, Muslim
Languages: Danish, Faroese, Greenlandic, English

Czechia (Czech Republic)

Area: 30,451 sq mi (78,867 sq km)
Population: 10,703,000
Capital: Prague, pop. 1,312,000
Currency: koruna (CZK)
Religion: Roman Catholic
Languages: Czech, Slovak

Djibouti

Area: 8,958 sq mi (23,200 sq km)
Population: 938,000
Capital: Djibouti, pop. 584,000
Currency: Djiboutian franc (DJF)
Religions: Muslim, Christian
Languages: French, Arabic, Somali, Afar

3 cool things about CZECHIA

1. Built in the ninth century, Prague Castle is the world's largest ancient castle and the official residence of Czechia's president.

2. Foraging for mushrooms in the forest is a popular pastime in Czechia.

3. Czech author Karel Čapek is credited for first using the word "robot" in his 1920 play *R.U.R.* about humanlike machines.

Dominica

Area: 290 sq mi (751 sq km)
Population: 75,000
Capital: Roseau, pop. 15,000
Currency: East Caribbean dollar (XCD)
Religions: Roman Catholic, Protestant
Languages: English, French patois

Dominican Republic

Area: 18,792 sq mi (48,670 sq km)
Population: 10,597,000
Capital: Santo Domingo, pop. 3,389,000
Currency: Dominican peso (DOP)
Religions: Roman Catholic, Protestant
Language: Spanish

Ecuador

Area: 109,483 sq mi (283,561 sq km)
Population: 17,093,000
Capital: Quito, pop. 1,901,000
Currency: U.S. dollar (USD)
Religions: Roman Catholic, Protestant
Languages: Spanish, Amerindian languages

The PEAK of Ecuador's MOUNT CHIMBORAZO is CLOSER TO THE SUN than ANYWHERE ELSE on Earth.

Egypt

Area: 386,662 sq mi (1,001,450 sq km)
Population: 106,437,000
Capital: Cairo, pop. 21,323,000
Currency: Egyptian pound (EGP)
Religions: Muslim, Oriental Orthodox
Languages: Arabic, English, French

El Salvador

Area: 8,124 sq mi (21,041 sq km)
Population: 6,528,000
Capital: San Salvador, pop. 1,107,000
Currency: U.S. dollar (USD)
Religions: Roman Catholic, Protestant
Language: Spanish

Equatorial Guinea

Area: 10,831 sq mi (28,051 sq km)
Population: 857,000
Capital: Malabo, pop. 297,000
Currency: CFA franc BEAC (XAF)
Religions: Roman Catholic, Muslim, Baha'i, animist, Indigenous beliefs
Languages: Spanish, Portuguese, French, Fang, Bubi

Eritrea

Area: 45,406 sq mi (117,600 sq km)
Population: 6,147,000
Capital: Asmara, pop. 998,000
Currency: nakfa (ERN)
Religions: Muslim, Oriental Orthodox, Roman Catholic, Protestant
Languages: Tigrinya, Arabic, English, Tigre, Kunama, Afar, other Cushitic languages

Estonia

Area: 17,463 sq mi (45,228 sq km)
Population: 1,220,000
Capital: Tallinn, pop. 449,000
Currency: euro (EUR)
Religions: Eastern Orthodox, Protestant
Languages: Estonian, Russian

Eswatini (Swaziland)

Area: 6,704 sq mi (17,364 sq km)
Population: 1,113,000
Capitals: Mbabane, pop. 68,000; Lobamba, pop. 11,000
Currency: lilangeni (SZL)
Religions: Roman Catholic, other Christian
Languages: English, siSwati

Ethiopia

Area: 426,372 sq mi (1,104,300 sq km)
Population: 110,871,000
Capital: Addis Ababa, pop. 5,006,000
Currency: birr (ETB)
Religions: Oriental Orthodox, Muslim, Protestant
Languages: Oromo, Amharic, Somali, Tigrinya, Afar

Fiji

Area: 7,056 sq mi (18,274 sq km)
Population: 940,000
Capital: Suva, pop. 178,000
Currency: Fijian dollar (FJD)
Religions: Protestant, Roman Catholic, other Christian, Hindu, Muslim
Languages: English, Fijian, Hindustani

Finland

Area: 130,558 sq mi (338,145 sq km)
Population: 5,587,000
Capital: Helsinki, pop. 1,317,000
Currency: euro (EUR)
Religion: Protestant
Languages: Finnish, Swedish

Germany

Area: 137,847 sq mi (357,022 sq km)
Population: 79,903,000
Capital: Berlin, pop. 3,567,000
Currency: euro (EUR)
Religions: Roman Catholic, Protestant, Muslim
Language: German

France

Area: 248,573 sq mi (643,801 sq km)
Population: 68,084,000
Capital: Paris, pop. 11,079,000
Currency: euro (EUR)
Religions: Roman Catholic, Muslim
Language: French

Ghana

Area: 92,098 sq mi (238,533 sq km)
Population: 32,373,000
Capital: Accra, pop. 2,557,000
Currency: cedi (GHC)
Religions: Protestant, Roman Catholic, other Christian, Muslim, traditional
Languages: Assanta, Ewe, Fante, English

Gabon

Area: 103,347 sq mi (267,667 sq km)
Population: 2,285,000
Capital: Libreville, pop. 845,000
Currency: CFA franc BEAC (XAF)
Religions: Roman Catholic, Protestant, other Christian, Muslim
Languages: French, Fang, Myene, Nzebi, Bapounou/Eschira, Bandjabi

Greece

Area: 50,949 sq mi (131,957 sq km)
Population: 10,570,000
Capital: Athens, pop. 3,153,000
Currency: euro (EUR)
Religion: Eastern Orthodox
Language: Greek

Gambia, The

Area: 4,363 sq mi (11,300 sq km)
Population: 2,221,000
Capital: Banjul, pop. 459,000
Currency: dalasi (GMD)
Religion: Muslim
Languages: English, Mandinka, Wolof, Fula

Grenada

Area: 133 sq mi (344 sq km)
Population: 114,000
Capital: St. George's, pop. 39,000
Currency: East Caribbean dollar (XCD)
Religions: Protestant, Roman Catholic
Languages: English, French patois

Georgia

Area: 26,911 sq mi (69,700 sq km)
Population: 4,934,000
Capital: Tbilisi, pop. 1,079,000
Currency: lari (GEL)
Religions: Eastern Orthodox, Muslim
Language: Georgian

Guatemala

Area: 42,042 sq mi (108,889 sq km)
Population: 17,423,000
Capital: Guatemala City, pop. 2,983,000
Currency: quetzal (GTQ)
Religions: Roman Catholic, Protestant, Indigenous beliefs
Languages: Spanish, Maya languages

COLOR KEY ● Africa ● Australia, New Zealand, and Oceania

Guinea

Area: 94,926 sq mi (245,857 sq km)
Population: 12,878,000
Capital: Conakry, pop. 1,991,000
Currency: Guinean franc (GNF)
Religions: Muslim, Christian
Languages: French, African languages

Guyana

Area: 83,000 sq mi (214,969 sq km)
Population: 788,000
Capital: Georgetown, pop. 110,000
Currency: Guyanese dollar (GYD)
Religions: Hindu, Protestant, Roman Catholic, other Christian, Muslim
Languages: English, Guyanese Creole, Amerindian languages, Indian languages, Chinese

Guinea-Bissau

Area: 13,948 sq mi (36,125 sq km)
Population: 1,976,000
Capital: Bissau, pop. 621,000
Currency: CFA franc BCEAO (XOF)
Religions: Muslim, Christian, animist
Languages: Crioulu, Portuguese, Pular, Mandingo

Haiti

Area: 10,714 sq mi (27,750 sq km)
Population: 11,198,000
Capital: Port-au-Prince, pop. 2,844,000
Currency: gourde (HTG)
Religions: Roman Catholic, Protestant, voodoo
Languages: French, Creole

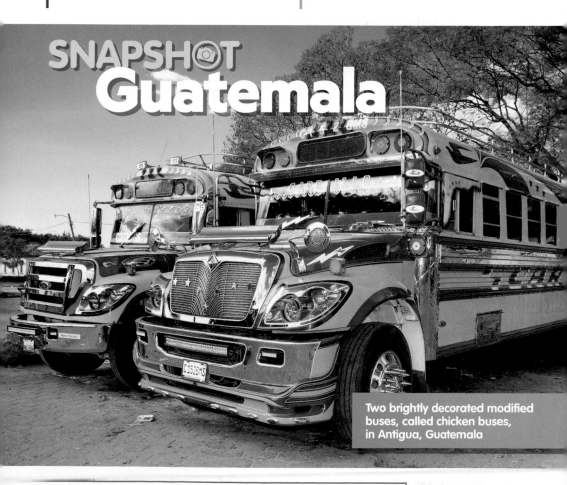

SNAPSHOT
Guatemala

Two brightly decorated modified buses, called chicken buses, in Antigua, Guatemala

Honduras

Area: 43,278 sq mi
(112,090 sq km)
Population: 9,346,000
Capital: Tegucigalpa,
pop. 1,485,000
Currency: lempira (HNL)
Religions: Roman Catholic, Protestant
Languages: Spanish, Amerindian dialects

Iceland

Area: 39,769 sq mi
(103,000 sq km)
Population: 354,000
Capital: Reykjavík, pop. 216,000
Currency: Icelandic krona (ISK)
Religion: Protestant
Languages: Icelandic, English, Nordic
languages, German

Hungary

Area: 35,918 sq mi (93,028 sq km)
Population: 9,728,000
Capital: Budapest, pop. 1,772,000
Currency: forint (HUF)
Religions: Roman Catholic, Protestant
Languages: Hungarian, English, German

India

Area: 1,269,219 sq mi (3,287,263 sq km)
Population: 1,339,331,000
Capital: New Delhi, pop. 31,181,000
Currency: Indian rupee (INR)
Religions: Hindu, Muslim
Languages: Hindi, English

SNAPSHOT
India

Doused in colorful powder and water,
friends celebrate Holi, an annual
festival in India commemorating spring.

COLOR KEY ● Africa ● Australia, New Zealand, and Oceania

Indonesia

Area: 735,358 sq mi (1,904,569 sq km)
Population: 275,122,000
Capital: Jakarta, pop. 10,915,000
Currency: Indonesian rupiah (IDR)
Religions: Muslim, Protestant
Languages: Bahasa Indonesia, English, Dutch, local dialects

Iran

Area: 636,371 sq mi (1,648,195 sq km)
Population: 85,889,000
Capital: Tehran, pop. 9,259,000
Currency: Iranian rial (IRR)
Religion: Muslim
Languages: Persian (Farsi), Turkic dialects, Kurdish

Iraq

Area: 169,235 sq mi (438,317 sq km)
Population: 39,650,000
Capital: Baghdad, pop. 7,323,000
Currency: Iraqi dinar (IQD)
Religion: Muslim
Languages: Arabic, Kurdish, Turkmen, Syriac, Armenian

Ireland (Éire)

Area: 27,133 sq mi (70,273 sq km)
Population: 5,225,000
Capital: Dublin (Baile Átha Cliath), pop. 1,242,000
Currency: euro (EUR)
Religion: Roman Catholic
Languages: English, Irish (Gaelic)

Israel

Area: 8,970 sq mi (23,232 sq km)
Population: 8,787,000
Capital: Jerusalem, pop. 944,000
Currency: new Israeli shekel (ILS)
Religions: Jewish, Muslim
Languages: Hebrew, Arabic, English

Italy

Area: 116,348 sq mi (301,340 sq km)
Population: 62,390,000
Capital: Rome, pop. 4,278,000
Currency: euro (EUR)
Religion: Roman Catholic
Languages: Italian, German, French, Slovene

Jamaica

Area: 4,244 sq mi (10,991 sq km)
Population: 2,817,000
Capital: Kingston, pop. 592,000
Currency: Jamaican dollar (JMD)
Religion: Protestant
Languages: English, English patois

Japan

Area: 145,914 sq mi (377,915 sq km)
Population: 124,687,000
Capital: Tokyo, pop. 37,340,000
Currency: yen (JPY)
Religions: Shinto, Buddhist
Language: Japanese

Jordan

Area: 34,495 sq mi (89,342 sq km)
Population: 10,910,000
Capital: Amman, pop. 2,182,000
Currency: Jordanian dinar (JOD)
Religion: Muslim
Languages: Arabic, English

Kazakhstan

Area: 1,052,089 sq mi (2,724,900 sq km)
Population: 19,246,000
Capital: Nur-Sultan (Astana), pop. 1,212,000
Currency: tenge (KZT)
Religions: Muslim, Eastern Orthodox
Languages: Kazakh (Qazaq), Russian, English

Kenya

Area: 224,081 sq mi (580,367 sq km)
Population: 54,685,000
Capital: Nairobi, pop. 4,922,000
Currency: Kenyan shilling (KES)
Religions: Protestant, Roman Catholic, other Christian, Muslim
Languages: English, Kiswahili, Indigenous languages

Laos

Area: 91,429 sq mi (236,800 sq km)
Population: 7,574,000
Capital: Vientiane, pop. 694,000
Currency: kip (LAK)
Religion: Buddhist
Languages: Lao, French, English, ethnic languages

Kiribati

Area: 313 sq mi (811 sq km)
Population: 113,000
Capital: Tarawa, pop. 64,000
Currency: Australian dollar (AUD)
Religions: Roman Catholic, Protestant, Mormon
Languages: I-Kiribati, English

Latvia

Area: 24,938 sq mi (64,589 sq km)
Population: 1,863,000
Capital: Riga, pop. 628,000
Currency: euro (EUR)
Religions: Protestant, Roman Catholic, Eastern Orthodox, Druze
Languages: Latvian, Russian

Kosovo

Area: 4,203 sq mi (10,887 sq km)
Population: 1,935,000
Capital: Pristina, pop. 217,000
Currency: euro (EUR)
Religion: Muslim
Languages: Albanian, Serbian, Bosnian

Lebanon

Area: 4,015 sq mi (10,400 sq km)
Population: 5,261,000
Capital: Beirut, pop. 2,435,000
Currency: Lebanese pound (LBP)
Religions: Muslim, Eastern Catholic
Languages: Arabic, French, English, Armenian

Kuwait

Area: 6,880 sq mi (17,818 sq km)
Population: 3,032,000
Capital: Kuwait City, pop. 3,177,000
Currency: Kuwaiti dinar (KWD)
Religions: Muslim, Christian
Languages: Arabic, English

Lesotho

Area: 11,720 sq mi (30,355 sq km)
Population: 2,178,000
Capital: Maseru, pop. 202,000
Currency: loti (LSL)
Religions: Protestant, Roman Catholic, other Christian
Languages: Sesotho, English, Zulu, Xhosa

Kyrgyzstan

Area: 77,201 sq mi (199,951 sq km)
Population: 6,019,000
Capital: Bishkek, pop. 1,060,000
Currency: Som (KGS)
Religions: Muslim, Eastern Orthodox
Languages: Kyrgyz, Uzbek, Russian

Liberia

Area: 43,000 sq mi (111,369 sq km)
Population: 5,214,000
Capital: Monrovia, pop. 1,569,000
Currency: Liberian dollar (LRD)
Religions: Christian, Muslim
Languages: English, Indigenous languages

COLOR KEY ● Africa ● Australia, New Zealand, and Oceania

Libya

Area: 679,362 sq mi
(1,759,540 sq km)
Population: 7,017,000
Capital: Tripoli, pop. 1,170,000
Currency: Libyan dinar (LYD)
Religion: Muslim
Languages: Arabic, Italian, English, Berber

Lithuania

Area: 25,212 sq mi
(65,300 sq km)
Population: 2,712,000
Capital: Vilnius, pop. 540,000
Currency: euro (EUR)
Religion: Roman Catholic
Language: Lithuanian

Liechtenstein

Area: 62 sq mi (160 sq km)
Population: 39,000
Capital: Vaduz, pop. 5,000
Currency: Swiss franc (CHF)
Religions: Roman Catholic, Protestant, Muslim
Language: German

Luxembourg

Area: 998 sq mi (2,586 sq km)
Population: 640,000
Capital: Luxembourg,
pop. 120,000
Currency: euro (EUR)
Religion: Roman Catholic
Languages: Luxembourgish, Portuguese,
French, German

SNAPSHOT
Kosovo

Kosovo's Old Stone Bridge, in the small
town of Prizren, is more than 500 years old.

Madagascar

Area: 226,658 sq mi (587,041 sq km)
Population: 27,534,000
Capital: Antananarivo, pop. 3,532,000
Currency: Malagasy ariary (MGA)
Religions: Christian, Indigenous beliefs, Muslim
Languages: French, Malagasy, English

Malawi

Area: 45,747 sq mi (118,484 sq km)
Population: 20,309,000
Capital: Lilongwe, pop. 1,171,000
Currency: Malawian kwacha (MWK)
Religions: Protestant, Roman Catholic, other Christian, Muslim
Languages: English, Chewa, other Bantu languages

Malaysia

Area: 127,355 sq mi (329,847 sq km)
Population: 33,519,000
Capital: Kuala Lumpur, pop. 8,211,000
Currency: ringgit (MYR)
Religions: Muslim, Buddhist, Christian, Hindu
Languages: Bahasa Malaysia (Malay), English, Chinese, Tamil, Telugu, Malayalam, Panjabi, Thai

Maldives

Area: 115 sq mi (298 sq km)
Population: 391,000
Capital: Male, pop. 177,000
Currency: rufiyaa (MVR)
Religion: Muslim
Languages: Dhivehi, English

Mali

Area: 478,841 sq mi (1,240,192 sq km)
Population: 20,138,000
Capital: Bamako, pop. 2,713,000
Currency: CFA franc BCEAO (XOF)
Religion: Muslim
Languages: French, Bambara, African languages

Malta

Area: 122 sq mi (316 sq km)
Population: 461,000
Capital: Valletta, pop. 213,000
Currency: euro (EUR)
Religion: Roman Catholic
Languages: Maltese, English

You can EXPLORE a 6,000-year-old UNDERGROUND BURIAL CHAMBER in Malta.

Marshall Islands

Area: 70 sq mi (181 sq km)
Population: 79,000
Capital: Majuro, pop. 31,000
Currency: U.S. dollar (USD)
Religions: Protestant, Roman Catholic, Mormon
Languages: Marshallese, English

Mauritania

Area: 397,955 sq mi (1,030,700 sq km)
Population: 4,079,000
Capital: Nouakchott, pop. 1,372,000
Currency: ouguiya (MRU)
Religion: Muslim
Languages: Arabic, Pulaar, Soninke, Wolof, French

Mauritius

Area: 788 sq mi (2,040 sq km)
Population: 1,386,000
Capital: Port Louis, pop. 149,000
Currency: Mauritian rupee (MUR)
Religions: Hindu, Muslim, Roman Catholic, other Christian
Languages: Creole, English

Mexico

Area: 758,449 sq mi
(1,964,375 sq km)
Population: 130,207,000
Capital: Mexico City,
pop. 21,919,000
Currency: Mexican peso (MXN)
Religions: Roman Catholic, Protestant
Language: Spanish

Micronesia, Federated States of

Area: 271 sq mi (702 sq km)
Population: 102,000
Capital: Palikir, pop. 7,000
Currency: U.S. dollar (USD)
Religions: Roman Catholic, Protestant
Languages: English, Chuukese, Kosrean, Pohnpeian,
other Indigenous languages

Moldova

Area: 13,070 sq mi
(33,851 sq km)
Population: 3,324,000
Capital: Chişinău,
pop. 494,000
Currency: Moldovan leu (MDL)
Religion: Eastern Orthodox
Languages: Moldovan, Romanian

Monaco

Area: 1 sq mi (2 sq km)
Population: 31,000
Capital: Monaco, pop. 31,000
Currency: euro (EUR)
Religion: Roman Catholic
Languages: French, English, Italian, Monegasque

Mongolia

Area: 603,908 sq mi
(1,564,116 sq km)
Population: 3,199,000
Capital: Ulaanbaatar,
pop. 1,615,000
Currency: tugrik (MNT)
Religion: Buddhist
Languages: Mongolian, Turkic, Russian

Montenegro

Area: 5,333 sq mi
(13,812 sq km)
Population: 607,000
Capital: Podgorica, pop. 177,000
Currency: euro (EUR)
Religions: Eastern Orthodox, Muslim
Languages: Serbian, Montenegrin

Morocco

Area: 276,662 sq mi
(716,550 sq km)
Population: 36,562,000
Capital: Rabat, pop. 1,907,000
Currency: Moroccan dirham (MAD)
Religion: Muslim
Languages: Arabic, Tamazight, other Berber
languages, French

3 cool things about MOROCCO

1. Morocco is the only African country to border both the Atlantic Ocean and the Mediterranean Sea.

2. Mint tea is the traditional drink of Morocco, served at meals and sipped throughout the day.

3. Morocco is one of just three kingdoms on the continent of Africa. (Eswatini and Lesotho are the others.)

Mozambique

Area: 308,642 sq mi
(799,380 sq km)
Population: 30,888,000
Capital: Maputo, pop. 1,122,000
Currency: metical (MZN)
Religions: Roman Catholic, Protestant, other Christian,
Muslim
Languages: Makhuwa, Portuguese, local languages

● Asia   ● Europe   ● North America   ● South America

Myanmar (Burma)

Area: 261,228 sq mi
(676,578 sq km)

Population: 57,069,000

Capital: Nay Pyi Taw,
pop. 640,000

Currency: kyat (MMK)

Religions: Buddhist, Christian

Language: Burmese

Nauru

Area: 8 sq mi (21 sq km)

Population: 10,000

Capital: Yaren, pop. 1,000

Currency: Australian
dollar (AUD)

Religions: Protestant, Roman Catholic

Languages: Nauruan, English

Namibia

Area: 318,261 sq mi
(824,292 sq km)

Population: 2,678,000

Capital: Windhoek, pop. 446,000

Currency: Namibian dollar (NAD)

Religions: Protestant, Indigenous beliefs

Languages: Indigenous languages, Afrikaans, English

Nepal

Area: 56,827 sq mi
(147,181 sq km)

Population: 30,425,000

Capital: Kathmandu, pop. 1,472,000

Currency: Nepalese rupee (NPR)

Religions: Hindu, Buddhist

Languages: Nepali, Maithali

SNAPSHOT
North Korea

North Koreans participate in a
mass dance in a Pyongyang square.

Netherlands

Area: 16,040 sq mi
(41,543 sq km)
Population: 17,337,000
Capitals: Amsterdam, pop. 1,158,000;
The Hague, pop. 704,000
Currency: euro (EUR)
Religions: Roman Catholic, Protestant, Muslim
Language: Dutch

North Korea

Area: 46,540 sq mi
(120,538 sq km)
Population: 25,831,000
Capital: Pyongyang,
pop. 3,108,000
Currency: North Korean won (KPW)
Religions: Buddhist, Confucianist, Christian,
syncretic Chondogyo
Language: Korean

New Zealand

Area: 103,799 sq mi
(268,838 sq km)
Population: 4,991,000
Capital: Wellington, pop. 417,000
Currency: New Zealand dollar (NZD)
Religions: Roman Catholic, Protestant
Languages: English, Maori

North Macedonia

Area: 9,928 sq mi
(25,713 sq km)
Population: 2,128,000
Capital: Skopje, pop. 601,000
Currency: Macedonian denar (MKD)
Religions: Macedonian Orthodox, Muslim
Languages: Macedonian, Albanian

Nicaragua

Area: 50,336 sq mi
(130,370 sq km)
Population: 6,244,000
Capital: Managua, pop. 1,073,000
Currency: cordoba oro (NIO)
Religions: Roman Catholic, Protestant
Language: Spanish

Norway

Area: 125,021 sq mi
(323,802 sq km)
Population: 5,510,000
Capital: Oslo, pop. 1,056,000
Currency: Norwegian krone (NOK)
Religion: Protestant
Languages: Bokmal Norwegian, Nynorsk Norwegian

Niger

Area: 489,191 sq mi (1,267,000 sq km)
Population: 23,606,000
Capital: Niamey, pop. 1,336,000
Currency: CFA franc BCEAO (XOF)
Religion: Muslim
Languages: French, Hausa, Djerma

Oman

Area: 119,499 sq mi
(309,500 sq km)
Population: 3,695,000
Capital: Muscat, pop. 1,590,000
Currency: Omani rial (OMR)
Religions: Muslim, Christian, Hindu
Languages: Arabic, English, Baluchi, Swahili, Urdu,
Indian dialects

Nigeria

Area: 356,669 sq mi
(923,768 sq km)
Population: 219,464,000
Capital: Abuja, pop. 3,464,000
Currency: naira (NGN)
Religions: Muslim, Roman Catholic, other Christian
Languages: English, Indigenous languages

Pakistan

Area: 307,374 sq mi
(796,095 sq km)
Population: 238,181,000
Capital: Islamabad, pop. 1,164,000
Currency: Pakistan rupee (PKR)
Religion: Muslim
Languages: Punjabi, Sindhi, Saraiki, Urdu, English

Palau

Area: 177 sq mi (459 sq km)
Population: 22,000
Capital: Ngerulmud, pop. 277
Currency: U.S. dollar (USD)
Religions: Roman Catholic, Protestant, Modekngei
Languages: Palauan, English, Filipino

Philippines

Area: 115,831 sq mi (300,000 sq km)
Population: 110,818,000
Capital: Manila, pop. 14,159,000
Currency: Philippine peso (PHP)
Religions: Roman Catholic, Protestant, Muslim
Languages: Filipino (Tagalog), English, Indigenous languages

Panama

Area: 29,120 sq mi (75,420 sq km)
Population: 3,929,000
Capital: Panama City, pop. 1,899,000
Currency: balboa (PAB)
Religions: Roman Catholic, Protestant
Languages: Spanish, Indigenous languages, English

Poland

Area: 120,728 sq mi (312,685 sq km)
Population: 38,186,000
Capital: Warsaw, pop. 1,790,000
Currency: zloty (PLN)
Religion: Roman Catholic
Language: Polish

Papua New Guinea

Area: 178,703 sq mi (462,840 sq km)
Population: 7,400,000
Capital: Port Moresby, pop. 391,000
Currency: kina (PGK)
Religions: Protestant, Roman Catholic, other Christian
Languages: Tok Pisin, English, Hiri Motu, other Indigenous languages

Portugal

Area: 35,556 sq mi (92,090 sq km)
Population: 10,264,000
Capital: Lisbon, pop. 2,972,000
Currency: euro (EUR)
Religion: Roman Catholic
Languages: Portuguese, Mirandese

Paraguay

Area: 157,048 sq mi (406,752 sq km)
Population: 7,273,000
Capital: Asunción (Paraguay), pop. 3,394,000
Currency: Guarani (PYG)
Religions: Roman Catholic, Protestant
Languages: Spanish, Guarani

Qatar

Area: 4,473 sq mi (11,586 sq km)
Population: 2,480,000
Capital: Doha, pop. 646,000
Currency: Qatari rial (QAR)
Religions: Muslim, Christian, Hindu
Languages: Arabic, English

Peru

Area: 496,224 sq mi (1,285,216 sq km)
Population: 32,201,000
Capital: Lima, pop. 10,883,000
Currency: nuevo sol (PEN)
Religions: Roman Catholic, Protestant
Languages: Spanish, Quechua, Aymara

Romania

Area: 92,043 sq mi (238,391 sq km)
Population: 21,230,000
Capital: Bucharest, pop. 1,794,000
Currency: leu (RON)
Religions: Eastern Orthodox, Protestant
Language: Romanian

COLOR KEY ● Africa ● Australia, New Zealand, and Oceania

Russia

Area: 6,601,665 sq mi
(17,098,242 sq km)
Population: 142,321,000
Capital: Moscow, pop. 12,593,000
Currency: Russian ruble (RUB)
Religions: Eastern Orthodox, Muslim
Language: Russian

Note: Russia is in both Europe and Asia, but its capital is in Europe, so it is classified here as a European country.

Rwanda

Area: 10,169 sq mi
(26,338 sq km)
Population: 12,943,000
Capital: Kigali, pop. 1,170,000
Currency: Rwandan franc (RWF)
Religions: Protestant, Roman Catholic
Languages: Kinyarwanda, French, English,
Kiswahili (Swahili)

Samoa

Area: 1,093 sq mi
(2,831 sq km)
Population: 205,000
Capital: Apia, pop. 36,000
Currency: tala (SAT)
Religions: Protestant, Roman Catholic, Mormon
Languages: Samoan (Polynesian), English

San Marino

Area: 24 sq mi (61 sq km)
Population: 34,000
Capital: San Marino, pop. 4,000
Currency: euro (EUR)
Religion: Roman Catholic
Language: Italian

SNAPSHOT
Samoa

A wooden ladder leads down
to the To Sua Ocean Trench
swimming hole in Upolu, Samoa.

Sao Tome and Principe

Area: 372 sq mi (964 sq km)
Population: 214,000
Capital: São Tomé, pop. 80,000
Currency: dobra (STN)
Religion: Roman Catholic
Languages: Portuguese, Forro

Saudi Arabia

Area: 830,000 sq mi (2,149,690 sq km)
Population: 34,784,000
Capital: Riyadh, pop. 7,388,000
Currency: Saudi riyal (SAR)
Religion: Muslim
Language: Arabic

Senegal

Area: 75,955 sq mi (196,722 sq km)
Population: 16,082,000
Capital: Dakar, pop. 3,230,000
Currency: CFA franc BCEAO (XOF)
Religion: Muslim
Languages: French, Wolof, other Indigenous languages

Serbia

Area: 29,913 sq mi (77,474 sq km)
Population: 6,974,000
Capital: Belgrade, pop. 1,402,000
Currency: Serbian dinar (RSD)
Religions: Eastern Orthodox, Roman Catholic
Language: Serbian

Seychelles

Area: 176 sq mi (455 sq km)
Population: 96,000
Capital: Victoria, pop. 28,000
Currency: Seychelles rupee (SCR)
Religions: Roman Catholic, Protestant
Languages: Seychellois Creole, English, French

Sierra Leone

Area: 27,699 sq mi (71,740 sq km)
Population: 6,807,000
Capital: Freetown, pop. 1,236,000
Currency: leone (SLL)
Religions: Muslim, Christian
Languages: English, Mende, Temne, Krio

Singapore

Area: 278 sq mi (719 sq km)
Population: 5,866,000
Capital: Singapore, pop. 5,866,000
Currency: Singapore dollar (SGD)
Religions: Buddhist, Christian, Muslim, Taoist, Hindu
Languages: English, Mandarin, other Chinese dialects, Malay, Tamil

3 cool things about SINGAPORE

1. Singapore's mascot is the merlion, a half-fish, half-lion mythical creature said to represent Singapore's name in Malay—Singapura—which means "Lion City."

2. The country's Changi Airport features a butterfly garden, an indoor waterfall, a movie theater, and Singapore's tallest slide at four stories high.

3. Singapore's Night Safari, the world's first nighttime zoo, welcomes guests to check out animals in the dark.

Slovakia

Area: 18,933 sq mi (49,035 sq km)
Population: 5,436,000
Capital: Bratislava, pop. 437,000
Currency: euro (EUR)
Religions: Roman Catholic, Protestant
Language: Slovak

Slovenia

Area: 7,827 sq mi
(20,273 sq km)
Population: 2,102,000
Capital: Ljubljana,
pop. 286,000
Currency: euro (EUR)
Religion: Roman Catholic
Language: Slovenian

Solomon Islands

Area: 11,157 sq mi
(28,896 sq km)
Population: 691,000
Capital: Honiara, pop. 82,000
Currency: Solomon Islands dollar (SBD)
Religions: Protestant, Roman Catholic
Languages: Melanesian pidgin, English,
Indigenous languages

Somalia

Area: 246,201 sq mi
(637,657 sq km)
Population: 12,095,000
Capital: Mogadishu, pop. 2,388,000
Currency: Somali shilling (SOS)
Religion: Muslim
Languages: Somali, Arabic, Italian, English

South Africa

Area: 470,693 sq mi (1,219,090 sq km)
Population: 56,979,000
Capitals: Pretoria (Tshwane),
pop. 2,655,000; Cape Town, pop.
4,710,000; Bloemfontein, pop. 578,000
Currency: rand (ZAR)
Religions: Christian, traditional or animist
Languages: isiZulu, isiXhosa, other Indigenous languages,
Afrikaans, English

South Korea

Area: 38,502 sq mi
(99,720 sq km)
Population: 51,715,000
Capital: Seoul, pop. 9,968,000
Currency: South Korean won (KRW)
Religions: Protestant, Buddhist, Roman Catholic
Languages: Korean, English

South Sudan

Area: 248,777 sq mi
(644,329 sq km)
Population: 10,984,000
Capital: Juba, pop. 421,000
Currency: South Sudanese pound (SSP)
Religions: animist, Christian, Muslim
Languages: English, Arabic, Dinka, Nuer, Bari,
Zande, Shilluk

Spain

Area: 195,124 sq mi (505,370 sq km)
Population: 47,261,000
Capital: Madrid, pop. 6,669,000
Currency: euro (EUR)
Religion: Roman Catholic
Languages: Castilian Spanish, Catalan,
Galician, Basque

Sri Lanka

Area: 25,332 sq mi
(65,610 sq km)
Population: 23,044,000
Capitals: Colombo, pop. 619,000;
Sri Jayewardenepura Kotte, pop. 103,000
Currency: Sri Lankan rupee (LKR)
Religions: Buddhist, Hindu, Muslim, Roman Catholic
Languages: Sinhala, Tamil, English

St. Kitts and Nevis

Area: 101 sq mi (261 sq km)
Population: 54,000
Capital: Basseterre, pop. 14,000
Currency: East Caribbean
dollar (XCD)
Religions: Protestant, Roman Catholic
Language: English

St. Lucia

Area: 238 sq mi (616 sq km)
Population: 167,000
Capital: Castries,
pop. 22,000
Currency: East Caribbean dollar (XCD)
Religions: Roman Catholic, Protestant
Languages: English, French patois

St. Vincent and the Grenadines

Area: 150 sq mi (389 sq km)
Population: 101,000
Capital: Kingstown, pop. 27,000
Currency: East Caribbean dollar (XCD)
Religions: Protestant, Roman Catholic
Languages: English, Vincentian Creole English, French patois

Switzerland

Area: 15,937 sq mi (41,277 sq km)
Population: 8,454,000
Capital: Bern, pop. 434,000
Currency: Swiss franc (CHF)
Religions: Roman Catholic, Protestant, other Christian, Muslim
Languages: German (Swiss German), French, Italian, Romansch

Sudan

Area: 718,723 sq mi (1,861,484 sq km)
Population: 46,751,000
Capital: Khartoum, pop. 5,989,000
Currency: Sudanese pound (SDG)
Religion: Muslim
Languages: Arabic, English, Nubian, Ta Bedawie, Fur

Syria

Area: 71,870 sq mi (186,142 sq km)
Population: 20,384,000
Capital: Damascus, pop. 2,440,000
Currency: Syrian pound (SYP)
Religions: Muslim, Eastern Orthodox, Oriental Orthodox, Eastern Catholic, other Christian
Languages: Arabic, Kurdish, Armenian, Aramaic, Circassian, French, English

SUDAN is home to MORE PYRAMIDS than EGYPT.

Tajikistan

Area: 55,637 sq mi (144,100 sq km)
Population: 8,991,000
Capital: Dushanbe, pop. 938,000
Currency: Tajikistani somoni (TJS)
Religion: Muslim
Languages: Tajik, Uzbek

Suriname

Area: 63,251 sq mi (163,820 sq km)
Population: 615,000
Capital: Paramaribo, pop. 239,000
Currency: Surinamese dollar (SRD)
Religions: Protestant, Hindu, Roman Catholic, Muslim
Languages: Dutch, English, Sranang Tongo, Caribbean Hindustani, Javanese

Tanzania

Area: 365,754 sq mi (947,300 sq km)
Population: 62,093,000
Capitals: Dar es Salaam, pop. 7,047,000; Dodoma, pop. 262,000
Currency: Tanzanian shilling (TZS)
Religions: Christian, Muslim
Languages: Kiswahili (Swahili), Kiunguja, English, Arabic, local languages

Sweden

Area: 173,860 sq mi (450,295 sq km)
Population: 10,262,000
Capital: Stockholm, pop. 1,657,000
Currency: Swedish krona (SEK)
Religion: Protestant
Language: Swedish

Thailand

Area: 198,117 sq mi (513,120 sq km)
Population: 69,481,000
Capital: Bangkok, pop. 10,723,000
Currency: baht (THB)
Religion: Buddhist
Languages: Thai, English

Timor-Leste

Area: 5,743 sq mi
(14,874 sq km)
Population: 1,414,000
Capital: Díli, pop. 281,000
Currency: U.S. dollar (USD)
Religion: Roman Catholic
Languages: Tetun, Mambai, Makasai, Portuguese, Indonesian, English

A record-setting average of **253 REEF FISH SPECIES** swim off the shores of TIMOR-LESTE'S ATAURO ISLAND.

Togo

Area: 21,925 sq mi (56,785 sq km)
Population: 8,283,000
Capital: Lomé, pop. 1,874,000
Currency: CFA franc BCEAO (XOF)
Religions: Christian, folk religion, Muslim
Languages: French, Ewe, Mina, Kabye, Dagomba

Tonga

Area: 288 sq mi (747 sq km)
Population: 106,000
Capital: Nuku'alofa,
pop. 23,000
Currency: pa'anga (TOP)
Religions: Protestant, Mormon, Roman Catholic
Languages: Tongan, English

Trinidad and Tobago

Area: 1,980 sq mi (5,128 sq km)
Population: 1,221,000
Capital: Port of Spain,
pop. 544,000
Currency: Trinidad and Tobago dollar (TTD)
Religions: Protestant, Roman Catholic, Hindu, Muslim
Languages: English, Creole, Caribbean Hindustani, Spanish, Chinese

Tunisia

Area: 63,170 sq mi
(163,610 sq km)
Population: 11,811,000
Capital: Tunis, pop. 2,403,000
Currency: Tunisian dinar (TND)
Religion: Muslim
Languages: Arabic, French, Berber

Turkey

Area: 302,535 sq mi
(783,562 sq km)
Population: 82,482,000
Capital: Ankara, pop. 5,216,000
Currency: Turkish lira (TRY)
Religion: Muslim
Languages: Turkish, Kurdish

Turkmenistan

Area: 188,456 sq mi
(488,100 sq km)
Population: 5,580,000
Capital: Ashgabat, pop. 865,000
Currency: Turkmenistani manat (TMT)
Religions: Muslim, Eastern Orthodox
Languages: Turkmen, Russian

Tuvalu

Area: 10 sq mi (26 sq km)
Population: 11,000
Capital: Funafuti,
pop. 7,000
Currency: Australian dollar (AUD)
Religion: Protestant
Languages: Tuvaluan, English, Samoan, Kiribati

Uganda

Area: 93,065 sq mi
(241,038 sq km)
Population: 44,712,000
Capital: Kampala, pop. 3,470,000
Currency: Ugandan shilling (UGX)
Religions: Protestant, Roman Catholic, Muslim
Languages: English, Ganda (Luganda), local languages, Swahili, Arabic

Ukraine

Area: 233,032 sq mi (603,550 sq km)
Population: 43,746,000
Capital: Kyiv, pop. 3,001,000
Currency: hryvnia (UAH)
Religions: Eastern Orthodox, Eastern Catholic, Roman Catholic, Protestant
Languages: Ukrainian, Russian

United Kingdom

Area: 94,058 sq mi (243,610 sq km)
Population: 66,052,000
Capital: London, pop. 9,426,000
Currency: pound sterling (GBP)
Religions: Protestant, Roman Catholic
Languages: English, Scots, Scottish Gaelic, Welsh, Irish, Cornish

United Arab Emirates

Area: 32,278 sq mi (83,600 sq km)
Population: 9,857,000
Capital: Abu Dhabi, pop. 1,512,000
Currency: UAE dirham (AED)
Religions: Muslim, Christian
Languages: Arabic, English, Hindi, Malayam, Urdu, Pashto, Tagalog, Persian

United States

Area: 3,796,741 sq mi (9,833,517 sq km)
Population: 334,998,000
Capital: Washington, D.C., pop. 5,378,000
Currency: U.S. dollar (USD)
Religions: Protestant, Roman Catholic
Languages: English, Spanish, Native American languages

SNAPSHOT
United Arab Emirates

The Burj Khalifa, the world's tallest building, soars above Dubai, U.A.E.

COLOR KEY ● Africa ● Australia, New Zealand, and Oceania

Uruguay

Area: 68,037 sq mi
(176,215 sq km)
Population: 3,398,000
Capital: Montevideo, pop. 1,760,000
Currency: Uruguayan peso (UYU)
Religions: Roman Catholic, other Christian
Language: Spanish

Vietnam

Area: 127,881 sq mi
(331,210 sq km)
Population: 102,790,000
Capital: Hanoi, pop. 4,875,000
Currency: dong (VND)
Religions: Buddhist, Roman Catholic
Languages: Vietnamese, English, French, Chinese, Khmer, Mon-Khmer, Malayo-Polynesian

Uzbekistan

Area: 172,742 sq mi
(447,400 sq km)
Population: 30,843,000
Capital: Tashkent,
pop. 2,545,000
Currency: Uzbekistan sum (UZS)
Religions: Muslim, Eastern Orthodox
Languages: Uzbek, Russian, Tajik

Yemen

Area: 203,850 sq mi
(527,968 sq km)
Population: 30,399,000
Capital: Sanaa, pop. 3,075,000
Currency: Yemeni rial (YER)
Religion: Muslim
Language: Arabic

Vanuatu

Area: 4,706 sq mi (12,189 sq km)
Population: 303,000
Capital: Port-Vila, pop. 53,000
Currency: Vatu (VUV)
Religions: Protestant, Roman Catholic
Languages: Local languages, Bislama, English, French

Zambia

Area: 290,587 sq mi
(752,618 sq km)
Population: 19,078,000
Capital: Lusaka, pop. 2,906,000
Currency: Zambian kwacha (ZMW)
Religions: Protestant, Roman Catholic
Languages: Bembe, Nyanja, Tonga, other Indigenous languages, English

Vatican City

Area: 0.2 sq mi (0.4 sq km)
Population: 1,000
Capital: Vatican City, pop. 1,000
Currency: euro (EUR)
Religion: Roman Catholic
Languages: Italian, Latin, French

You can spot
TERMITE HILLS
as **TALL** as a
HOUSE in ZAMBIA.

Venezuela

Area: 352,144 sq mi
(912,050 sq km)
Population: 29,069,000
Capital: Caracas, pop. 2,946,000
Currency: bolivar soberano (VES)
Religion: Roman Catholic
Languages: Spanish, Indigenous languages

Zimbabwe

Area: 150,872 sq mi
(390,757 sq km)
Population: 14,830,000
Capital: Harare, pop. 1,542,000
Currency: Zimbabwean dollar (ZWL)
Religions: Protestant, Roman Catholic, other Christian
Languages: Shona, Ndebele, English, Indigenous languages

THE POLITICAL UNITED STATES

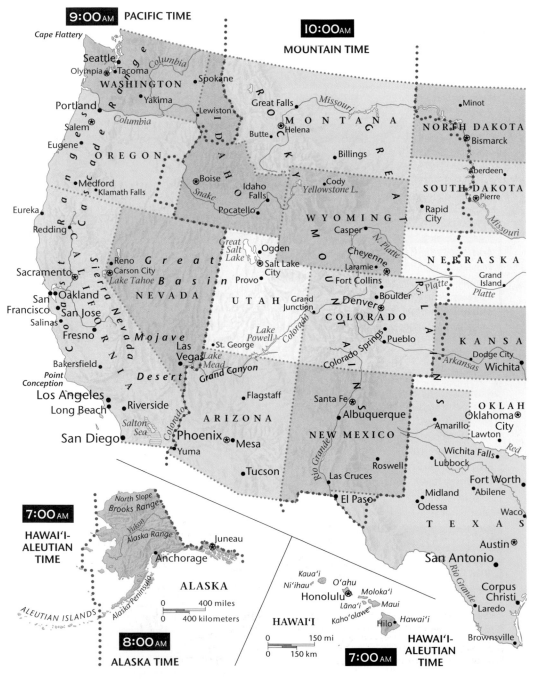

9:00AM **PACIFIC TIME**

10:00AM
MOUNTAIN TIME

Cape Flattery

Seattle
Olympia • Tacoma
WASHINGTON • Spokane
Portland • Yakima
Salem • Columbia • Lewiston
Eugene • OREGON
Medford • Boise
Klamath Falls • Idaho Falls
Eureka • Redding • Pocatello

Great Falls • Missouri
MONTANA
Butte • Helena
Billings

Minot
NORTH DAKOTA
• Bismarck
Aberdeen
SOUTH DAKOTA
Pierre

Cody
Yellowstone L.
WYOMING
Casper • N. Platte
Cheyenne
Laramie
Fort Collins

Rapid City
Missouri

NEBRASKA
Grand Island
Platte

Reno • Great
Carson City
Lake Tahoe • Basin
NEVADA
San Francisco • Oakland
San Jose
Salinas
Fresno • Sierra Nevada
Mojave

Great Salt Lake • Ogden
Salt Lake City
Provo
UTAH • Grand Junction
Lake Powell • Colorado
Denver • Boulder
COLORADO
Colorado Springs • Pueblo

S. Platte

KANSAS
Dodge City
Arkansas • Wichita

Bakersfield
Point Conception
Desert • Colorado
Las Vegas • Lake Mead
Grand Canyon

St. George

Los Angeles
Long Beach • Riverside
San Diego • Salton Sea
Phoenix • Mesa
Yuma
Tucson

Flagstaff
ARIZONA

Santa Fe
Albuquerque
NEW MEXICO

Las Cruces
El Paso

Roswell

Amarillo
Lawton
Wichita Falls
Lubbock

OKLAH
Oklahoma City
Red

Fort Worth
Midland • Abilene
Odessa • Waco
TEXAS
Austin

San Antonio
Rio Grande
Corpus Christi
Laredo

Brownsville

7:00AM
HAWAI'I-ALEUTIAN TIME

North Slope
Brooks Range
Yukon
Alaska Range • Juneau
Anchorage
ALASKA
Alaska Peninsula
ALEUTIAN ISLANDS

0 400 miles
0 400 kilometers

8:00AM
ALASKA TIME

Kaua'i
Ni'ihau • O'ahu
Honolulu • Moloka'i
Lāna'i • Maui
Kaho'olawe
Hilo • Hawai'i
HAWAI'I

0 150 mi
0 150 km

7:00AM
HAWAI'I-ALEUTIAN TIME

The United States is made up of 50 states joined like a giant quilt. Each is unique, but together they make a national fabric held together by a constitution and a federal government. State boundaries, outlined in dotted lines on the map, set apart internal political units within the country. The national capital—Washington, D.C.—is marked by a star in a double circle. The capital of each state is marked by a star in a single circle.

11:00 AM
CENTRAL TIME

12:00 NOON
EASTERN TIME

0   300 miles
0   300 kilometers
Albers Conic Equal-Area Projection

TIME ZONES: Earth is divided into 24 time zones, each about 15 degrees of longitude wide, reflecting the distance Earth turns from west to east each hour. The U.S. is divided into six time zones, indicated by red dotted lines on the map.

THE PHYSICAL UNITED STATES

Mt. St. Helens+
(2,549 m) 8,363 ft

+Mt. Rainier
14,411 ft
(4,392 m)
Columbia

Mt. Hood
11,240 ft
(3,426 m)

CASCADE RANGE

COLUMBIA RANGE

Snake

Flathead
Lake

Bitterroot Range

Blue Mountains

Great Sandy Desert

Columbia Plateau

Salmon River
Mountains

Snake

Snake River Plain

Yellowstone
Lake

ROCKY

Absaroka Range

Milk

Fort Peck
Lake

Missouri

Yellowstone

Bighorn Mts.

Grand
Teton
13,770 ft
(4,197 m)

GREAT

Little Missouri

Missouri

Heart

Missouri

Lake
Sakakawea

White
Butte
3,506 ft
(1,069 m)

Lake
Oahe

Black
Hills

Geographical Center
of the 50 United States

Black Elk
Peak
7,242 ft
(2,207 m)

White

James

Great
Salt
Lake

Wasatch Range

Great Divide
Basin

MOUNTAINS

Laramie Mts.

Front Range

Niobrara

N. Platte

Sand Hills

Platte

Sierra Nevada

Lake
Tahoe

Great

Basin

Uinta Mts.

Geographical Center
of the 48
Contiguous United States.

S. Platte

Smoky Hills

Sacramento Valley

San Joaquin

San Joaquin Valley

Mt. Whitney
14,494 ft
(4,418 m)

Death
Valley

Mojave

Desert

Lake
Mead

Lake
Powell

Colorado

Mt. Elbert
(4,399 m) 14,433 ft+

San Juan Mts.

Sangre de Cristo Mts.

+Pikes Peak
14,110 ft
(4,301 m)

PLAINS

Arkansas

Red Hills

Lowest Point in
North America
(-86 m) -282 ft

Grand
Canyon

Colorado

Colorado

Plateau

Painted Desert

Black Mesa
4,973 ft
(1,516 m)

Cimarron

Canadian

Channel
Islands

Salton
Sea

Imperial
Valley

Gila

Colorado

Humphreys Peak+
12,635 ft
(3,851 m)

Sonoran

Desert

Salt

Sacramento Mts.

Rio Grande

Llano
Estacado

Brazos

Colorado

+Guadalupe Peak
8,749 ft
(2,667 m)

Pecos

Edwards
Plateau

Rio Grande

0 ____ 400 miles
0 ____ 400 kilometers

North Slope

Brooks Range

Yukon

(Mt. McKinley) Denali
(6,190 m) 20,310 ft+

Highest Point in
North America

Alaska Range

Alexander
Archipelago

Aleutian Islands

Alaska Peninsula

Kaua'i

Ni'ihau

O'ahu

Moloka'i

Lāna'i

Kaho'olawe

Maui

Mauna Kea+
13,796 ft
(4,205 m)

Hawai'i

0 ____ 150 miles
0 ____ 150 kilometers

ALASKA AND HAWAII:
In addition to the states
located on the main landmass,
the U.S. has two states—Alaska
and Hawaii—that are not directly
connected to the other 48 states.
If Alaska and Hawaii were shown in
their correct relative sizes and locations,
the map would not fit on these pages.

Stretching from the Atlantic Ocean in the east to the Pacific Ocean in the west, the United States is the third largest country (by area) in the world. Its physical diversity ranges from mountains to fertile plains to dry deserts. Shading on the map indicates changes in elevation, while colors show different vegetation patterns.

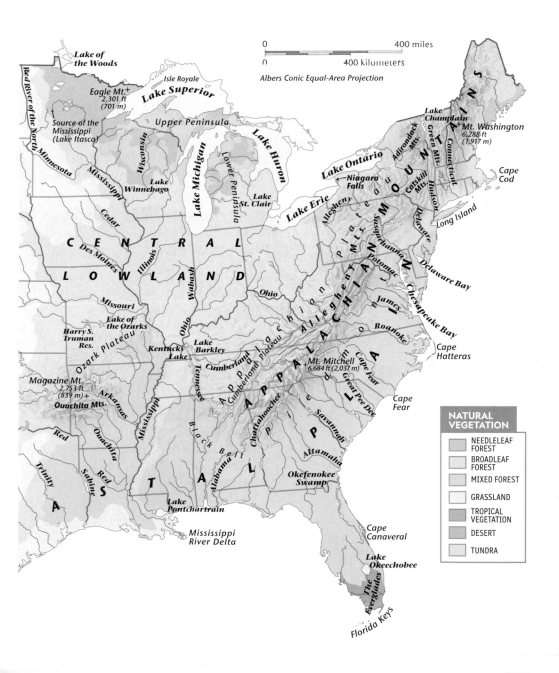

0   400 miles
0   400 kilometers

Albers Conic Equal-Area Projection

NATURAL VEGETATION

- NEEDLELEAF FOREST
- BROADLEAF FOREST
- MIXED FOREST
- GRASSLAND
- TROPICAL VEGETATION
- DESERT
- TUNDRA

THE STATES

From sea to shining sea, the United States of America is a nation of diversity. In the 244 years since its creation, the nation has grown to become home to a wide range of peoples, industries, and cultures. The following pages present a general overview of all 50 states in the United States.

The country is generally divided into five large regions: the Northeast, the Southeast, the Midwest, the Southwest, and the West. Though loosely defined, these zones tend to share important similarities, including climate, history, and geography. The color key below provides a guide to which states are in each region.

The flag of each state and highlights of demography and industry are also included. These details offer a brief overview of each state.

In addition, each state's official flower and bird are identified.

Color Key by Region

Alabama

Nickname: Heart of Dixie
Area: 52,420 sq mi (135,767 sq km)
Population: 4,922,000
Capital: Montgomery; population 360,000
Statehood: December 14, 1819; 22nd state
State flower/bird: Camellia/yellowhammer (northern flicker)

Residents of MAGNOLIA SPRINGS, ALABAMA, get their MAIL DELIVERED BY BOAT.

Alaska

Nickname: Last Frontier
Area: 665,384 sq mi (1,723,337 sq km)
Population: 731,000
Capital: Juneau; population 32,000
Statehood: January 3, 1959; 49th state
State flower/bird: Forget-me-not/ willow ptarmigan

Arizona

Nickname: Grand Canyon State
Area: 113,990 sq mi (295,234 sq km)
Population: 7,421,000
Capital: Phoenix; population 4,584,000
Statehood: February 14, 1912; 48th state
State flower/bird: Saguaro cactus blossom/ cactus wren

Arkansas

Nickname: Natural State
Area: 53,179 sq mi (137,732 sq km)
Population: 3,031,000
Capital: Little Rock; population 521,000
Statehood: June 15, 1836; 25th state
State flower/bird: Apple blossom/ mockingbird

California

Nickname: Golden State
Area: 163,695 sq mi (423,967 sq km)
Population: 39,368,000
Capital: Sacramento; population 2,155,000
Statehood: September 9, 1850; 31st state
State flower/bird: California poppy/ California quail

Colorado

Nickname: Centennial State
Area: 104,094 sq mi (269,601 sq km)
Population: 5,808,000
Capital: Denver; population 2,862,000
Statehood: August 1, 1876; 38th state
State flower/bird: Rocky Mountain columbine/ lark bunting

Connecticut

Nickname: Constitution State
Area: 5,543 sq mi (14,357 sq km)
Population: 3,557,000
Capital: Hartford; population 1,004,000
Statehood: January 9, 1788; 5th state
State flower/bird: Mountain laurel/American robin

Delaware

Nickname: First State
Area: 2,489 sq mi (6,446 sq km)
Population: 987,000
Capital: Dover; population 38,000
Statehood: December 7, 1787; 1st state
State flower/bird: Peach blossom/blue hen chicken

DELAWARE's state colors, blue and buff, were inspired by George Washington's military UNIFORM.

Florida

Nickname: Sunshine State
Area: 65,758 sq mi (170,312 sq km)
Population: 21,733,000
Capital: Tallahassee; population 195,000
Statehood: March 3, 1845; 27th state
State flower/bird: Orange blossom/mockingbird

Georgia

Nickname: Peach State
Area: 59,425 sq mi (153,910 sq km)
Population: 10,710,000
Capital: Atlanta; population 5,911,000
Statehood: January 2, 1788; 4th state
State flower/bird: Cherokee rose/brown thrasher

Hawaii

Nickname: Aloha State
Area: 10,932 sq mi (28,313 sq km)
Population: 1,407,000
Capital: Honolulu; population 898,000
Statehood: August 21, 1959; 50th state
State flower/bird: Pua aloalo/Nene (Hawaiian goose)

Idaho

Nickname: Gem State
Area: 83,569 sq mi (216,443 sq km)
Population: 1,827,000
Capital: Boise; population 455,000
Statehood: July 3, 1890; 43rd state
State flower/bird: Syringa/mountain bluebird

Illinois

Nickname: Prairie State
Area: 57,914 sq mi (149,995 sq km)
Population: 12,588,000
Capital: Springfield; population 114,000
Statehood: December 3, 1818; 21st state
State flower/bird: Violet/northern cardinal

Indiana

Nickname: Hoosier State
Area: 36,420 sq mi (94,326 sq km)
Population: 6,755,000
Capital: Indianapolis; population 1,833,000
Statehood: December 11, 1816; 19th state
State flower/bird: Peony/northern cardinal

Iowa

Nickname: Hawkeye State
Area: 56,273 sq mi (145,746 sq km)
Population: 3,164,000
Capital: Des Moines; population 552,000
Statehood: December 28, 1846; 29th state
State flower/bird: Wild prairie rose/American goldfinch

Kansas

Nickname: Sunflower State
Area: 82,278 sq mi (213,100 sq km)
Population: 2,914,000
Capital: Topeka; population 125,000
Statehood: January 29, 1861; 34th state
State flower/bird: Wild native sunflower/ western meadowlark

Kentucky

Nickname: Bluegrass State
Area: 40,408 sq mi (104,656 sq km)
Population: 4,477,000
Capital: Frankfort; population 28,000
Statehood: June 1, 1792; 15th state
State flower/bird: Goldenrod/northern cardinal

Louisiana

Nickname: Pelican State
Area: 52,378 sq mi (135,659 sq km)
Population: 4,645,000
Capital: Baton Rouge; population 746,000
Statehood: April 30, 1812; 18th state
State flower/bird: Magnolia/brown pelican

Maine

Nickname: Pine Tree State
Area: 35,380 sq mi (91,633 sq km)
Population: 1,350,000
Capital: Augusta; population 19,000
Statehood: March 15, 1820; 23rd state
State flower/bird: White pine cone and tassel/ black-capped chickadee

Maryland

Nickname: Old Line State
Area: 12,406 sq mi (32,131 sq km)
Population: 6,056,000
Capital: Annapolis; population 39,000
Statehood: April 28, 1788; 7th state
State flower/bird: Black-eyed Susan/ Baltimore oriole

Massachusetts

Nickname: Bay State
Area: 10,554 sq mi (27,336 sq km)
Population: 6,894,000
Capital: Boston; population 4,315,000
Statehood: February 6, 1788; 6th state
State flower/bird: Mayflower/ black-capped chickadee

Michigan

Nickname: Wolverine State
Area: 96,714 sq mi (250,487 sq km)
Population: 9,967,000
Capital: Lansing; population 326,000
Statehood: January 26, 1837; 26th state
State flower/bird: Apple blossom/ American robin

> You're never more than 85 miles (137 km) away from a **GREAT LAKE IN MICHIGAN.**

Minnesota

Nickname: North Star State
Area: 86,936 sq mi (225,163 sq km)
Population: 5,657,000
Capital: St. Paul; population 2,946,000
Statehood: May 11, 1858; 32nd state
State flower/bird: Pink and white lady slipper/ common loon

Mississippi

Nickname: Magnolia State
Area: 48,432 sq mi (125,438 sq km)
Population: 2,967,000
Capital: Jackson; population 426,000
Statehood: December 10, 1817; 20th state
State flower/bird: Magnolia/mockingbird

Missouri

Nickname: Show-Me State
Area: 69,707 sq mi (180,540 sq km)
Population: 6,152,000
Capital: Jefferson City; population 43,000
Statehood: August 10, 1821; 24th state
State flower/bird: Hawthorn blossom/eastern bluebird

Montana

Nickname: Treasure State
Area: 147,040 sq mi (380,831 sq km)
Population: 1,081,000
Capital: Helena; population 33,000
Statehood: November 8, 1889; 41st state
State flower/bird: Bitterroot/western meadowlark

A 1959 EARTHQUAKE in MONTANA created a lake five miles (8 km) long.

Nebraska

Nickname: Cornhusker State
Area: 77,348 sq mi (200,330 sq km)
Population: 1,938,000
Capital: Lincoln; population 289,000
Statehood: March 1, 1867; 37th state
State flower/bird: Goldenrod/western meadowlark

Nevada

Nickname: Silver State
Area: 110,572 sq mi (286,380 sq km)
Population: 3,138,000
Capital: Carson City; population 56,000
Statehood: October 31, 1864; 36th state
State flower/bird: Sagebrush/mountain bluebird

New Hampshire

Nickname: Granite State
Area: 9,349 sq mi (24,214 sq km)
Population: 1,366,000
Capital: Concord; population 44,000
Statehood: June 21, 1788; 9th state
State flower/bird: Purple lilac/purple finch

New Jersey

Nickname: Garden State
Area: 8,723 sq mi (22,591 sq km)
Population: 8,882,000
Capital: Trenton; population 331,000
Statehood: December 18, 1787; 3rd state
State flower/bird: Violet/Eastern goldfinch

New Mexico

Nickname: Land of Enchantment
Area: 121,590 sq mi (314,917 sq km)
Population: 2,106,000
Capital: Santa Fe; population 85,000
Statehood: January 6, 1912; 47th state
State flower/bird: Yucca/greater roadrunner

New York

Nickname: Empire State
Area: 54,555 sq mi (141,297 sq km)
Population: 19,337,000
Capital: Albany; population 632,000
Statehood: July 26, 1788; 11th state
State flower/bird: Rose/eastern bluebird

North Carolina

Nickname: Tar Heel State
Area: 53,819 sq mi (139,391 sq km)
Population: 10,601,000
Capital: Raleigh; population 1,498,000
Statehood: November 21, 1789; 12th state
State flower/bird: Flowering dogwood/northern cardinal

North Dakota

Nickname: Peace Garden State
Area: 70,698 sq mi (183,108 sq km)
Population: 765,000
Capital: Bismarck; population 74,000
Statehood: November 2, 1889; 39th state
State flower/bird: Wild prairie rose/ western meadowlark

Ohio

Nickname: Buckeye State
Area: 44,826 sq mi (116,098 sq km)
Population: 11,693,000
Capital: Columbus; population 1,666,000
Statehood: February 19, 1803; 17th state
State flower/bird: Scarlet carnation/ northern cardinal

Oklahoma

Nickname: Sooner State
Area: 69,899 sq mi (181,037 sq km)
Population: 3,981,000
Capital: Oklahoma City; population 998,000
Statehood: November 16, 1907; 46th state
State flower/bird: Oklahoma rose/ scissor-tailed flycatcher

3 cool things about OKLAHOMA

1. The world's first parking meter, known as Park-O-Meter No. 1, was installed in Oklahoma City in 1935.

2. Oklahoma's Cimarron County is the only county in the U.S. that touches four states: Colorado, New Mexico, Texas, and Kansas.

3. The swimming pool in the backyard of the governor's mansion is shaped like the state of Oklahoma.

Oregon

Nickname: Beaver State
Area: 98,379 sq mi (254,799 sq km)
Population: 4,242,000
Capital: Salem; population 174,000
Statehood: February 14, 1859; 33rd state
State flower/bird: Oregon grape/ western meadowlark

Pennsylvania

Nickname: Keystone State
Area: 46,054 sq mi (119,280 sq km)
Population: 12,783,000
Capital: Harrisburg; population 550,000
Statehood: December 12, 1787; 2nd state
State flower/bird: Mountain laurel/ ruffed grouse

Rhode Island

Nickname: Ocean State
Area: 1,545 sq mi (4,001 sq km)
Population: 1,057,000
Capital: Providence; population 1,200,000
Statehood: May 29, 1790; 13th state
State flower/bird: Violet/ Rhode Island red

South Carolina

Nickname: Palmetto State
Area: 32,020 sq mi (82,933 sq km)
Population: 5,218,000
Capital: Columbia; population 730,000
Statehood: May 23, 1788; 8th state
State flower/bird: Yellow jessamine/ Carolina wren

South Dakota

Nickname: Mount Rushmore State
Area: 77,116 sq mi (199,729 sq km)
Population: 893,000
Capital: Pierre; population 14,000
Statehood: November 2, 1889; 40th state
State flower/bird: American pasque/ ring-necked pheasant

COLOR KEY Northeast Southeast

Tennessee

Nickname: Volunteer State
Area: 42,144 sq mi (109,153 sq km)
Population: 6,887,000
Capital: Nashville; population 1,272,000
Statehood: June 1, 1796; 16th state
State flower/bird: Iris/mockingbird

Texas

Nickname: Lone Star State
Area: 268,596 sq mi (695,662 sq km)
Population: 29,361,000
Capital: Austin; population 2,117,000
Statehood: December 29, 1845; 28th state
State flower/bird: Bluebonnet/mockingbird

Utah

Nickname: Beehive State
Area: 84,897 sq mi
(219,882 sq km)
Population: 3,250,000
Capital: Salt Lake City; population 1,180,000
Statehood: January 4, 1896; 45th state
State flower/bird: Sego lily/California gull

Vermont

Nickname: Green Mountain State
Area: 9,616 sq mi (24,906 sq km)
Population: 623,000
Capital: Montpelier; population 7,000
Statehood: March 4, 1791; 14th state
State flower/bird: Red clover/hermit thrush

Virginia

Nickname: Old Dominion
Area: 42,775 sq mi (110,787 sq km)
Population: 8,591,000
Capital: Richmond; population 1,117,000
Statehood: June 25, 1788; 10th state
State flower/bird: American dogwood/
northern cardinal

Washington

Nickname: Evergreen State
Area: 71,298 sq mi (184,661 sq km)
Population: 7,694,000
Capital: Olympia; population 53,000
Statehood: November 11, 1889; 42nd state
State flower/bird: Coast rhododendron/
American goldfinch

West Virginia

Nickname: Mountain State
Area: 24,230 sq mi (62,756 sq km)
Population: 1,785,000
Capital: Charleston; population 47,000
Statehood: June 20, 1863; 35th state
State flower/bird: Rhododendron/
northern cardinal

In the late 1950s, the U.S. government built a **TOP SECRET BUNKER BENEATH A HOTEL** in **WHITE SULPHUR SPRINGS, WEST VIRGINIA.**

Wisconsin

Nickname: Badger State
Area: 65,496 sq mi (169,635 sq km)
Population: 5,833,000
Capital: Madison; population 494,000
Statehood: May 29, 1848; 30th state
State flower/bird: Wood violet/
American robin

Wyoming

Nickname: Equality State
Area: 97,813 sq mi (253,335 sq km)
Population: 582,000
Capital: Cheyenne; population 64,000
Statehood: July 10, 1890; 44th state
State flower/bird: Indian paintbrush/
western meadowlark

 Midwest Southwest ● West

THE TERRITORIES

The United States has 14 territories— political divisions that are not states. Three of these are in the Caribbean Sea, and the other 11 are in the Pacific Ocean.

St. John, U.S. Virgin Islands

Convention Center, San Juan, Puerto Rico

Talofofo Falls, Guam

U.S. CARIBBEAN TERRITORIES

Puerto Rico
Area: 5,325 sq mi (13,791 sq km)
Population: 3,143,000
Capital: San Juan; population 2,445,000
Languages: Spanish, English

U.S. Virgin Islands
Area: 733 sq mi (1,898 sq km)
Population: 106,000
Capital: Charlotte Amalie; population 52,000
Languages: English, Spanish, French

U.S. PACIFIC TERRITORIES

American Samoa
Area: 581 sq mi (1,505 sq km)
Population: 46,000
Capital: Pago Pago; population 49,000
Language: Samoan, English

Guam
Area: 571 sq mi (1,478 sq km)
Population: 169,000
Capital: Hagåtña (Agana); population 147,000
Languages: English, Filipino, Chamorro, other Pacific island and Asian languages

Northern Mariana Islands
Area: 1,976 sq mi (5,117 sq km)
Population: 52,000
Capital: Capital Hill; population 51,000
Languages: Philippine languages, Chinese, Chamorro, English

Other U.S. Territories
Baker Island, Howland Island, Jarvis Island, Johnston Atoll, Kingman Reef, Midway Islands, Palmyra Atoll, Wake Island, Navassa Island (in the Caribbean)

Figures for capital cities vary widely between sources because of differences in the way areas are defined and other projection methods.

THE U.S. CAPITAL

District of Columbia

Area: 68 sq mi (177 sq km)
Population: 5,378,000

Abraham Lincoln, who was president during the Civil War and an opponent of slavery, is remembered in the Lincoln Memorial, located at the opposite end of the National Mall from the U.S. Capitol Building.

The Lincoln Memorial celebrated its 100th anniversary in 2022.

COLOR KEY ● Territories ● Northeast

weird but true!

Check out these outrageous U.S.A. facts.

JELL-O is the **official state snack** of **UTAH.**

Ghost fireflies of the southeastern United States **glow blue.**

So many peeps!

THERE ARE **600 TIMES MORE CHICKENS** THAN HUMANS IN DELAWARE.

ACCORDING TO NEW JERSEY FOLKLORE, the **JERSEY DEVIL** is a creature with the head of a goat, bat wings, and a forked tail.

The trunk of the **LARGEST TREE,** located in California, weighs as much as **200 AFRICAN ELEPHANTS.**

It's tree-rific!

GENERAL SHERMAN

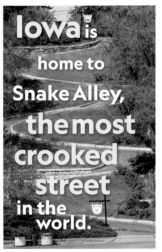

Iowa is home to **Snake Alley,** the most **crooked street** in the world.

At the Georgia State Fair, the **winning pig** in the pig races **gets an Oreo cookie.**

THE **INK** USED TO PRINT U.S. PAPER MONEY IS **MAGNETIC.**

NUTTY NARROWS BRIDGE in Longview, Washington, was built so **SQUIRRELS CAN SAFELY CROSS A BUSY ROAD.**

WHAT WEIRD DESTINATION IS RIGHT FOR YOU?

Do you like your weirdness from a distance?

Lake Hillier, Middle Island, western Australia
Researchers think that bacteria in this pink lake give it its rosy color. But because the island is used only for research, your visit will be from the air.

Spotted Lake, British Columbia, Canada
The water of this lake evaporates in summer, leaving behind small mineral pools of varying color. They're best viewed from far enough away that you can see all the quirky circles at once.

Skylodge Adventure Suites, Cusco, Peru
Get cozy in your transparent bedroom capsule 1,000 feet (305 m) up—hanging from the side of a cliff in Peru's Sacred Valley.

Or do you prefer your weirdness up close?

Bonne Terre Mine, Missouri, U.S.A.
Scuba dive to your heart's content in this flooded underground lead mine—now the world's largest freshwater dive resort.

RACING ROLLER COASTER

Get ready for a supercharged ride!
Kingda Ka at Six Flags Great Adventure in New Jersey, U.S.A., is not only the world's tallest roller coaster—it's the world's second fastest, too! Hang on tight and check out these heart-pumping facts about the ride.

DROP
418 FEET
(127 M)

PEAK
129- (39-M)
FEET-TALL
CAMEL HUMP

HEIGHT
456 FEET
(142 M)
THAT'S AS TALL AS A 45-STORY BUILDING!

SPEED
128 (206 KM/H)
MILES AN HOUR
HAVE A NEED FOR SPEED? RIDERS REACH TOP SPEED IN JUST 3.5 SECONDS!

RIDE DURATION
50.6 SECONDS

CLIMB ANGLE
90°

LENGTH ## 3,118 FEET (950 M)

347

15 AMAZING FACTS ABOUT THE WORLD

Earth **ROTATES** on its **AXIS 1.5 MILLISECONDS SLOWER EVERY CENTURY.**

CHINA'S MOUNTAINOUS BAMBOO FORESTS can rise sharply—but **GIANT PANDAS** can easily **CLIMB AS HIGH AS 13,000 FEET** (3,962 m) up the slopes.

About **12,000 years ago,** the **Sahara** was covered with millions of trees.

In Jordan's **ANCIENT CITY OF PETRA,** buildings were carved directly into cliff walls.

The **SURFACE** of the **PACIFIC OCEAN** is **LARGER** than all of **EARTH'S CONTINENTS** combined.

CANADA'S THOR PEAK IS THOUGHT TO HAVE THE WORLD'S LONGEST UNINTERRUPTED CLIFF FACE.

More people live in **TAMPA, FLORIDA, U.S.A.,** than in all of **ICELAND.**

Greetings from **TAMPA** FLORIDA

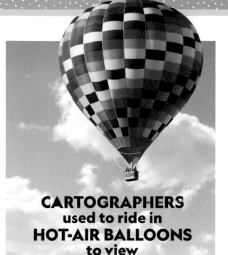

CARTOGRAPHERS used to ride in **HOT-AIR BALLOONS** to view and map land.

When forests **FLOOD ALONG SOUTH AMERICA'S AMAZON RIVER,** river dolphins sometimes swim around trees.

The **Dead Sea's water level drops** more than **3 FEET (0.9 M) EACH YEAR.**

One CAVE in MALAYSIA is big enough to hold eight **JUMBO JETS.**

INDONESIA'S REMOTE FOJA MOUNTAINS ARE HOME TO BIZARRE SPECIES SUCH AS THE PINOCCHIO FROG.

The **CHOCOLATE HILLS** in the **PHILIPPINES** are shaped like giant **Hershey's KISSES.**

KISSES®

The United Arab Emirates has two artificial islands **SHAPED LIKE PALM TREES.**

The SCORCHING DESERTS of NORTH AFRICA don't hurt the SAND CAT—the animal's PAW PADS ARE COVERED IN FUR to protect its feet from heat.

Bizarre Beaches

THE WORLD'S COOLEST COASTLINES OFFER SO MUCH MORE THAN SANDY SHORES.

BLACK-OUT

WHAT: Punalu'u Black Sand Beach
WHERE: Big Island, Hawaii, U.S.A.
WHY IT'S BIZARRE: The jet-black sand on this skinny stretch of beach is made up of tiny bits of hardened lava, produced over centuries by the nearby (and still active) Kilauea volcano. This cool spot is also a popular nesting place for hawksbill and green sea turtles.

GLASS FROM THE PAST

WHAT: Glass Beach
WHERE: Fort Bragg, California, U.S.A.
WHY IT'S BIZARRE: Decades ago, the water along this beach was a dumping ground for glass bottles and other debris. Now what was once tossed in the ocean has washed up as a rainbow of shimmering sea glass covering the coves.

FOR THE BIRDS

WHAT: Boulders Beach
WHERE: Harbour Island, Bahamas
WHY IT'S BIZARRE: You might expect to see penguins on an icy coast. But these birds like it hot! African penguins splash in the warm waters of this national park next to 540-million-year-old granite boulders.

TIP-OFF

WHAT: Zlatni Rat
WHERE: Bol, Croatia
WHY IT'S BIZARRE: This narrow beach is a real shape-shifter. Its tip—which sticks out as much as 1,640 feet (500 m) into the crystal blue water—shifts in different directions as a result of wind, waves, and currents.

THE 7 ORIGINAL WONDERS of the WORLD

More than 2,000 years ago, many travelers wrote about sights they had seen on their journeys. Over time, seven of those places made history as the "wonders of the ancient world." There are seven because the Greeks, who made the list, believed the number seven to be magical.

THE PYRAMIDS OF GIZA, EGYPT

BUILT: ABOUT 2600 B.C.
MASSIVE TOMBS OF EGYPTIAN PHARAOHS LIE INSIDE THIS ANCIENT WONDER—THE ONLY ONE STILL STANDING TODAY.

HANGING GARDENS OF BABYLON, IRAQ

BUILT: DATE UNKNOWN
LEGEND HAS IT THAT THIS GARDEN PARADISE WAS PLANTED ON AN ARTIFICIAL MOUNTAIN, BUT MANY EXPERTS SAY IT NEVER REALLY EXISTED.

TEMPLE OF ARTEMIS AT EPHESUS, TURKEY

BUILT: SIXTH CENTURY B.C.
THIS TOWERING TEMPLE WAS BUILT TO HONOR ARTEMIS, THE GREEK GODDESS OF THE HUNT.

STATUE OF ZEUS, GREECE

BUILT: FIFTH CENTURY B.C.
THIS 40-FOOT (12-M) STATUE DEPICTED THE KING OF THE GREEK GODS.

MAUSOLEUM AT HALICARNASSUS, TURKEY

BUILT: FOURTH CENTURY B.C.
THIS ELABORATE TOMB WAS BUILT FOR KING MAUSOLUS.

COLOSSUS OF RHODES, RHODES (AN ISLAND IN THE AEGEAN SEA)

BUILT: FOURTH CENTURY B.C.
A 110-FOOT (34-M) STATUE HONORING THE GREEK SUN GOD HELIOS.

LIGHTHOUSE OF ALEXANDRIA, EGYPT
BUILT: THIRD CENTURY B.C.
THE WORLD'S FIRST LIGHTHOUSE, IT USED MIRRORS TO REFLECT SUNLIGHT FOR MILES OUT TO SEA.

THE 7 NEW WONDERS of the WORLD

Why name new wonders of the world? Most of the original ancient wonders no longer exist. To be eligible for the new list, the wonders had to be human-made before the year 2000 and in preservation. They were selected through a poll of more than 100 million voters!

TAJ MAHAL, INDIA

COMPLETED: 1648
THIS LAVISH TOMB WAS BUILT AS A FINAL RESTING PLACE FOR THE BELOVED WIFE OF EMPEROR SHAH JAHAN.

PETRA, SOUTHWEST JORDAN

COMPLETED: ABOUT 200 B.C.
SOME 30,000 PEOPLE ONCE LIVED IN THIS ROCK CITY CARVED INTO CLIFF WALLS.

MACHU PICCHU, PERU

COMPLETED: ABOUT 1450
OFTEN CALLED THE "LOST CITY IN THE CLOUDS," MACHU PICCHU IS PERCHED 7,710 FEET (2,350 M) HIGH IN THE ANDES.

THE COLOSSEUM, ITALY

COMPLETED: A.D. 80
WILD ANIMALS—AND HUMANS—FOUGHT EACH OTHER TO THE DEATH BEFORE 50,000 SPECTATORS IN THIS ARENA.

CHRIST THE REDEEMER STATUE, BRAZIL

COMPLETED: 1931
TOWERING ATOP CORCOVADO MOUNTAIN, THIS STATUE IS TALLER THAN A 12-STORY BUILDING AND WEIGHS ABOUT 2.5 MILLION POUNDS (1.1 MILLION KG).

CHICHÉN ITZÁ, MEXICO

COMPLETED: 10TH CENTURY
ONCE THE CAPITAL CITY OF THE ANCIENT MAYA EMPIRE, CHICHÉN ITZÁ IS HOME TO THE FAMOUS PYRAMID OF KUKULCÁN.

GREAT WALL OF CHINA, CHINA

COMPLETED: 1644
THE LONGEST HUMAN-MADE STRUCTURE EVER BUILT, IT WINDS OVER AN ESTIMATED 4,500 MILES (7,200 KM).

QUIZ WHIZ

Is your geography knowledge off the map? Quiz yourself to find out!

Write your answers on a piece of paper. Then check them below.

1 **Where in the world is Glass Beach?**
a. Koh Samui, Thailand
b. Fort Bragg, California, U.S.A.
c. St. George, Bermuda
d. Fort Fisher, North Carolina, U.S.A.

2 **What stands out about Lake Hillier in western Australia?**
a. its depth
b. its abundance of fish
c. its pink water
d. its heart shape

3 **What caused Australia's wangarru population to dwindle?**
a. drought
b. poaching
c. cold weather
d. They hopped away to New Zealand.

4 **True or false?** The United Arab Emirates has two artificial islands shaped like pine trees.

5 **In Singapore, there are plans underway to plant _____ new trees by 2030.**
a. 100
b. 1,000
c. 100,000
d. 1,000,000

Not **STUMPED** yet? Check out the *NATIONAL GEOGRAPHIC KIDS QUIZ WHIZ* collection for more crazy **GEOGRAPHY** questions!

ANSWERS: 1. b; 2. c; 3. a; 4. False: They're shaped like palm trees.; 5. d

HOMEWORK HELP

Finding Your Way Around

LATITUDE AND LONGITUDE lines help us determine locations on Earth. Every place on Earth has a special address called absolute location. Imaginary lines called lines of latitude run west to east, parallel to the Equator. These lines measure distance in degrees north or south from the Equator (0° latitude) to the North Pole (90° N) or to the South Pole (90° S). One degree of latitude is approximately 70 miles (113 km).

Lines of longitude run north to south, meeting at the poles. These lines measure distance in degrees east or west from 0° longitude (prime meridian) to 180° longitude. The prime meridian runs through Greenwich, England.

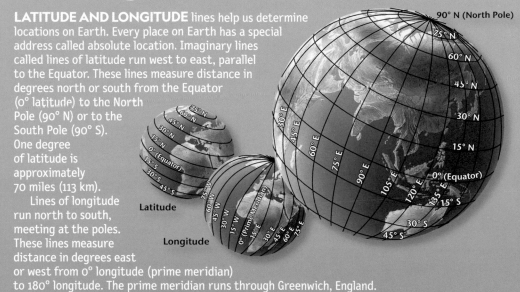

Latitude

Longitude

ABSOLUTE LOCATION. Suppose you are using latitude and longitude to play a game of global scavenger hunt. The clue says the prize is hidden at absolute location 30° S, 60° W. You know that the first number is south of the Equator, and the second is west of the prime meridian. On the map at right, find the line of latitude labeled 30° S. Now find the line of longitude labeled 60° W. Trace these lines with your fingers until they meet. Identify this spot. The prize must be located in northern Argentina (see arrow, right).

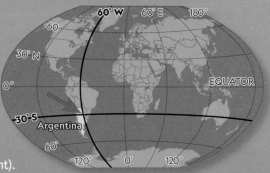

CHALLENGE!

1. Look at the map of Africa on pp. 282–283. Which country can you find at 10° S, 20° E?

2. Look at the map of Asia on pp. 290–291. Which country can you find at 20° N, 80° E?

3. On the map of Europe on pp. 298–299, which country is found at 50° N, 30° E?

4. Look at the map of North America on pp. 302–303. Which country can you find at 20° N, 100° W?

ANSWERS: 1. Angola; **2.** India; **3.** Ukraine; **4.** Mexico

GAME ANSWERS

What in the World?
page 133

Top row: **spider, scorpion, beetle**
Middle row: **termites, centipede, cockroach**
Bottom row: **worms, salamander, slug**

Signs of the Times
page 134

Signs **3** and **6** are fake.

Noun Town
page 136

The 12 compound nouns are:
1. **sleeping bag,** 2. **eggplant,** 3. **catfish,**
4. **bellhop,** 5. **ladybug,** 6. **housework,**
7. **butterfly,** 8. **limelight,** 9. **arrowhead,**
10. **full moon,** 11. **tree house,**
12. **coffee table**

Find the Hidden Animals
page 137

1. **A,** 2. **E,** 3. **C,** 4. **D,** 5. **B,** 6. **F**

What in the World?
page 138

Top row: **surfboards, Great Barrier Reef, kangaroo**
Middle row: **cassowary, boomerang, Uluru**
Bottom row: **flag, koala, Sydney Opera House**

Stump Your Parents
page 139

1. **D,** 2. **B,** 3. **A,** 4. **A,** 5. **B,** 6. **C,** 7. **A,** 8. **C,** 9. **D,**
10. **A-3; B-4 ; C-5; D-2; E-1**

What in the World?
page 142

Top row: **palm tree, sandcastle, snorkel and mask**
Middle row: **swimsuit, beach ball, seaweed**
Bottom row: **seashell, beach towel, umbrella**

Find the Hidden Animals
page 143

1. **E,** 2. **F,** 3. **D,** 4. **B,** 5. **A,** 6. **C**

Stump Your Parents
page 145

1. **C,** 2. **D,** 3. **B,** 4. **A,** 5. **D,** 6. **C,** 7. **B,** 8. **C,** 9. **A,** 10. **C**

What in the World?
page 146

Top row: **raspberries, bicycle, ruby**
Middle row: **gloves, red fox, peppers**
Bottom row: **sneaker, pomegranate, cardinal**

Want to Learn More?

Find more information about topics in this book in these National Geographic Kids resources.

Brain Candy series

Weird But True! series

Just Joking series

5,000 Awesome Facts (About Everything!) series

Beastly Bionics
Jennifer Swanson
June 2020

Ultimate U.S. Road Trip Atlas, 2nd edition
Crispin Boyer
April 2020

Fetch! A How to Speak Dog Training Guide
Aubre Andrus
August 2020

Girls Can!
Marissa Sebastian,
Tora Shae Pruden,
Paige Towler
October 2020

Breaking the News
Robin Terry Brown
October 2020

Cutest Animals on the Planet
National Geographic Kids
March 2021

Top Secret
Crispin Boyer
April 2021

Ultimate Rockopedia
Steve Tomecek
December 2020

NASA; 93 (LO), Alice Brereton; 94, Mondolithic Studios; 95 (UP), Allexxandar/IS/GI; 95 (Jupiter), rtype/AS; 95 (eclipse), Igor Kovalchuk/SS; 95 (supermoon), JSirlin/AS; 96 (UP), NGIC; 96 (LO), Joe Rocco; 97 (UP), Ralph Lee Hopkins/NGIC; 97 (andesite), Iosmandarinas/SS; 97 (porphyry), MarekPhotoDesign/AS; 97 (schist), Yes058 Montree Nanta/SS; 97 (gneiss), Dirk Wiersma/ Science Source; 97 (limestone), Charles D. Winters/Photo Researchers, Inc.; 97 (halite), Theodore Clutter/Science Source; 98 (UP LE), raiwa/IS; 98 (UP RT), MarcelC/IS; 98 (CTR RT), Anatoly Maslennlkov/SS; 98 (LO RT), IS; 98 (LO LE), Albert Russ/SS; 99 (UP RT), Mark A. Schneider/Science Source; 99 (UP LE), didyk/ IS; 99 (Talc), Ben Johnson/Science Source; 99 (Gypsum), Meetchum/DS; 99 (Calcite), Kazakovmaksim/DS; 99 (Fluorite), Albertruss/ DS; 99 (Apatite), Ingemar Magnusson/DS; 99 (Orthoclase), Joel Arem/Science Source; 99 (Topaz), Igorkali/DS; 99 (Corundum), oldeez/ DS; 99 (Diamond), 123dartist/DS; 101, Exp 351 Science Team/Leeds University; 102, Frank Ippolito; 103 (UP LE), Gary Fiegehen/All Canada Photos/Alamy; 103 (UP RT), Salvatore Gebbia/ NGIC; 103 (CTR LE), NASA; 103 (CTR RT), Diane Cook & Len Jenshel/NGIC; 104-105, Nicolas Marino/mauritius images GmbH/AL; 105 (UP), Chris Philpot; 105 (CTR LE), Taiga/AS; 105 (LO RT), Mazur Travel/AS; 106 (UP RT), Charles D. Winters/Photo Researchers, Inc.; 106 (CTR LE), Igor Kovalchuk/SS; 106 (LO RT), CGiHeart/AS; 107, pixhook/E+/GI

Awesome Exploration (108-129)

108-109, Westend61/AL; 111, Diego Camilo Carranza Jimenez/Anadolu Agency/GI; 112 (CTR LE), Roger Winstead; 112 (CTR RT), Michael Nolan/robertharding/GI; 112 (LO), Meg Lowman; 113 (UP), Smileus/AS; 113 (CTR), AVTG/AS; 113 (binoculars), Nataliya Hora/DS; 113 (paper), Photo_SS/SS; 113 (pencil), photastic/SS; 113 (LO), Aditi Sundar; 114 (UP), Thomas Marent./ MP; 114 (CTR RT), Jonathan Byers; 114 (CTR LE), Robert Liddell; 115 (UP), Sora Devore/ NGIC; 115 (CTR), Carsten Peter/NGIC; 115 (CTR RT), Carsten Peter/NGIC; 116-117 (ALL), Gab Mejia; 118-119 (UP), Aga Nowack; 118 (Jungblut), Arwyn Edwards; 118 (Wynn-Grant), Christine Jean Chambers; 118 (LO), Tibor Bognar/GI; 119 (Somaweera), Ruchira Somaweera 119 (UP RT), Nilu Gunarathne; 119 (Medici), Liana John; 119 (LO RT), Marina Klink; 119 (Daniel Dick), Max Chipman; 119 (CTR LE), Daniel Dick; 120-121 (ALL), Joel Sartore, National Geographic Photo Ark/NGIC; 122, Mattias Klum/NGIC; 123 (UP), Brian J. Skerry/NGIC; 123 (LO), Michael Nichols/ NGIC; 124 (LE), Gabby Wild; 124 (UP RT), Rebecca Hale/NG Staff; 124 (LO RT), Theo Allofs/MP; 125 (BACKGROUND), Arctic-Images/Corbis/GI; 125 (UP RT), ARCTIC IMAGES/AL; 125 (LO LE), ARCTIC IMAGES/AL; 126 (UP), Daniel Milchev/GI; 126 (LO), Laurence Griffiths/GI; 127 (UP LE), Robert Mora/GI; 127 (UP RT), Zapata Racing; 127 (CTR RT), Don Bartletti/Los Angeles Times via GI; 127 (LO RT), ohrim/SS; 127 (LO LE), Mathieu Belanger/The New York Times/Redux Pictures; 127 (CTR LE), JVT/GI; 128 (UP RT), Zapata Racing; 128 (CTR LE), Thomas Marent/MP; 128 (CTR RT), Diego Camilo Carranza Jimenez/Anadolu Agency/GI; 128 (LO LE), Theo Allofs/MP; 129, Grady Reese/IS

Fun and Games (130-149)

130-131, Thichaa/SS; 132 (UP), Sean Crane/ MP; 132 (moose), Scott Suriano/GI; 132 (grouse), pchoui/iStock/GI; 132 (lynx), Michael Quinton/MP; 132 (hare), Jim Cumming/GI; 132 (profile), Mark Raycroft/MP; 132 (male grouse), Wayne Lynch/All Canada Photos/AL; 132 (tufts), Michael Quinton/MP; 132 (swim- ming), Ron Sanford/GI; 132 (snow), Diana Robinson Photography/GI; 132 (fur), Jurgen and Christine Sohns/MP; 133 (UP LE), Antonio Veraldi/DS; 133 (UP CTR), Ghm Meuffels/DS; 133 (UP RT), Sweetcrisis/DS; 133 (CTR LE), Sydeen/DS; 133 (CTR), Antonio Veraldi/DS; 133 (CTR RT), Unteroffizier/DS; 133 (LO LE), Mikhail Kokhanchikov/DS; 133 (LO CTR), Fotosutra/DS; 133 (LO RT), Derrick Neill/DS; 134 (UP LE), Travel Pictures/AL; 134 (UP RT), Thomas Winz/GI; 134 (CTR RT), Richard Newstead/GI; 134 (LO RT), MyLoupe/Universal Images Group via GI; 134 (LO CTR), Andrew Holt/GI; 134 (LO LE), Owaki/ Kulla/GI; 134 (CTR LE), Charles Gullung/GI; 135, Jason Tharp; 136, Joren Cull; 137 (UP CTR), Fabio Liverani/Nature Picture Library; 137 (UP RT), John Cancalosi/Nature Picture Library; 137 (CTR LE), atese/GI; 137 (CTR RT), Jurgen Freund/Nature Picture Library; 137 (LO LE), Terry Andrewartha/Nature Picture Library; 137 (LO RT), Jose B. Ruiz/Nature Picture Library; 138 (UP LE), surflover/SS; 138 (UP CTR), Felix Martinez/GI; 138 (UP RT), age fotostock/ Superstock; 138 (CTR LE), Andy Gehrig/GI; 138 (CTR), Kharidehal Abhirama Ashwin/SS; 138 (CTR RT), Ikpro/SS; 138 (LO LE), Nils Versemann/ SS; 138 (LO CTR), Gary Bell/oceanwideimages; 138 (LO RT), age fotostock/Stuperstock; 139 (UP), Pltphotography/DS; 139 (CTR RT), Charles Krebs/GI; 139 (LO RT), Ryan McVay/GI; 139 (LO LE), Markstout/GI; 139 (tree), Cornelia Doerr/ GI; 139 (compass), Kisan/SS; 139 (CTR LE), Kevin Kelley/GI; 140, Dan Sipple; 141, Chris Ware; 142 (UP LE), image100/AL; 142 (UP CTR), Subbotina Anna/AS; 142 (UP RT), Kletr/SS; 142 (CTR LE), Ron Levine/Photodisc Red/GI; 142 (CTR), koosen/SS; 142 (CTR RT), Gary Bell/GI; 142 (LO LE), Alexander Raths/SS; 142 (UP LE), Wendy Carrig/GI; 142 (LO RT), Kalabi Yau/SS; 143 (UP CTR), Brandon Cole; 143 (UP RT), Kevin Schafer/ GI; 143 (CTR LE), Chris Mattison/FLPA/MP; 143 (CTR RT), Andy Mann/GI; 143 (LO LE), Thomas Marent/MP; 143 (LO RT), David Fleetham/ Nature Picture Library; 144, Jason Tharp; 145 (UP), Eric Isselee/SS; 145 (CTR LE), J.-L. Klein & M.-L. Hubert/MP; 145 (CTR RT), godrick/SS; 145 (LO RT), Smit/SS; 145 (LO LE), Suzi Eszterhas/ MP; 146 (UP LE), Sergii Kolesnyk/DS; 146 (UP CTR), Sorachar Tangjitjaroen/DS; 146 (UP RT), Andrii Mykhailov/DS; 146 (CTR LE), Aleksandr Bryliaev/SS; 146 (CTR), Brian Sedgbeer/DS; 146 (CTR RT), Saltcityphotography/DS; 146 (LO LE), matka_Wariatka/SS; 146 (LO CTR), Katerina Kovaleva/DS; 146 (LO RT), Brian Kushner/DS; 147 (UP), imageBROKER/Jurgen & Christine Sohns/GI; 147 (kangaroo), D. Parer and E. Parer-Cook/MP; 147 (platypus), Tom McHugh/Science Source; 147 (spider), ©Jürgen Otto; 147 (skink), Gerry Ellis/MP; 147 (pouch), Yva Momatiuk and John Eastcott/MP; 147 (swimming), Dave Watts/MP; 147 (dancing), ©Jürgen Otto; 147 (mob), Malcolm Schuyl/MP; 148-149, Strika Entertainment

20 Things to Make You Happy (150-165)

150-151, Chendongshan/SS; 152, Pete Pahham/SS; 153 (UP), Peter Augustin/GI; 153 (LO), Voronin76/SS; 154 (UP), Gts/SS; 154 (LO), Krakenimages/SS; 155, Zaretska Olga/ SS; 156, Daniel Milchev/GI; 157, Flashpop/ GI; 158 (fishing), Jupiterimages/SuperStock; 158 (planting), Sofiaworld/SS; 158 (baking), Bashutskyy/SS; 158 (photography), Marian Stanca/AL; 158 (golf), vm/GI; 158-159 (LO), Image Source Plus/AL; 160, Ivory27/SS; 161 (UP), Yury Zap/AL; 161 (LO), SuperStock; 162 (UP), Ariel Skelley/GI; 162 (LO), Potapov Alexander/SS; 163 (UP), MM Productions/GI; 163 (LO), Vinko93/SS; 164, Beskova Ekaterina/ SS; 165, Hello World/GI

Culture Connection (166-189)

166-167, Prisma by Dukas Presseagentur GmbH/AL; 168 (UP LE), CreativeNature.nl/SS; 168 (UP RT), Roka/SS; 168 (CTR LE), Phoenix Tenebra/SS; 168 (CTR RT), Orchid photho/ SS; 168 (LO LE), Tubol Evgeniya/SS; 169 (UP), SylvainB/SS; 169 (CTR RT), Dinodia Photos; 169 (CTR LE), Zee/Alamy; 169 (LO), wacpan/ SS; 170 (UP), Scott Keeler/Tampa Bay Times/ ZUMA Wire/AL; 170 (LO), Marie1969/SS; 171 (UP LE), VisitBritain/John Coutts/GI; 171 (UP RT), lev radin/SS; 171 (CTR RT), Viviane Ponti/GI; 171 (CTR LE), CR Shelare/GI; 171 (LO RT), Carol M. Highsmith/Library of Congress Prints and Photographs Division; 171 (LO LE), epa european pressphoto agency b.v./AL; 172, Chonnanit/SS; 173, Eric Isselee/SS; 175, Claus Bjoern Larsen/Ritzau Scanpix/AFP via GI; 176 (UP), Kate Pritchett; 176 (CTR RT), the_bakek- ing/Cover Images/Newscom; 176 (LO LE), Molly Robbins; 177 (UP), Serdar Yener of Yeners Way, Online Cake Tutorials; 177 (CTR LE), Studio Cake; 177 (LO CTR), Serdar Yener of Yeners Way, Online Cake Tutorials; 177 (LO RT), Studio Cake; 178-179 (BACKGROUND), Subbotina Anna/SS; 178-179 (cartoons), JOE ROCCO; 178 (CTR RT), adit_ajie/SS; 179 (CTR RT), Retro AdArchives/ Alamy; 180 (UP LE), Radomir Tarasov/DS; 180 (UP CTR), maogg/GI; 180 (UP RT), Paul Poplis/GI; 180 (CTR LE), Mlenny/iStock/GI; 180 (CTR RT), JACK GUEZ/AFP/GI; 180 (LO LE), Glyn Thomas/ Alamy; 180 (LO RT), Brian Hagiwara/GI; 181 (UP LE), Georgios Kollidas/Alamy; 181 (UP RT), Joe Pepler/Rex USA/SS; 181 (pig), Igor Stramyk/SS; 181 (CTR LE), Mohamed Osama/DS; 181 (CTR RT), Daniel Krylov/DS; 181 (LO LE), Colin Hampden-White 2010; 181 (LO RT), Kelley Miller/NGS Staff; 182 (Ton), Nguyen Dai Duong; 182 (CTR RT), Ho Trung Lam; 182 (LO LE), Mark Thiessen/NGP; 182 (Narayanan), RANDALL SCOTT/NGIC; 183 (UP LE), Jeremy Fahringer; 183 (Harrison), Mark Thiessen/NGIC; 183 (Barfield), Robert Massee; 183 (CTR RT), Catherine Cofré; 183 (CTR LE), K. Bista; 183 (Perlin), Mark Thiessen/NG Staff; 183 (Rapacha), Jeevan Sunuwar Kirat; 183 (LO RT), Jeevan Sunuwar Kirat; 184 (UP RT), Jose Ignacio Soto/SS; 184 (UP LE), liquidlibrary/GI Plu/GI; 184 (LO), Photosani/SS; 185 (LE), Corey Ford/DS; 185 (RT), IS; 186 (UP), Randy Olson; 186 (LO RT), Sam Panthaky/AFP/GI; 186 (LO LE), Martin Gray/NGIC; 187 (UP), Mayur Kakade/GI; 187 (LO RT), Richard Nowitz/NGIC; 187 (LO LE), Reza/NGIC; 188 (UP LE), Carol M. Highsmith/

Library of Congress Prints and Photographs Division; 188 (CTR RT), Daniel Krylov/DS; 188 (CTR LE), adit_ajie/SS; 188 (LO RT), Studio Cake; 189 (bird stamp), spatuletail/SS; 189 (Brazil stamp), PictureLake/E+/GI; 189 (money), cifotart/SS; 189 (CTR), zydesign/SS

Science and Technology (190-213)

190-191, AndreasReh/GI; 193, James Moy Photography/GI; 194 (UP), Jetpack Aviation; 194 (LO), Johny Kristensen; 195 (UP LE), REX USA; 195 (UP RT), REX USA; 195 (LO LE), Waverly Labs; 195 (LO RT), Origami Labs; 196, Ted Kinsman/Science Source; 197 (1), Sebastian Kaulitzki/SS; 197 (2), Eye of Science/Photo Researchers, Inc.; 197 (3), Volker Steger/Christian Bardele/Photo Researchers, Inc.; 197 (fungi), ancelpics/GI; 197 (protists), sgame/SS; 197 (plants), puwanai/SS; 197 (animals), kwest/SS; 198, Craig Tuttle/Corbis/GI; 199 (UP), Isabelle/AS; 199 (CTR), Berndt Fischer/Biosphoto; 199 (LO LE), naturediver/AS; 199 (LO CTR), M Andy/SS; 200 (UP), SciePro/SS; 200 (LO LE), Makovsky Art/SS; 200 (LO CTR), EFKS/SS; 200 (LO RT), Lightspring/SS; 202 (UP), Odua Images/SS; 202 (peanuts), Hong Vo/SS; 202 (allergies), Africa Studio/SS; 202 (mites), Sebastian Kaulitzki/SS; 202 (penicillin), rebcha/SS; 202 (pollen), Brian Maudsley/SS; 203 (UP LE), juan moyano/AL; 203 (UP RT), William West/AFP via GI; 203 (LO RT), Pasieka/Science Source; 203 (LO LE), VikramRaghuvanshi/GI; 204 (UP LE), kittipong053/SS; 204 (UP RT), Luisa Leal Photography/SS; 204 (swiss), PictureP./AS; 204 (french), nmarques74/AS; 204 (CTR RT), Kei Shooting/SS; 204 (LO RT), SciePro/SS; 204 (LO LE), Alf Ribeiro/SS; 205 (UP LE), chert28/SS; 205 (UP RT), NASA/JSC; 205 (pillow), New Africa/SS; 205 (pattern), piolka/IS/GI; 205 (LO RT), Underwood Archives/GI; 205 (LO RT), Michael Cocita/AS; 205 (LO LE), Sorrapong Apidech/EyeEm/GI; 205 (CTR LE), FG Trade/GI; 206 (LE), Eric Isselee/SS; 206 (RT), sdominick/GI; 207 (UP), Jean-Pierre Clatot/AFP/GI; 207 (CTR), kryzhov/SS; 207 (LO), Lane V. Erickson/SS; 208-209, Mondolithic Studios; 210-211, Mondolithic Studios; 212 (UP LE), M Andy/SS; 212 (UP RT), sdominick/GI; 212 (LO RT), kittipong053/SS; 212 (LO LE), REX USA; 213, Klaus Vedfelt/GI

Wonders of Nature (214-235)

214-215, Stuart Westmorland/Danita Delimont/AS; 216 (LE), AVTG/IS; 216 (RT), Brad Wynnyk/SS; 217 (UP LE), Rich Carey/SS; 217 (UP RT), Richard Walters/IS; 217 (LO RT), Michio Hoshino/MP/NGIC; 217 (LO RT), Karen Graham/IS; 218, Debra James/SS; 219 (UP), Pniesen/DS; 219 (CTR), Pablo Cogollos; 220-221 (BACKGROUND), Chris Anderson/SS; 220 (LE), cbpix/SS; 220 (RT), Mike Hill/Photographer's Choice/GI; 221 (CTR LE), Wil Meinderts/Buiten-beeld/MP; 221 (CTR RT), Paul Nicklen/NGIC; 221 (LO RT), Jan Vermeer/MP; 223 (UP), Stuart Armstrong; 223 (LO), Franco Tempesta; 224, Steve Mann/SS; 225 (UP), Chasing Light-Photography by James Stone/GI; 225 (RT), James Balog/NGIC; 227, Anna_Om/GI; 228 (UP LE), Richard T. Nowitz/Corbis; 228 (UP RT), gevende/IS/GI; 228 (CTR RT), Brand X; 228 (LO RT), Eric Nguyen/Corbis; 228 (LO LE), Alan and Sandy Carey/GI; 229 (1), Leonid Tit/SS; 229 (2), Frans Lanting/NGIC; 229 (3), Lars Christensen/SS; 229 (4) Daniel Loretto/SS; 229 (LO), Richard Peterson/SS; 230, 3dmotus/SS; 231 (UP LE), Lori Mehmen/Associated Press; 231 (EFo), Susan Law Cain/SS; 231 (EF1), Brian Nolan/IS; 231 (EF2), Susan Law Cain/SS; 231 (EF3), Judy Kennamer/SS; 231 (EF4), jam4travel/SS; 231 (EF5), jam4travel/SS; 231 (LO LE), Jim Reed; 232 (UP LE), The Asahi Shimbun via GI; 232 (UP RT), The Asahi Shimbun via GI; 232 (CTR), Thomas Black; 232 (LO), Thomas Ryan Allison/Bloomberg via GI; 233 (UP LE), donyanedomam/AS; 233 (LO LE), Chelsea Stein Engberg; 233 (LO RT), Jessica Bartlett/University Photographer/CSU Chico; 234 (UP), Daniel Loretto/SS; 234 (CTR LE), Thomas Black; 234 (CTR RT), Debra James/SS; 234 (LO), James Balog/NGIC

History Happens (236-267)

236-237, Menahem Kahana/AFP via GI; 238 (UP), Sanjida Rashid/NG Staff; 238 (CTR RT), Merydolla/SS; 238 (LO RT), Gift of Theodore M. Davis, 1909/Metropolitan Museum of Art; 238 (LO LE), Mr Crosson/SS; 238 (CTR LE), Enrico Montanari/SS; 239 (ALL), Alice Brereton; 240-241 (UP), Mondolithic Studios; 241 (INSET), Seamas Culligan/Zuma/CORBIS; 241 (LO), Roger Ressmeyer/CORBIS; 243, Tetra Images/GI; 244 (UP LE), Metropolitan Museum of Art, Munsey Fund, 1932; 244 (UP RT), DEA/A. De Gregorio/De Agostini/GI; 244 (LO), Look and Learn/Bridgeman Images; 245 (UP), Metropolitan Museum of Art; 245 (CTR), Purchase, Arthur Ochs Sulzberger Gift, and Rogers, Acquisitions and Fletcher Funds, 2016/Metropolitan Museum of Art; 245 (LO), Heritage Images/GI; 246 (UP), Jim Zuckerman/GI; 246 (CTR), Dinodia Photo/GI; 247 (UP), David Keith Jones/AL; 247 (CTR), NG Maps; 248-249 (BACKGROUND), Matjaz Slanic/E+/GI; 248 (LO), Mari Lobos; 247 (frame), Afateev/GI; 249 (UP), Mari Lobos; 249 (oval frame), Winterling/DS; 249 (LO), Marí Lobos; 249 (square frame), Iakov Filimonov/SS; 250, U.S. Air Force photo/Staff Sgt. Alexandra M. Boutte; 251 (UP), akg-images; 251 (LO), Heritage Auctions, Dallas; 252, Scott Rothstein/SS; 253 (UP), SS; 253 (CTR), Zack Frank/SS; 253 (LO), Gary Blakely/SS; 254 (UP), grandriver/E+/GI; 254 (CTR), Stan Honda/AFP via GI; 254 (LO), grandriver/GI; 255-259 (ALL PORTRAITS), White House Historical Association; 255 (ice cream), Layland Masuda/SS; 256 (baby), Gladskikh Tatiana/SS; 259 (Biden), David Lienemann/The White House; 259 (cow), Elisabeth Aardema/SS; 260 (UP LE), White House Photo/AL; 260 (UP RT), AP Photo/Carolyn Kaster; 260 (LO RT), Tory Kallman/SS; 260 (LO LE), Everett Collection Historical/AL; 261 (UP LE), Niday Picture Library/AL; 261 (UP RT), Science History Images/AL; 261 (LO RT), Bettmann/GI; 261 (LO LE), White House Photo/AL; 262 (UP), Bettmann/CORBIS/GI; 262 (INSET), Science Source/GI; 263 (UP), Charles Kogod/NGIC; 263 (LO), Saul Loeb/AFP via GI; 264, Bettmann Archive/GI; 265 (UP LE), Pat Benic/UPI/Alamy Live News; 265 (UP RT), Chris Pizzello/Invision/AP; 265 (LO), Bettmann/GI; 266 (UP LE), Seamas Culligan/Zuma/CORBIS; 266 (CTR RT), Jim Zuckerman/GI; 266 (CTR LE), Metropolitan Museum of Art; 266 (LO), Marí Lobos; 267, Christopher Furlong/GI

Geography Rocks (268-353)

268-269, Roberto Moiola/Sysaworld/GI; 275 (UP), Mark Thiessen/NGP; 275 (LO), NASA; 277 (BACKGROUND), Fabiano Rebeque/Moment/GI; 277 (UP LE), Thomas J. Abercrombie/NGIC; 277 (UP CTR), Maria Stenzel/NGIC; 277 (UP RT), Gordon Wiltsie/NGIC; 277 (LO LE), James P. Blair/NGIC; 277 (LO CTR), Bill Hatcher/NGIC; 277 (LO RT), Carsten Peter/NGIC; 279, Didier Marti/GI; 280, Londolozi Images/Mint Images/GI; 281 (UP), AdemarRangel/GI; 281 (CTR LE), Frank Glaw; 281 (CTR RT), image-BROKER/SS; 281 (LO RT), eAlisa/SS; 284, Klein & Hubert/Nature Picture Library; 285 (UP), Achim Baque/SS; 285 (CTR LE), Mark Conlon, Antarctic Ice Marathon; 285 (CTR RT), Flipser/SS; 285 (LO RT), Ashley Cooper/DPA Picture Alliance/Avalon; 288, P Deliss/The Image Bank/GI; 289 (UP), Grant Rooney Premium/; 288 (CTR LE), estherpoon/AS; 288 (CTR RT), Nate Allen/EyeEm/GI; 289 (LO RT), slowmotiongli/AS; 292, Arun Roisri/Moment RF/GI; 293 (UP), Andrew Watson/John Warburton-Lee Photography Ltd/GI; 293 (CTR LE), Ken/AS; 293 (CTR RT), WITTE-ART/AS; 293 (LO RT), Dmitry/AS; 296, Yasonya/AS; 297 (UP RT), Roy Pedersen/SS; 297 (CTR LE), Thomas Lohnes/GI; 297 (CTR RT), sucharat/AS; 297 (LO RT), Cover Images via AP Images; 300, John A. Anderson/SS; 301 (UP), Dina Julayeva/SS; 301 (CTR LE), Beth Zaiken; 301 (CTR RT), Daniel Prudek/AS; 301 (LO RT), Mint Images RF/GI; 304, hadynyah/IS/GI; 305 (UP), SOBERKA Richard/hemis.fr/GI; 305 (CTR LE), buteo/AS; 305 (CTR RT), Ernesto Ryan/Getty Image; 305 (LO RT), Keren Su/GI; 310, Cheryl Ramalho/AS; 313, Uros Ravbar/DS; 317, Aleksandar Todorovic/SS; 318, ferrantraite/E+/GI; 321, DaveLongMedia/IS/GI; 324, Adam Howard/AL; 327, Michael Runkel/AL; 332, dblight/GI; 344 (UP), SeanPavonePhoto/IS/GI; 344 (CTR LE), TexPhoto/E+/GI; 344 (CTR RT), Harold G Herradura/GI; 344 (LO), PhotoDisc; 345 (UP LE), Africa Studio/AS; 345 (UP RT), Imageman/SS; 345 (CTR RT), Quad-City Times/Zuma Press; 345 (LO RT), Anton Chernenko/SS; 345 (money), Eti Swinford/DS; 345 (magnet), Mega Pixel/SS; 345 (LO LE), Sonsedska Yuliia/SS; 345 (devil), Nikulina Tatiana/SS; 345 (wings), BlueRingMedia/SS; 345 (CTR), haveseen/SS; 346 (UP), Auscape International Pty Ltd/AL; 346 (CTR LE), Bruce Obee/Newscom; 346 (CTR RT), CB2/ZOB/Supplied by WENN/Newscom; 346 (LO), Alastair Pollock Photography/GI; 347, Six Flags; 348 (UP LE), Pete Oxford/MP; 348 (UP RT), Radu Razvan Gheorghe/DS; 348 (CTR RT), Wrangel/DS; 348 (LO RT), MICHAEL NICHOLS/NGIC; 348 (water), Chen Po Chuan/DS; 348 (LO CTR), Callahan/SS; 348 (CTR LE), Christin Farmer/DS; 349 (UP LE), Vladimir Ovchinnikov/DS; 349 (UP RT), Kevin Schafer/MP; 349 (Dead Sea), Strange/DS; 349 (candy), Richard Watkins/AL; 349 (LO RT), Photononstop/AL; 349 (LO LE), Renault Philippe/Hemis/AL; 349 (CTR LE), Tim Laman/NGIC; 350 (UP LE), Danita Delimont/AL; 350 (UP RT), ArtyAlison/IS/GI; 350 (LO RT), Gardel Bertrand/GI; 350 (LO LE), Ian Cumming/ZUMApress/Newscom; 351 (A), sculpies/GI; 351 (B), Archives Charmet/Bridgeman Images; 351 (C), Archives Charmet/Bridgeman Images; 351 (D), Archives Charmet/Bridgeman Images; 351 (E), Bridgeman Images; 351 (F), Archives Charmet/Bridgeman Images; 351 (G), DEA PICTURE LIBRARY/GI; 351 (H), Holger Mette/SS; 351 (I), Holger Mette/SS; 351 (J), Jarno Gonzalez Zarraonandia/SS; 351 (K), David Iliff/SS; 351 (L), ostill/SS; 351 (M), Hannamariah/SS; 351 (N), Jarno Gonzalez Zarraonandia/SS; 352 (UP), ArtyAlison/IS/GI; 352 (LE), Ken/AS; 352 (LO), Nate Allen/EyeEm/GI

NATIONAL GEOGRAPHIC and Yellow Border Design are trademarks of the
National Geographic Society, used under license.

Since 1888, the National Geographic Society has funded more than
14,000 research, conservation, education, and storytelling projects around
the world. National Geographic Partners distributes a portion of the funds
it receives from your purchase to National Geographic Society to support
programs including the conservation of animals and their habitats.
To learn more, visit natgeo.com/info.

For more information, visit nationalgeographic.com,
call 1-877-873-6846, or write to the following address:

National Geographic Partners, LLC
1145 17th Street N.W.
Washington, DC 20036-4688 U.S.A.

For librarians and teachers:
nationalgeographic.com/books/librarians-and-educators

More for kids from National Geographic: natgeokids.com

National Geographic Kids magazine inspires children to explore their world
with fun yet educational articles on animals, science, nature, and more.
Using fresh storytelling and amazing photography, *Nat Geo Kids* shows kids
ages 6 to 14 the fascinating truth about the world—and why they should care.
natgeo.com/subscribe

For rights or permissions inquiries, please contact National Geographic
Books Subsidiary Rights: bookrights@natgeo.com

Designed by Kathryn Robbins and Ruthie Thompson

The publisher would like to thank everyone who worked to make this book
come together: Mary Jones, project editor; Angela Modany, editor;
Sarah Wassner Flynn, writer; Michelle Harris, researcher; Sarah J. Mock,
senior photo editor; Mike McNey, map production; Anne LeongSon and Gus Tello,
design production assistants; Joan Gossett, editorial production manager;
and Molly Reid, production editor.

Trade paperback ISBN: 978-1-4263-7283-4
Trade hardcover ISBN: 978-1-4263-7336-7

Printed in the United States of America
22/WOR/1